FUNDRAISING GUIDES

The Foundation Center's

GUIDE TO PROPOSAL WRITING

Sixth Edition

Jane C. Geever

Library of Congress Cataloging-in-Publication Data
Geever, Jane C.
   The Foundation Center's guide to proposal writing—6th ed.
      p. cm.
   ISBN 978-1-59542-404-4 (alk. paper)
   1. Proposal writing for grants—United States—Handbooks, manuals, etc.
   I. Foundation Center. II. Title.
   HG177.5.U6G44 2012
   658.15'224—dc23
      2012010895

About The Foundation Center

Established in 1956, the Foundation Center is the leading source of information about philanthropy worldwide. Through data, analysis, and training, it connects people who want to change the world to the resources they need to succeed. The Center maintains the most comprehensive database on U.S. and, increasingly, global grantmakers and their grants—a robust, accessible knowledge bank for the sector. It also operates research, education, and training programs designed to advance knowledge of philanthropy at every level. Thousands of people visit the Center's web site each day and are served in its five regional library/learning centers and its network of more than 450 funding information centers located in public libraries, community foundations, and educational institutions nationwide and around the world. For more information, please visit foundationcenter.org or call (212) 620-4230.

Table of Contents

Preface

For many years, grantseekers using Foundation Center libraries, our web site, and print and electronic directories have been asking us for help beyond research into potential funders for their work. They need assistance in writing the proposal and advice on the proper way to submit it, given the widely differing policies and preferences among foundations and corporate grantmakers. To respond to this demand, in 1993 we commissioned Jane C. Geever and Patricia McNeill of the firm J. C. Geever, Inc., to write a guide for us, based on their many years of fundraising experience and knowledge of a great variety of grantmakers. Several editions followed, and the *Guide* as well as seminars we offer based on the advice herein have proven very popular with our audiences. This sixth edition includes responses to a series of interview questions by 40 grantmakers and excerpts from actual proposals to illustrate the text.

We hope this guide to proposal writing proves useful to all of you who are seeking grants, and we would welcome your comments and reactions to it.

We wish to thank the following grantmakers who participated in the interviews for their time and the valuable insights they provided:

Jessamine Chin,
   Philanthropy Program Manager*
Adobe Foundation
San Jose, CA

Jane B. O'Connell, President
Karen L. Rosa, Vice President and
   Executive Director
Altman Foundation
New York, NY

Laura H. Gilbertson, Chief Administrator
The William Bingham Foundation
Cleveland, OH

Matthew Klein, Executive Director
Blue Ridge Foundation New York
Brooklyn, NY

Marilyn Gelber, President
Brooklyn Community Foundation
Brooklyn, NY

David A. Odahowski, President and CEO
Edyth Bush Charitable Foundation, Inc.
Winter Park, FL

Karen Kinney, Program Officer
The Morris & Gwendolyn Cafritz
   Foundation
Washington, DC

Dianne Yamashiro-Omi, Program Manager
The California Endowment
Oakland, CA

Amy B. Scop, Director of Grants
   Management
The California Wellness Foundation
Woodland Hills, CA

Doug Bauer, Executive Director
The Clark Foundation
New York, NY

Kathleen Cerveny, Director of Institutional
   Learning and Arts Initiatives
The Cleveland Foundation
Cleveland, OH

Lita Ugarte Pardi, Senior Program Officer
The Community Foundation for
   Greater Atlanta
Atlanta, GA

Julie Farkas, Senior Program Officer*
Consumer Health Foundation
Washington, DC

Victoria Kovar, Program Officer
Cooper Foundation
Lincoln, NE

J. Andrew Lark, Trustee
The Frances L. & Edwin L. Cummings
   Memorial Fund
New York, NY

A. Thomas Hildebrandt, Director
The Davenport-Hatch Foundation
Penfield, NY

David D. Weitnauer, President
R. Howard Dobbs, Jr. Foundation, Inc.
Atlanta, GA

Matt Carpenter, Senior Vice President/
   Grants
El Pomar Foundation
Colorado Springs, CO

Peter F. Bird, Jr., President and CEO
The Frist Foundation
Nashville, TN

Darin McKeever, Deputy Director,
   Charitable Sector Support Policy &
   Government Affairs
The Bill & Melinda Gates Foundation
Seattle, WA

Susan M. Carter, Executive Director
Georgia Power Foundation, Inc.
Atlanta, GA

Robert B. Jaquay, Associate Director
The George Gund Foundation
Cleveland, OH

*Formerly

We also wish to thank the following nonprofit organizations whose leaders graciously permitted us to use excerpts from their proposals to illustrate the text:

Big Brothers of Nashville
Nashville, TN
Jann Seymour, Executive Director

Center for the Visually Impaired
Atlanta, GA
Susan B. Green, President

The Children's Institute
Verona, NJ
Bruce Ettinger, Executive Director and
   Superintendent/CEO

The CityKids Foundation
New York, NY
Kirsten Connor, Executive Director

Claremont Neighborhood Centers, Inc.
Bronx, NY
Abraham Jones, Executive Director

East Side House, Inc.
Bronx, NY
John A. Sanchez, Co-founder and
   Executive Director

ENACT, Inc.
New York, NY
Diana Feldman, President

Exalt Youth
Brooklyn, NY
Sonja Okun, Founder and
   Executive Director

Fernbank Museum of Natural History
Atlanta, GA
Susan E. Neugent, President and CEO

The Frazer Center
Atlanta, GA
Trace Haythorn, Executive Director

Goddard Riverside Community Center
New York, NY
Stephan Russo, Executive Director

Green City Force
Brooklyn, NY
Lisbeth Shepherd, Executive Director

Ingenuity Festival of Art + Technology
Cleveland, OH
Paula Grooms, Executive Director

King Manor Association of Long Island
Jamaica, NY
Mary Anne Mrozinski, Executive Director

Lincoln Symphony Orchestra
Lincoln, NE
Barbara Zach, Executive Director

Lollypop Farm, Humane Society of
   Greater Rochester
Fairport, NY
Alice Calabrese, President and CEO

New York Cares
New York, NY
Gary Bagley, Executive Director

New York City Outward Bound
Long Island City, NY
Richard Stopol, President

Operation Exodus Inner City
New York, NY
Mathew Mahoney, Executive Director

Project H Design
Windsor, NC
Emily Pilloton, Executive Director

Read Alliance
New York, NY
Yvonne Petrasovits, President

Rochester Area Crime Stoppers
Rochester, NY
Paul Hawkins, Chairperson

Sanctuary for Families, Inc.
New York, NY
Laurel W. Eisner, Executive Director

St. John's Foundation
Rochester, NY
Catherine (Kit) Pollicove, President

Tri-County Scholarship Fund
Parsippany, NJ
Gregory Floyd, President

WINGS
Charleston, SC
Bridget Laird, Chief Executive Officer

From the Author

Proposal writing is essential to the fundraising process, but it can be intimidating for the novice. There is nothing worse than staring at a blank piece of paper or computer screen with the sinking feeling that so much is riding on the prose you must create. Yet, if you follow the step-by-step process described in this book, you can create a proposal with a minimum of anxiety.

Take the steps one at a time. You will be successful in writing exciting and compelling proposals, proposals that will capture the interest of foundations and corporations, proposals that will generate grant support for your nonprofit organization.

In preparing this book, I interviewed a cross section of foundation and corporate representatives to find out their current thoughts on what should go into a proposal. While this material reinforces the steps I describe for writing a proposal, it also presents some notable insights into how grantmakers do their work, the challenges facing funders today, and how they are responding. These insights are a distinguishing feature of this book: They show the reality of the fundraising process from the funder's side of the proposal.

The 40 funding representatives interviewed include a geographic mix of local and national grantmakers, as well as representatives of independent, corporate, and community foundations and grantmaking public charities. Some of the funders represented have been in existence for many years.

Others are fairly new. One foundation does not have paid staff; some have at least one person on staff; others employ many people.

While the grantmakers interviewed reflect a relatively broad spectrum, it is important to remember that there are nearly 80,000 grantmaking private and community foundations in the United States. The majority of these have no staff and in fact are so small that the few local grants they award each year can be handled by trustees, lawyers, or family members. Therefore, the comments made here do not necessarily apply to all funders, but they do provide an indication of how some of the larger funders operate and how they evaluate the proposals they receive.

A series of questions was designed for the interview sessions in order to elicit views not only on proposal writing but also on the entire funding process and particularly on the impact of the economy on this process. Interviews were conducted via the telephone, following a questionnaire format. Questions were posed as to desired proposal contents, layout, length, and presentation. Funders were asked how proposals captured and kept their attention, what the characteristics of a successful proposal are, and what red flags are raised when they read proposals. Discussion ensued about their due diligence and the proposal review process. They weighed in on follow-up strategies once an agency receives a grant and whether, and how, to resubmit a rejected proposal. They were also asked to describe trends they perceived in the current funding climate.

Information and quotes gleaned from these interviews are used throughout the text. Chapter 17, "What the Funders Have to Say," reflects the substance of the interviews. Here, the reader will find specific questions asked of each grantmaking representative with some of their responses. The goal in presenting this information is clearly not to focus on particular funders but rather to provide a more general sense of grantmakers' perspectives on proposal writing. The funders interviewed have spoken frankly. They have all granted permission to the Foundation Center to use their quotes.

Acknowledgements

I would like to express appreciation to the staff of J. C. Geever, Inc., particularly to Kit Chan and Cheryl Austin, who helped prepare the manuscript; to Jonah Cardillo, Columbia University, Masters of Science in Fundraising Management Program, for boundless support, energy, and ideas, and to JuWon Choi, Marie DeAeth, and Betty Saronson of the Foundation Center, who saw this guide through production.

Introduction

If you are reading this book, you probably have already decided that foundations should be part of your fundraising strategy. You should be aware that, together, foundations and corporations historically have provided less than 20 percent of private gift support to nonprofit institutions, compared to nearly 75 percent by living individuals (see annual *Giving USA* reports, published by the Giving USA Foundation). Foundation and corporate support, however, can be extremely important in augmenting other forms of income, in permitting major new initiatives, or simply in promoting the mission of your agency.

Unfortunately, competition for these grant dollars has increased. There are many nonprofits competing for dollars and every year new nonprofits are created to respond to new or heightened social needs. Recent cutbacks in government funding for nonprofit services and activities have meant that many groups that previously relied primarily on government funds are now turning to private sources to support their work. Meanwhile, private foundations have experienced significant reductions in their own assets due to stock market losses.

What you need to attract donors to your agency is a comprehensive fundraising strategy that includes a variety of sources and approaches. This book focuses on how to create proposals to win foundation and corporate support. You need to tell your story clearly, keeping the interests of those you are approaching in mind. You will want to recognize the potential for long-term partnerships with foundations and corporations.

The Proposal Is Part of a Process

The subject of this book is proposal writing. But the proposal does not stand alone. It must be part of a process of planning and of research on, outreach to, and cultivation of potential foundation and corporate donors.

This process is grounded in the conviction that a partnership should develop between the nonprofit and the donor. When you spend a great deal of your time seeking money, it is hard to remember that it can also be difficult to give money away. In fact, the dollars contributed by a foundation or corporation have no value until they are attached to solid programs in the nonprofit sector.

This truly *is* an ideal partnership. The nonprofits have the ideas and the capacity to solve problems, but no dollars with which to implement them. The foundations and corporations may have the financial resources but not necessarily the other resources needed to create programs. Bring the two together effectively, and the result is a dynamic collaboration. Frequently, the donor is transformed into a stakeholder in the grantee organization, becoming deeply interested and involved in what transpires.

Roxanne Ford of W. M. Keck Foundation says: "I lucked into one of the greatest jobs in the world. I am eternally grateful that there are people out there willing to take a chance and bring us some of their best ideas to look at and see if Keck would be interested in funding them. The fact that people do that with good humor and grace and intelligence day after day amazes me."

You need to follow a step-by-step process in the search for private dollars. As Nancy Wiltsek of the Pottruck Family Foundation admonished us in the past, "Abide by the process!" It takes time and persistence to succeed. After you have written a proposal, it could take a year or more to obtain the funds needed to carry it out. And even a perfectly written proposal submitted to the right prospect might be rejected for any number of reasons.

Raising funds is an investment in the future. Your aim should be to build a network of foundation and corporate funders, many of which give small gifts on a fairly steady basis, and a few of which give large, periodic grants. By doggedly pursuing the various steps of the process, each year you can retain most of your regular supporters and strike a balance with the comings and goings of larger donors. The distinctions between support for basic, ongoing operations and special projects are discussed elsewhere in this book. For now, keep in mind that corporate givers and small family foundations tend to be better prospects for annual support than the larger, national foundations.

The recommended process is not a formula to be rigidly adhered to. It is a suggested approach that can be adapted to fit the needs of any nonprofit and the peculiarities of each situation. Fundraising is an art, not a science. You must bring your own creativity to it and remain flexible.

An example might help. It is recommended that you attempt to speak with the potential funder prior to submitting your proposal. The purpose of your call is to test your hypothesis gleaned from your research about the potential match between your nonprofit organization and the funder. Be sure to have specific questions regarding the core elements of your project and that funder's interest and previous giving. Board member assistance, if you are fortunate enough to have such contacts, ordinarily would not come into play until a much later stage. But what do you do if a board member indicates that his law partner is chairman of the board of a foundation you plan to approach? He offers to submit the proposal directly to his partner. You could refuse the offer and plod through the next steps, or you could be flexible in this instance, recognizing that your agency's likelihood of being funded by this foundation might have just risen dramatically. Don't be afraid to take the risk.

Recognizing the importance of the process to the success of your agency's quest for funds, let's take a look at each step.

Step One: Setting Funding Priorities

In the planning phase, you need to map out all of your agency's priorities, whether or not you will seek foundation or corporate grants for them. Ideally these priorities are determined in an annual planning session. The result of the meeting should be a solid consensus on the funding priorities of your organization for the coming year. Before seeking significant private sector support, you need to decide which of your organization's funding priorities will translate into good proposals. These plans or projects are then developed into funding proposals, and they form the basis of your foundation and corporate donor research.

Step Two: Drafting the Basic Proposal

You should have at least a rough draft of your proposal in hand before you proceed, so that you can be really clear about what you'll be asking funders to support. In order to develop this core proposal, you will need to assemble detailed background information on the project, select the proposal writer, and write the actual components of the document, including the executive summary, statement of need, project description, budget, and organizational information.

Step Three: Packaging the Proposal

At this juncture you have laid the groundwork for your application. You have selected the projects that will further the goals of your organization. You have written the basic proposal, usually a "special project" proposal, or a variation, such as one for a capital campaign or endowment fund.

Before you can actually put the document together and get it ready to go out the door, you will need to tailor your basic proposal to the specific funder's priorities. When you have taken that step, you will need to add a cover letter and, where appropriate, an appendix, paying careful attention to the components of the package and how they are put together.

Step Four: Researching Potential Funders

You are now ready to identify those sources that are most likely to support your proposal. You will use various criteria for developing your list, including the funders' geographic focus and their demonstrated interest in the type of project for which you are seeking funds. This research process will enable you to prepare different finished proposal packages based on the guidelines of specific funders.

Step Five: Contacting and Cultivating Potential Funders

This step saves you unnecessary or untimely submissions. Taking the time to speak with a funder about your organization and your planned proposal submission sets the tone for a potentially supportive future relationship, *if* they show even a glimmer of interest in your project. This step includes judicious use of phone and/or e-mail communication, face-to-face meetings, board contacts, and written updates and progress reports. Each form of cultivation is extremely important and has its own place in the fundraising process. Your goal in undertaking this cultivation is to build a relationship with the potential donor and to communicate important information while your request is pending. Persistent cultivation keeps your agency's name in front of the foundation or corporation. By helping funders learn more about your group and its programs, you make it easier for them to come to a positive response on your proposal—or, failing that, to work with you in the future.

Step Six: Responding to the Result

No matter what the decision from the foundation or corporation, you must assume responsibility for taking the next step. If the response is positive, good follow-up is critical to turning a mere grant into a true partnership.

Unfortunately, even after you have followed all of the steps in the process, statistically the odds are that you will learn via the mail or a phone call that your request was denied. Follow-up is important here, too, either to find out if you might try again at another time or with another proposal or to learn how to improve your chances of getting your proposal funded by others.

1

Getting Started: Establishing a Presence and Setting Funding Priorities

Every nonprofit organization needs to raise money. That is a given. Yet some nonprofits believe that their group must look special or be doing something unique before they are in a position to approach foundations and corporate grantmakers for financial support. This assumption is mistaken. If your organization is meeting a valid need, you are more than likely ready to seek foundation or corporate support.

But three elements should already be in place. First, your agency should have a written mission statement. Second, your organization should have completed the process of officially acquiring nonprofit status, or you need to have identified an appropriate fiscal agent to receive the funds on your behalf. Finally, you should have credible program or service achievements or plans in support of your mission.

Mission Statement

When your agency was created, the founders had a vision of what the organization would accomplish. The mission statement is the written summary of that vision. It is the global statement from which all of your nonprofit's programs and services flow. Such a statement enables you to convey the excitement of the purpose of your nonprofit, especially to a potential funder who has not previously heard of your work. Of course, for you to procure a grant, the foundation or corporation must agree that the needs being addressed are important ones.

Acquiring Nonprofit Status

The agency should be incorporated in the state in which you do business. In most states this means that you create bylaws and have a board of directors. It is easy to create a board by asking your close friends and family members to serve. A more effective board, though, will consist of individuals who care about the cause and are willing to work to help your organization achieve its goals. They will attend board meetings, using their best decision-making skills to build for success. They will actively serve on committees. They will support your agency financially and help to raise funds on its behalf. Potential funders will look for this kind of board involvement.

In the process of establishing your nonprofit agency, you will need to obtain a designation from the federal Internal Revenue Service that allows your organization to receive tax-deductible gifts. This designation is known as 501(c)(3) status. A lawyer normally handles this filing for you. Legal counsel can be expensive. However, some lawyers are willing to provide free help or assistance at minimal cost to organizations seeking 501(c)(3) status from the IRS. It is helpful if you request a letter that indicates 509(a) status as well because some grantmakers require both statements. 509(a) indicates that your organization is "not a private foundation."

Once your nonprofit has gone through the filing process, you can accept tax-deductible gifts. If you do not have 501(c)(3) status and are not planning to file for it in the near future, you can still raise funds. You will need to find another nonprofit with the appropriate IRS designation willing to act as a fiscal agent for grants received by your agency. How does this work? Primary contact will be between your organization and the funder. The second agency, however, agrees to be responsible for handling the funds and providing financial reports. The funder will require a formal written statement from the agency serving as fiscal agent. Usually the fiscal agent will charge your organization a fee for this service.

Credible Programs

Potential funders will want to know about programs already in operation. They will invest in your agency's future based on your past achievements. You will use the proposal to inform the funder of your accomplishments, which should also be demonstrable if an on-site visit occurs.

If your organization is brand new or the idea you are proposing is unproven, the course you plan to take must be clear and unambiguous. Your plan must be achievable and compelling. The expertise of those involved must be relevant. Factors such as these must take the place of a track record when one does not yet exist. Funders are often willing to take a risk on a new idea, but be certain that you can document the importance of the idea and the strength of the plan.

Like people, foundations have different levels of tolerance for risk. Some will invest in an unknown organization because the proposed project looks particularly innovative. Most, however, want assurance that their money is going to an agency with strong leaders who have proven themselves capable of implementing the project described in the proposal.

What really makes the difference to the potential funder is that your nonprofit organization has a sense of direction and is implementing, or has concrete plans to implement, programs that matter in our society. You have to be able to visualize exciting programs and to articulate them via your proposal. Once you've got these three elements in place, you're ready to raise money from foundations and corporations!

Setting Funding Priorities

Once your organization has established a presence, the first step of the proposal process is determining the priorities of your organization. Only after you do that can you select the right project or goals to turn into a proposal.

YOUR PRIORITIES

There is one rule in this process: You must start with your organization's needs and then seek funders that will want to help with them. Don't start with a foundation's priorities and try to craft a project to fit them. Chasing the grant dollar makes little sense from the perspectives of fundraising, program design, or agency development.

When you develop a program tailored to suit a donor, you end up with a project that is critically flawed. First, in all likelihood the project will be funded only partially by the grant you receive. Your organization is faced with the dilemma of how to fund the rest of it. Further, it will likely be hard to manage the project as part of your total program without distorting your other activities. Scarce staff time and scarcer operating funds might have to be diverted from the priorities you have already established. At worst, the project might conflict with your mission statement.

START WITH A PLANNING SESSION

A planning session is an excellent way to identify the priorities for which you will seek foundation grants and to obtain agency-wide consensus on them. Key board members, volunteers, and critical staff, if your agency has staff, should come together for a several-hour discussion. Such a meeting will normally occur when the budget for the coming fiscal year is being developed. In any case, it cannot be undertaken until the overall plan and priorities for your organization are established.

The agenda for the planning session is simple. With your organization's needs and program directions clearly established, determine which programs, needs, or activities can be developed in proposal form for submission to potential funders.

Phillip Henderson of Surdna Foundation, Inc. gives us some very important insights: "The thing that always strikes me is that poor proposal packages are much less about the detail of which documents and elements are weak. Usually poor proposals are the result of poor thinking and a lack of clarity in what the organization wants to do, what outcomes it wants to achieve, and how that works with what the foundation is trying to do."

The projects you take to grantmakers will come directly from your planning.

APPLY FUNDABILITY CRITERIA

Before moving ahead with the design of project proposals, test them against a few key criteria:

1. *The money cannot be needed too quickly.* It takes time for funders to make a decision about awarding a grant. If the foundation or corporate grantmaker does not know your agency, a cultivation period will probably be necessary.

   A new program can take several years to be fully funded, unless specific donors have already shown an interest in it. If your new program needs to begin immediately, foundation and corporate donors might not be logical sources to pursue. You should begin with other funding—from individuals, churches, or civic groups; from earned income; or from your own operating budget—or else you should delay the start-up until funding is secured from a foundation or corporate grantmaker.

A project that is already in operation and has received foundation and corporate support stands a better chance of attracting additional funders within a few months of application. Your track record will provide a new funder with an easy way to determine that your nonprofit can deliver results.

2. ***Specific projects tend to be of greater interest to most foundation and corporate funders than are general operating requests.*** This fundraising fact of life can be very frustrating for nonprofits that need dollars to keep their doors open and their basic programs and services intact. There is no doubt, though, that it is easier for the foundation or corporate funder to make a grant when the trustees will be able to see precisely where the money is going, and the success of their investment can be more readily assessed.

Keep in mind the concerns of the foundation and corporate funders about this question when you are considering how to develop your proposals for them. You may have to interpret the work of your organization according to its specific functions. For example, one nonprofit agency uses volunteers to advocate in the courts on behalf of children in the foster care system. Its goal is to bring about permanent solutions to the children's situations. When this agency first secured grants from foundations and corporations, it did so for general support of its program. Finding supporters reluctant to continue providing general support once the program was launched, the staff began to write proposals for specific aspects of the agency's work, such as volunteer recruitment, volunteer training, and advocacy, thus making it easier for donors to continue to fund ongoing, core activities.

Some foundations do give general operating support. You will use the print and electronic directories, web sites, annual reports, the foundations' own 990-PFs, and other resources described elsewhere in this book to target those that are true candidates for operating and annual support requests, if you find that your funding priorities cannot be packaged into projects. Alternatively, your general operating dollars might have to come from non-foundation sources.

3. *Support from individual donors and/or government agencies might be better sources for some of the priorities you are seeking to fund.* Moreover, having a diverse base of funding support is beneficial to the financial well-being of your nonprofit agency and is important to foundation and corporate prospects. They look for the sustainability of organizations beyond receipt of their own gifts. Foundation and corporation support usually will not take the place of support from individuals in the form of personal gifts raised via face-to-face solicitation, special events, direct mail, and/or by earned income in the form of fees or dues.

You know the priorities of your organization. You have determined which ones should be developed for submission to foundations and corporations in the form of a proposal. You are now ready to move on to the proposal-writing step.

2

Developing the Proposal: Preparation, Tips on Writing, Overview of Components

One advantage of preparing your proposal before you approach any funders is that all of the details will have been worked out. You will have the answers to just about any question posed to you about this project.

You can then take steps to customize your basic proposal with a personalized cover letter and revisions or adjustments to the document to reflect the overlapping interests of each particular grantmaker and your nonprofit. If a prospective funder requires a separate application form or an online application, it will be much easier to respond to the questions once you have your basic proposal all worked out.

Gathering Background Information

The first thing you will need to do in writing your proposal is to gather the documentation for it. You will require background documentation in three areas: concept, program, and expenses.

If all of this information is not readily available to you, determine who will help you gather each type of information. If you are part of a small nonprofit with no staff, a knowledgeable board member will be the logical choice. If you are in a larger agency, there should be program and financial support staff who can help you. Once you know with whom to talk, identify the questions to ask.

This data-gathering process makes the actual writing much easier. And by involving other stakeholders in the process, it also helps key people within your agency seriously consider the project's value to the organization.

CONCEPT

It is important that you have a good sense of how the project fits into the philosophy and mission of your agency. The need that the proposal is addressing must also be documented. These concepts must be well articulated in the proposal. Funders want to know that a project reinforces the overall direction of an organization, and they might need to be convinced that the case for the project is compelling. You should collect background data on your organization and on the need to be addressed so that your arguments are well documented.

PROGRAM

Here is a checklist of the program information you require:

- the nature of the project and how it will be conducted;

- the timetable for the project;

- the anticipated outcomes and how best to evaluate the results; and

- staffing and volunteer needs, including deployment of existing staff and new hires.

EXPENSES

You will not be able to pin down all of the expenses associated with the project until the program details and timing have been worked out. Thus, the main financial data gathering takes place after the narrative part of the proposal has been written. However, at this stage you do need to sketch out the broad outlines of the budget to be sure that the costs are in reasonable proportion to the outcomes you anticipate. If it appears that the costs will be prohibitive, even anticipating a foundation grant, you should then scale back your plans or adjust them to remove the least cost-effective expenditures.

Deciding Who Will Write the Proposal

While gathering data, you can make the decision about who will actually write the document. You might decide to ask someone else to draft it for you. This is a tough decision. If the obvious staff member you identify to write the first draft will have to put aside some other major task, it might not be cost-effective for the agency, and you might consider whether someone else on staff is a skilled writer or a willing learner and could be freed up from routine assignments.

If you lack a staff member with the skills and time to take on the task, a volunteer or board member might be an excellent alternative. You will need to identify someone who knows the agency and writes well. You will spend substantial time with this person, helping to describe the kind of document you want. In the long run, this can be time well spent, because you now have identified a willing and skilled volunteer proposal writer.

If you have found your writer on staff or among your volunteer ranks, you are all set. The information for the proposal has been gathered, and work can commence. Should you fail to find someone this way, then an outsider will be needed. Bear in mind, before you choose this option, that the most successful proposals are often "homegrown," even if they aren't perfect. A too-slick proposal obviously written by an outsider can be a real turnoff to funders.

On the other hand, while someone inside your agency will always know your organization better than a consultant, an outsider can bring objectivity to the process and may write more easily, especially with the data gathering already complete. Once the decision is made to use a consultant, you will need to make a list of prospective consultants, interview the leading candidates, check references, and make your selection.

You and the consultant will develop a contract that adequately reflects the proposed relationship. This document should include:

- details on the tasks to be performed by the consultant;

- the date when the contract becomes effective and the date of its expiration;

- a cancellation clause that can be exercised by either party within a specific number of days' notice, usually not less than 30 or more than 90 days;

- a statement that the agency owns the resulting proposal;

- information on the fee that the consultant will be paid and when it is to be paid (perhaps tying it to delivery of the product or completion of specified tasks);

- details on reimbursement of out-of-pocket expenses or on an expense advance on which the consultant may draw; and

- a provision for the contract to be signed both by the consultant and by an officer of the nonprofit.

If possible, your nonprofit organization should use legal counsel in developing the contract. At a minimum, an attorney should review the document to see that the agency's interests are protected. Seek out pro bono legal assistance, if need be. Do not consider oral agreements to be binding on either side. Put everything in writing.

Tips on Writing the Proposal

Regardless of who writes the proposal, grant requests are unique documents. They are unlike any other kind of writing assignment.

For many grantseekers, the proposal is the only opportunity to communicate with a foundation or corporate donor. The written document is the one thing that remains with a funder after all the meetings and telephone calls have taken place. It must be self-explanatory. It must reflect the agency's overall image. Your proposal will educate the funder about your project and agency. It should motivate the potential funder to make a gift.

You do need to put as much care into preparing your proposal as you have put into designing the project and as you are planning to put into operating it. You have spent a fair amount of time determining priorities for raising funds and gathering the appropriate information for the proposal. The information you have collected should be thoroughly woven into an integrated whole that dramatically depicts your agency's project for the funder.

There are some basic rules that apply to all writing and a few that are unique to proposals to foundations and corporations. Here are some tips for the proposal writer:

GET YOUR THOUGHTS SORTED OUT

A proposal must deliver critical ideas about your project quickly and easily. Your writing must be clear if you want others to understand your project and become excited by it. It will be hard to accomplish this if you have not clarified your thoughts in advance.

This means identifying the central point of your proposal. All of your subsequent points should flow easily from it. Once you have clearly thought through the broad concepts of the proposal, you are ready to prepare an outline.

OUTLINE WHAT YOU WANT TO SAY

You understand the need for the program. You have already gathered the facts about how it will unfold, if funded. You have identified the benchmarks of success and the financial requirements. With this information in hand, outline what should be said and in what order. If you take the time to create this outline, the process of writing will be much easier, and the resulting proposal will be stronger. Rushing to write a document without an outline only leads to frustration, confusion, and a poorly articulated proposal.

AVOID JARGON

Jargon confuses the reader and hampers his or her ability to comprehend your meaning. It impedes your style. It may be viewed as pretentious. With so much at stake in writing a proposal, it makes sense to avoid words (and acronyms) that are not generally known and to select words for their precision.

BE COMPELLING, BUT DON'T OVERSTATE YOUR CASE

People give to people. While your proposal has to present the facts, it must let the human element shine through. Personify the issue. Tell your story with examples. Illuminate your vision so that the funder can share it with you. Don't be afraid to humanize the materials once the facts are in place. But never assume that your writing is so compelling that programmatic details are unnecessary. A number of the grantmakers interviewed for this guide indicated a preference for real-life examples to enhance the text of a proposal. Doug Bauer of The Clark Foundation indicates: "One of the things we are looking for is a narrative story, one that is backed up with good data." Laura H. Gilbertson of The William Bingham Foundation adds: "If there is a little story, it helps. It illustrates what you do better than trying to describe it sometimes."

Try to be realistic in presenting your case. Take care that in your enthusiasm you do not overstate the need, the projected outcomes, or the basic facts about your organization. It is dangerous to promise more than you can deliver. The proposal reviewer is sure to raise questions, and the result could be damaged credibility with the funder. Worse, if the proposal is funded, and the results do not live up to the exaggerated expectations, future support is jeopardized.

KEEP IT SIMPLE

In the old days, fundraisers believed that the longer the document and the more detail it had, the better it was and the more money could be requested. Today, foundation and corporate funders look for concisely presented ideas. Eliminate wordiness. Simply present the key thoughts.

KEEP IT GENERIC

As you progress through the fundraising process, you may well approach a number of different potential funders with the same or a similar proposal. Thus, it makes sense to develop a basic proposal that, with certain customizing touches, can be submitted to a number of sources, including those favoring electronic submissions.

In some areas of the country, groups of foundations have agreed to adopt a common application form. It makes sense to inquire as to whether one exists in your geographic area and whether the funder you are applying to accepts proposals in this form. The very same careful research that goes into identifying appropriate funders pertains to contacting those that accept common application forms. Examples of common application forms can be found at the Foundation Center's web site at foundationcenter.org.

COMPONENTS OF A PROPOSAL

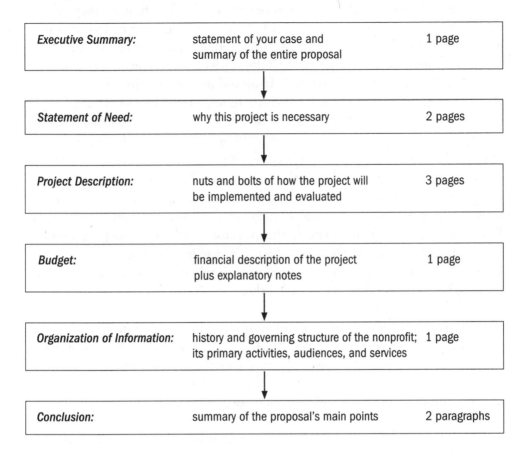

Executive Summary:	statement of your case and summary of the entire proposal	1 page
Statement of Need:	why this project is necessary	2 pages
Project Description:	nuts and bolts of how the project will be implemented and evaluated	3 pages
Budget:	financial description of the project plus explanatory notes	1 page
Organization of Information:	history and governing structure of the nonprofit; its primary activities, audiences, and services	1 page
Conclusion:	summary of the proposal's main points	2 paragraphs

REVISE AND EDIT

Once you have completed the proposal, put it away temporarily. Then in a day or two, reread it with detachment and objectivity, if possible. Look for the logic of your arguments. Are there any holes? Move on to analyzing word choices and examining the grammar. Karen Kinney of The Morris & Gwendolyn Cafritz Foundation suggests: "Have three people who are not familiar with your program review the proposal. Have them read it. Ask if they understand it because if they do not, we might not. Having an outside perspective can help you avoid jargon, repetitiveness, and too many pages." As the grantmaker suggests, give the document to someone else to read. Select someone with well-honed communication skills who can point out areas that remain unclear and raise unanswered questions. Ask for a critical review of the case and of the narrative flow. This last step will be most helpful in closing any gaps, in eliminating jargon, and in heightening the overall impact of the document.

A well-crafted document should result from all these hours of gathering, thinking and sifting, and writing and rewriting. Carol Robinson, former executive director of the Isaac H. Tuttle Fund, previously provided us with an ideal to strive for that is still very telling today: "To me a proposal is a story. You speak to the reader and tell the reader a story, something you want him/her to visualize, hear, feel. It should have dimension, shape and rhythm and, yes, it should 'sing'" (private letter, December 30, 1985). Current interviewee Robert B. Jaquay of The George Gund Foundation notes: "Preparing proposals is a 'sense-making activity.' It includes: the ability to bring order to a complicated set of events; a sense of proportion of the activity to the large description of community; and the sense of how the grant will help further the mission of the organization. Those kinds of sense-making expressions are really really helpful." Victoria Kovar of Cooper Foundation challenges us: "The applicant must clearly state the purpose of the grant right up front. That puts the rest of the information in context. One of the signs of a great grant application is when the distinctive sections of an application really relate to each other."

The following chapters include many examples to assist you in better understanding the points being made. All are excerpts from actual proposals and are reprinted with permission from the issuing agency. Please note that to keep the design of the book as straightforward as possible, we did not always reproduce these examples in their original formats.

No two proposals are precisely the same in their execution, and no single proposal is absolutely perfect. In fact, some of the examples presented here have flaws. These examples are used to underscore a specific point, but together they illustrate the more general one that flexibility on the part of the proposal writer is essential. In a winning proposal, often the nature of the issues being addressed overrides rules about format.

A full sample proposal appears in Appendix A.

Developing the Proposal: The Executive Summary

This first page of the proposal is the most important section of the entire document. Here you will provide the reader with a snapshot of what is to follow. Specifically, it summarizes all of the key information and is a sales document designed to convince the reader that this project should be considered for support. Be certain to include:

Need—a brief statement of the reason or rationale for your project, in other words, the problem or issue your agency is prepared to address (one or two paragraphs);

Project—a short description of the project, including what will take place and how many people will benefit from the program, how and where it will operate, for how long, and who will staff it (one or two paragraphs);

Ask—a request for a specific grant amount for your project (one paragraph); and

Organization and its expertise—a brief statement of the name, history, purpose, and activities of your agency and its capacity to carry out this program (one paragraph).

How will the executive summary be used? First, in the initial due diligence review of your request, it will enable the funder to determine that the proposal is within its guidelines. Then it is often forwarded to other staff or board members to assist in their general review of the request. If you don't provide a summary, someone at the funder's office may well do it for you and emphasize the wrong points. Karen Kinney of The Morris & Gwendolyn Cafritz Foundation makes an excellent point: "My advice to anybody writing a proposal, whether the format requires it or not, is to put a beginning paragraph that states clearly the requested amount and purpose of the project for which you are requesting support."

Here's a tip: It is easier to write the executive summary *last*. You will have your arguments and key points well in mind. It should be concise. Ideally, the summary should be no longer than one page or 300 words.

What follows is an example of an executive summary, taken from a proposal submitted by East Side House to The Frances L. & Edwin L. Cummings Memorial Fund. The summary immediately identifies the financial request. It explains clearly about the organization and the project.

EXECUTIVE SUMMARY

East Side House requests a $40,000 grant from the Frances L. and Edwin L. Cummings Memorial Fund to support the full-time salary of a **College and Career Advisor (CCA) at the Bronx Haven High School (BHHS)**.

Serving the greater Mott Haven/South Bronx community, East Side House has been helping people out of poverty for years by enabling them to invest in their education. We remain relevant in this work today particularly in addressing the educational attainment and employability of our at-risk adolescent/young adult population. BHHS is one of our three core educational programs that work with this difficult-to-serve youth population.

First opened in September 2008, BHHS targets students ages 16 to 21 who have at least one year of NYC public school experience, but who are over-aged and under-credited for their grade level. BHHS uses an accelerated, individualized curriculum coupled with specialized support. Our initial success has facilitated a move to the Alfred E. Smith Educational Campus, allowing us to increase our service capacity by 25 percent for a total of 125 students annually.

Studies show that college completion rates increase dramatically if a young person completes their first year of college on time. We recently created the CCA position to provide intense college access support to students during the 3 critical phases—acceptance, matriculation and first-year completion—in order to increase college success rates amongst our BHHS graduates.

Support from the Cummings Memorial Fund will allow East Side House to sustain this new critical position for the 2011/2012 program year and address college access/career development in a more meaningful way for long-term impact.

This second example is excerpted from a proposal of The CityKids Foundation. Once again, the request to the grantmaker is prominent. There is a straightforward explanation of the project, the reason for the request, and information about the applicant.

EXECUTIVE SUMMARY

Established in 1985 with the vision of bringing high-quality arts experiences to underserved young people, CityKids transformed its free programmatic offerings to meet the evolving needs of young people. We added leadership and community service opportunities, as well as needed academic support, job readiness, and mental health services to enhance the artistic, intellectual, and leadership development of our participants. CityKids teens work with staff to design, implement, and evaluate each program area. Now in its 27th year of service, CityKids has been an anchor in the downtown community since its inception, helping more than 25,000 young people makes a successful transition into adulthood annually.

Neither example contains every element of the ideal executive summary, but both persuasively make the case for reading further.

4

Developing the Proposal:
The Statement of Need

If the funder reads beyond the executive summary, you have successfully piqued his or her interest. Your next task is to build on this initial interest in your project by enabling the funder to understand the problem that the project will remedy.

The statement of need enables the reader to learn more about the issues. It presents the facts and evidence that support the need for the project and establishes that your nonprofit understands the problems and therefore can reasonably address them. The information used to support the case can come from authorities in the field, as well as from your agency's own experience.

Like a good debater, you must assemble all the arguments and then present them in a logical sequence that will readily convince the reader of their importance. You want the need section to be persuasive, yet succinct. Keep in mind that some of our current interviewees suggest that this part of the document be extremely brief because they are experts in the particular area and do not need you to recount information they know. Dianne Yamashiro-Omi of The California Endowment indicates: "I usually tell folks to spend less time on the need section. We are more interested in the strategy and how it would fit with our foundation's strategic plan and mission."

As you marshal your arguments, consider the following six points: First, decide which facts or statistics best support the project. Be sure the data you present are accurate. There are few things more embarrassing than to have the funder tell you that your information is out of date or incorrect. Information that is too generic or broad will not help you develop a winning argument for your project. Information that does not relate to your organization or the project you are presenting will cause the funder to question the entire proposal. There should be a balance between the information presented and the scale of the program. Here is a list of possible sources to call upon when compiling facts, figures, and statistics to back up your case:

- needs assessments conducted by objective outside parties or by your own agency

- surveys—local or regional or national, conducted by your organization or by others

- focus groups with representatives of key audiences

- interviews with stakeholders

- usage statistics

- media coverage of the problem or lack of service

- reports from government agencies or other nonprofits

- demographic studies

- projections for the future, suggesting how bad things will get if this problem is not addressed, and/or how good things will be if it is.

These should all derive from authorities with impeccable credentials and be as up-to-date as possible.

An example might be helpful here. Your nonprofit organization plans to initiate a program for battered women, for which you will seek support from foundations and corporations in your community. You have impressive national statistics on hand. You can also point to an increasing number of local women and their children seeking help. However, local data are limited. Given the scope of the project and the base of potential supporters, you should probably use the more limited local information only. It is far more relevant to the interests of funders close to home. If you were to seek support from more nationally oriented funders, then the broader information would be helpful, supplemented by details based on local experience.

Second, give the reader hope. The picture you paint should not be so grim that the situation appears hopeless. The funder will wonder whether an investment in a solution will be worthwhile. Here's an example of a solid statement of need: "Breast cancer kills. But statistics prove that regular checkups catch most breast cancer in the early stages, reducing the likelihood of death. Hence, a program to encourage preventive checkups will reduce the risk of death due to breast cancer." Avoid overstatement and overly emotional appeals.

Third, decide if you want to put your project forward as a model. This could expand the base of potential funders, but serving as a model works only for certain types of projects. Don't try to make this argument if it doesn't really fit. Funders may well expect your agency to follow through with a replication plan if you present your project as a model.

If the decision about a model is affirmative, you should document how the problem you are addressing occurs in other communities. Be sure to explain how your solution could be a solution for others as well.

Fourth, determine whether it is reasonable to portray the need as acute. You are asking the funder to pay attention to your proposal because either the problem you address is worse than others or the solution you propose makes more sense than others. Here is an example of a balanced but weighty statement: "Drug abuse is a national problem. Each day, children all over the country die from drug overdose. In the South Bronx the problem is worse. More children die here than any place else. It is an epidemic. Hence, our drug prevention program is needed more in the South Bronx than in any other part of the city."

Fifth, decide whether you can demonstrate that your program addresses the need differently or better than other projects that preceded it. It is often difficult to describe the need for your project without being critical of the competition. But you must be careful not to do so. Being critical of other nonprofits will not be well received by the funder. It may cause the funder to look more carefully at your own project to see why you felt you had to build your case by demeaning others. The funder may have invested in these other projects or may begin to consider them, now that you have brought them to its attention.

If possible, you should make it clear that you are cognizant of, and on good terms with, others doing work in your field. Keep in mind that today's funders are very interested in collaboration. They may even ask why you are not collaborating with those you view as key competitors. So at the least you need to describe how your work complements, but does not duplicate, the work of others.

Sixth, avoid circular reasoning. In circular reasoning, you present the absence of your solution as the actual problem. Then your solution is offered as the way to solve the problem. For example, the circular reasoning for building a community swimming pool might go like this: "The problem is that we have no pool in our community. Building a pool will solve the problem." A more persuasive case would cite what a pool has meant to a neighboring community, permitting it to offer recreation, exercise, and physical therapy programs. The statement might refer to a survey that underscores the target audience's planned usage of the facility and conclude with the connection between the proposed usage and potential benefits to enhance life in the community.

To make your need statement compelling, you'll want to put a human face on the problem. There are a number of ways you might do this:

- use anecdotes, succinctly related

- provide real-life examples (with fictitious names if need be) to make those you serve come alive

- supply actual quotes from those who have benefited or will benefit from your services

- emphasize the needs of those you serve, not your own

- always make the funder feel that there is hope that the problem will be solved.

The statement of need does not have to be long and involved. Short, concise information captures the reader's attention. This is the case in the following example from the Read Alliance to Altman Foundation.

NEED AND TARGET POPULATION

As revealed by recent test scores, New York City students continue to face significant reading challenges, and the achievement gap in reading persists. Only 47 percent of third graders citywide, and only one-third of Black and Hispanic New York City third graders, met or exceeded reading standards on the most recent New York State English Language Arts exam. While this is partially due to higher standards set for the state, New York City 4th graders scored 10 percentage points lower than their peers statewide. Read Alliance provides children with the early reading achievement critical for continued academic success and future high school graduation.

According to the Wharton Business School's online publication, "Teens gain critical skills from early work experiences; without widespread teen employment opportunity, the future workforce will be compromised... Working as a team, completing tasks and taking responsibility. Kids learn these skills through employment... While getting a foothold in the labor market is especially important for teens who enter the workforce directly after high school, it is also true for those who attend four-year colleges." The employment rates of minority teens have steadily declined over the past decade and are consistently below those of White teens (US Bureau of Labor Statistics, 2009). By providing formal training, early work experience, and ongoing support, Read Alliance prepares hundreds of teens each year for future college and career success.

The next example comes from a proposal to Blue Ridge Foundation New York from Green City Force. Note the use of footnotes.

Green jobs are the focus of much attention these days. President Obama has made the fight against global warming, weaning our dependence on foreign oil, and creation of "green jobs" centerpieces of his administration. The American Recovery and Reinvestment Act includes nearly $62 billion in energy-related investments, which are expected to generate hundreds of thousands of jobs in areas such as green construction, energy efficiency, and renewable energy. In the private sector, while the economy continues to plummet, investments in alternative energy and clean technologies were up 40 percent since 2007[1].

How many of these green jobs will go to young people growing up in poverty? It is a time of crisis for young people: more than 50 percent young people of color do not finish high school; 65 percent of young people who drop out of school end up in jail; and 65 percent exiting jail will return, perpetuating cycles of poverty. The green wave may pass young people by, if the infrastructure does not exist to prepare them for next-generation jobs. It is urgent to expose young people to the opportunities for family-supporting careers in trades related to expanding green industries, and create bridges for those who wish to pursue apprenticeships or employment. Green jobs advocacy has made phenomenal headway over the past 18 months. Leading environmental and political organizations from 1Sky, to the Sierra Club to MoveOn, have made green jobs a rallying cry. Green for All founder and green pathways out of poverty advocate Van Jones is soon to join the White House as special advisor, and our Labor Secretary is green jobs champion Hilda Solis. The issue now is implementation: building the green economy, and connecting young people to career opportunities.

[1]"Alternative Energy Companies Grow Even as Others Falter", by Simona Covel, Wall Street Journal, January 13th.

A third example was submitted to The Community Foundation for Greater Atlanta by the Center for the Visually Impaired.

During the next 12 months, CVI will continue to face the challenge of serving more individuals impacted by vision loss with less funding than ever before. In the past few years, CVI has faced significant budget cuts from the United Way and government sources, while simultaneously addressing increasing vision rehabilitation needs due to an increased number of babies born prematurely, which may result in retinopathy of prematurity; complications from diabetes, a growing epidemic; or age-related eye diseases that plague our aging community. In spite of the challenges facing individuals with vision loss, many of these people want to continue to live independently, having real jobs and real lives. Therefore, a significant opportunity for the coming year is the establishment of a contact center on our premises and the creation of a customer service training program at CVI. By establishing a contact center, CVI will be able to offer jobs for people who are blind or visually impaired while earning revenue to extend its programs for the increasing number of people who need vision rehabilitation.

The last example was submitted to The William Bingham Foundation by WINGS.

We are the only U.S. organization solely focused on social and emotional learning in after school programming—it's crucial we replicate our program because more kids need WINGS. By the time they reach high school, as many as 40 to 60 percent of all students - urban, suburban and rural are chronically disengaged from school, according to national research. Not only does this disengagement bring declines in academic performance, but also increases the likelihood of risky behavior across all racial, ethnic and income groups.

WINGS serves the most at-risk kids in at-risk schools in Charleston County, where the dropout rate has reached alarming levels among African-American families: nearly 1 out of 2 boys and 1 out of 4 girls leave high school before graduation. The research shows that students who do not feel connected to school are more likely to drop out before graduation, exhibit disruptive and violent behavior, carry or use a weapon, experiment with tobacco, alcohol or drugs, engage in early sexual involvement, and consider or attempt suicide.

As you can see from all four examples, the need statement begins the process whereby the organization builds its case and tells its story. This process continues in the next section of the proposal, which describes how the project will address the need.

5

Developing the Proposal: The Project Description

In this section, your goal is to describe the nuts and bolts of the project in a way that excites the reader, while making a compelling case for the approach you have adopted. It is worth stating right up front that your plan is not written in stone. It might change based on feedback on your proposal and the experience you gain through implementation. It is not worth putting your organization in a defensive position in negotiating with grantmakers, and you certainly don't want to surprise a funder if in the project's final report you state that you changed your approach.

This section of your proposal should have five subsections: objectives, methods, staffing/administration, evaluation, and sustainability. Together, objectives and methods dictate staffing and administrative requirements. They then become the focus of the evaluation to assess the results of the project. The project's sustainability flows directly from its success, hence its ability to attract other support. The five subsections present an interlocking picture of the total project.

Objectives

Objectives are the measurable outcomes of the program. They help delineate your methods. Your objectives must be tangible, specific, concrete, measurable, and achievable in a specified time period. Grantseekers often confuse objectives with goals, which are conceptual and more abstract. For the purpose of illustration, here is the goal of a project with a subsidiary objective:

Goal: Our afterschool program will help children read better.

Objective: Our afterschool remedial education program will assist 50 children in improving their reading scores by one grade level as demonstrated on standardized reading tests administered after participating in the program for six months.

The goal in this case is abstract: improving reading, while the objective is much more specific. It is achievable in the short term (six months) and measurable (improving 50 children's reading scores by one grade level).

With competition for dollars so great, well-articulated objectives are increasingly critical to a proposal's success.

Calling upon a different example, there are at least four types of objectives:

1. Behavioral—A human action is anticipated.
   Example: Fifty of the 70 children participating will learn to swim.

2. Performance—A specific time frame within which a behavior will occur, at an expected proficiency level, is anticipated.
   Example: Fifty of the 70 children will learn to swim within six months and will pass a basic swimming proficiency test administered by a Red Cross-certified lifeguard.

3. Process—The manner in which something occurs is an end in itself.
   Example: We will document the teaching methods utilized, identifying those with the greatest success.

4. Product—A tangible item will result.
   Example: A manual will be created to be used in teaching swimming to this age and proficiency group in the future.

As you will see in Chapter 6, the types of objectives you develop for your project will determine the kind of evaluation you will conduct.

Here is an example with both goals and objectives. It was submitted by the Goddard Riverside Community Center to The Frances L. & Edwin L. Cummings Memorial Fund.

SPECIFIC AND MEASURABLE GOALS

The new Director of Training will be part of an expanded Options team that will realize the ambitious goals of the Options Strategic Plan over the next five years.

Goal 1. The Options Institute will increase the amount and effectiveness of financial aid counseling in schools and community-based organizations in New York State.

Objectives:

a. Design and implement an outreach campaign to increase enrollment at financial aid trainings.

b. Expand and deepen the financial aid curriculum.

c. Train and support over 150 college access and success providers annually on financial aid issues.

d. Equip 50 college access providers annually to run effective financial aid workshops for young people and their families.

Goal 2. The Options Institute will expand and deepen its curricula to meet the needs of college counselors from multiple settings.

Objectives:

a. Further develop the Institute's curricula to address all the core competencies college access counselors need.

b. Develop partnerships to customize the curricula for college access providers in community-based organizations (CBOs), traditional schools, alternative schools (YABC and Transfer), GED programs, Administration for Children's Services (ACS) and other foster care agencies.

c. Create training guides with their associated materials and resources for all curricula.

Goal 3. The Options Institute will establish an interactive online resource center for college access and success providers across the nation.

> **Objectives:**
>
> a. Design, implement, and maintain a website featuring all of the Institute's resources as well as national research and best practices.
>
> b. Develop interactive features within the online resource center to support working counselors around financial aid counseling and best practices.

In any given proposal, you will find yourself setting forth one or more of these types of objectives, depending on the nature of your project. Be certain to present the objectives very clearly. Make sure that they do not become lost in verbiage and that they stand out on the page. You might, for example, use numbers, bullets, or indentations to denote the objectives in the text. Above all, be realistic in setting objectives. Don't promise what you can't deliver. Remember, the funder will want to be told in the final report that the project actually accomplished these objectives.

The example that follows is excerpted from a proposal to the Brooklyn Community Foundation submitted by Exalt Youth. It states the project's objectives succinctly.

Funding from the Brooklyn Community Foundation will enable us to continue the launch of an expanded version of our program model serving 150 court-involved youth in the next year, as well as fully implement the comprehensive performance measurement system we designed through a Theory of Change process last fall. The Foundation's contribution will play a key role in exalt's pivotal next phase in which infrastructure development will be one of our most important steps towards becoming a nationally recognized and influential model. Specifically, support will help us achieve the following outcomes:

- Exalt will serve 150 youth in the next year.
- 75 percent of youth enrolled will complete the 6-week training component of the program.
- 55 percent of youth enrolled will complete pre-internship training, internships and the second phase of classroom training and thus be considered "graduates".
- Fewer than 8 percent of graduates will recidivate within 2 years of program completion.
- 85 percent of program graduates will continue pursuing educational goals (e.g. by advancing in grade levels, obtaining a GED, graduating high school, enrolling in college, etc.).
- 100 percent of program graduates will show improvements in their comprehension and application of exalt's four core skills through a newly designed pre and post test.
- 100 percent of graduates will demonstrate increased employability as measured by successful completion of internships, employer evaluations, and increased score on four core skill and employment readiness post tests.

Methods

By means of the objectives, you have explained to the funder what will be achieved by the project. The methods section describes the specific activities that will take place to achieve the objectives. It might be helpful to divide our discussion of methods into the following: how, when, and why.

How: This is the detailed description of what will occur from the time the project begins until it is completed. Your methods should match the previously stated objectives. In our example about teaching 50 children to swim, appropriate methods would describe 1) how the youngsters will be recruited, 2) how they will be taught to enhance their skills, and 3) how their swimming skills will be measured. There would be no reason to describe an extraneous activity like helping the parents learn to enjoy swimming with their children, because using swimming to bring the family together in wholesome exercise is not a stated objective of the project.

In the next example from Green City Force's proposal to Blue Ridge Foundation New York, we learn very succinctly how the agency will implement its program.

> Green City Corps will use a national service model to engage, support and train young people, and connect them to career-track employment in expanding green sectors. Working closely with employers, community-based green jobs training providers, weatherization agencies, youth-serving organizations, and others, Green City Corps will create a youth corps dedicated to greening the city and to preparing young people to be successful in green economy careers such as energy efficiency, renewable energy, and sales and marketing of products for green construction.

Project H Design, in its proposal for Studio H to Adobe Foundation, describes a series of very clear activities aimed at accomplishing its objectives.

> For the purposes of Studio H, our goals are to:
> - Inspire critical thinking and creative problem solving within the next generation.
> - Provide a more holistic, relevant, locally responsive approach to public education.
> - Give underserved students an opportunity to broaden their perspective of the world.
> - Integrate core subject learning into project-based design projects.

- Provide transferable college credit and usable industry skills for college-bound and job-seeking high school students.
- Construct full-scale transformative architecture for the community, by the hands of high school students.
- Support the new programming that will exist within the structures we build (i.e. the farmers market).
- Build long-term creative capital in resource-poor communities in need of new solutions.
- Make all lesson plans, teaching modules, and learnings transparent and openly available to educators around the country.
- Collaborate with additional schools and districts to bring the program (or components of it) to new locations.

During the first year of Studio H, we have seen much progress towards achieving these goals both individually for our students, and for the broader community. We believe that in underserved communities such as Bertie County (the poorest and most racially divided county in the state), education and creative capital are two drastically under-supported assets that require constant investment and fresh vision. Our stated goals inspire creative solutions to societal issues by teaching youth the skills they need to address such societal issues themselves, and to execute such solutions in a democratic, beautiful, and physical manner through architecture and design. If we meet our goals, we hope that our students will be better equipped to tackle acute social needs when they become the next small businessmen, mayors, tradespeople, or town councilmen of their communities.

Specifically, we are working towards our goals using the following mechanics:

- Over the course of one school year, students earn 17 college credits, high school elective credit, and approximately $3000 in wages during the summer construction phase.

- 16 junior-year high school students per year are enrolled in Studio H as an elective, which is held for 3 hours every school day, during school hours (2 block periods). The Studio H facility is a free-standing barn on the site of Bertie High School, which Project H converted into a wood/metal shop, design studio, and classroom.

- Instructors are Project H's founder/executive director Emily Pilloton and project manager Matthew Miller, who are employed as adjunct faculty at Pitt Community College (through which we are able to both offer college credit and teach on the high school campus through a cooperative agreement with the Board of Education).

- Studio H is offered at no cost to the Bertie County School District and is entirely self-funded by Project H (including all construction costs, classroom materials, transportation, student and instructor salaries, etc).

- Our second year's full-scale project will be either a) an animal rescue shelter and education center, or b) three smaller farmers market annexes in neighboring towns. We anticipate that either project will benefit close to 1000 residents.

Lastly, our operational goals are to build capacity around Studio H, as the cornerstone initiative of our organization. As we continue the program year after year, we believe each built project will feed off of the previous, and will allow us as an organization to more deeply and thoroughly assess and document our learnings around high school design education and community-driven design.

Another example is from New York Cares' proposal to The Frances L. & Edwin L. Cummings Memorial Fund.

How they will be selected: In the 11-12 school year, New York Cares' Sophomore Skills, SAT Prep, College Prep and FAFSA programs will target more than 1,400 disadvantaged high school students, grades 10 through 12, throughout New York City. New York Cares creates and distributes to our partner schools and agencies the student applications for the SAT Prep program. Next, our partners collect and evaluate the student applications, and ultimately select the participants. Our partners also select the students they feel would benefit from the Sophomore Skills, College Prep and FAFSA programs. We look for students who are motivated to attend college, but who require additional support to strengthen their skills in literacy, math and test-taking - and who need individualized attention in order to complete college admissions and aid applications. We prefer students who have a good attendance record and will commit to attending weekly sessions over the course of a semester (for Sophomore Skills) or a school year (SAT Prep and College Prep). The FAFSA program involves a one-time session for the students and their parents/guardians.

How the students will benefit: Our Sophomore Skills volunteers will help tenth-grade students to build their basic math, English and test-taking skills so they can succeed in their core classes and prepare to participate in our SAT Prep tutoring the next year. Our specially trained SAT Prep volunteers will use the Kaplan curriculum to prepare high school juniors to take the SAT test (our program boosts student scores by an average of more than 200 points). Our College Prep volunteers will help the high school seniors who are graduates of the SAT Prep program to complete college admissions, scholarship and financial aid applications - increasing the students' chances of getting into a range of colleges with the aid and scholarships they need to attend. Further, through our new FAFSA program, New York Cares volunteers will help students and their families to complete the FAFSA (Free Application for Federal Student Aid) in time to make informed decisions about financial aid packages and college acceptances.

Think about how you can most readily construct a logical sequence from each objective to its relevant method. This can be accomplished in a number of ways, some relating simply to visual placement on the page.

One means of organizing this section is to write out each objective and to list beneath it the method(s) that will make the objective possible. For example, it might look like this:

Objective: to recruit 70 children

Methods:

• Put up signs in the Y.

• Go to each school and address classes on the fun of swimming.

• Put ads in the local paper.

• Enclose a flyer about the program with the next mailer sent out to each family in the community.

The methods should match the magnitude of the objectives. Once you are sure that each objective has related methods that describe how the objective will be achieved, you should check that the emphasis given each method matches the importance of the related objective. In our swimming example, recruitment of 70 children is probably the least important objective; demonstrating that 50 of them can pass the Red Cross test is more critical. To match the magnitude of the objectives with appropriate detail about the project, more emphasis should be placed on the testing than on recruiting. This refining and highlighting of information will enable the reader to understand the project and to have confidence in your agency.

The methods should appear doable; otherwise, you lose credibility. For example, if the swimming course is to be taught by an Olympic swimmer who remains anonymous, the reader might question whether the organization can deliver what it has promised. However, if the Olympic star is identified by name and has already agreed to run the program, the reader will likely be convinced.

When: The methods section should present the order and timing for the various tasks. It might make sense to provide a timetable so that the reader does not have to map out the sequencing on his or her own. The timetable could look like this one, excerpted from the Arts & Business Council of Miami's proposal. Note that the anticipated number of months to undertake each task is provided in parentheses.

PROJECT TIMELINE

1. Work directly with arts groups to reach over 100,000 patrons, donors, sponsors and arts participants by applying new ticketing solutions to venues throughout the tri-county. This will not require any additional investment on the part of the venue and will help support cultural activity by making it easier for performing groups to present at a variety of venues in the region. (12 months)

2. Leverage existing infrastructure to reduce total regional spending on ticketing operations throughout the cultural sector. (12 months)

3. Reach over 100 arts executives and broaden arts managers' understanding of customer service and audience development through a variety of training events offered through the Arts & Business Council. (6 to 9 months)

4. Enhance service levels for patrons of the arts by providing 24/7 Internet ticketing and a fully functioning call center open 7 days per week. (Final 3 months)

5. Encourage collaboration among 100 arts groups to help reach new audiences and attract new sources of funding via the web site. (Final 3 months)

6. Develop an Amplifying Arts Audiences task force made up of arts executives, arts board members, business executives and partners from local chambers, arts councils and related nonprofits. (Final 3 months of project)

Another presentation of a solid work plan comes from a proposal submitted to the Flinn Foundation by the Hualapai Tribal Health Department for the prior edition of this *Guide*. The timeline depicts a one-year project.

TIMELINE

	Oct	Nov	Dec	Jan	Feb	Mar	Apr	May	Jun	July	Aug	Sept
Planning for Diabetes Conference	⊢——⊣											
Schedule Work Site/School Site Screening	⊢———⊣											
Implement Diabetes Conference			|									
Conduct Monthly Work Site/ School Site Screenings			⊢————————————————————⊣									
Expand Individual Care Form					⊢——⊣							
Place Expanded Form into Practice					⊢———————————————⊣							
Develop Data Entry System					⊢——⊣							
Staff Training for Data Entry						⊢———⊣						
Data Entry							⊢—————————————⊣					
Data Analysis									⊢———————⊣			
Final Report											|	

The current staff member who works half time will be hired to work full time. No additional time is needed for hiring or training.

The timetable tells the reader "when" and provides another summary of the project that supports the rest of the methods section.

Why: You need to defend your chosen methods, especially if they are new or unorthodox. Why will the planned work lead to the outcomes you anticipate? You can answer this question in a number of ways, including using examples of other projects that work and expert testimony.

The methods section enables the reader to visualize the implementation of the project. It should convince the reader that your agency knows what it is doing, thereby establishing credibility.

Staffing/Administration

In describing the methods, you will have mentioned staffing for the project. You now need to devote a few sentences to discussing the number of staff, their qualifications, and specific assignments. Details about individual staff members involved in the project can be included either as part of this section or in the appendix, depending on the length and importance of this information.

"Staffing" can refer to volunteers, board members, or consultants, as well as to paid staff. Most proposal writers do not develop staffing sections for projects that are primarily volunteer-run. Describing tasks that volunteers will undertake, however, can be most helpful to the proposal reader. Such information underscores the value added by the volunteers and the cost-effectiveness of the project.

For a project with paid staff, be certain to describe which staff will work full time and which will work part time on the project. Identify staff already employed by your nonprofit and those to be recruited specifically for the project. How will you free up the time of an already fully deployed individual?

Salary and project costs are affected by the qualifications of the staff. Delineate the practical experience you require for key staff, as well as level of expertise and educational background. If an individual has already been selected to direct the program, summarize his or her credentials and include a brief biographical sketch in the appendix. A strong project director can help influence a grant decision.

Explain anything unusual about the proposed staffing for the project. It is better to include such information in the proposal narrative than to have the funder raise questions once the proposal review begins.

Three samples of staffing sections follow. The first is part of a proposal from Exalt Youth to the Brooklyn Community Foundation.

STAFFING

Exalt currently employs 7 full-time staff and 3 part-time staff. We have one part time Senior Teacher position vacant and are interviewing candidates.

Exalt is headed by founder/Executive Director, Sonja Okun, who developed exalt's award-winning, best-practices model at CASES, New York's oldest alternative-to-incarceration agency, in 1997. The Internship Program and its evaluation is overseen by our Director of Program Operations/External Relations, Gisele Castro. Program cycles are managed by the following additional staff members, all who have experience working with at risk youth: Program Coordinators Molly Birnbaum and Gabriel Higuera, Senior Teacher Nathaniel Quinn, and External Partner & Alumni Liaison, Alessandra DeAlmeida. All our staff members hold a minimum of a Bachelor Degree in areas ranging from business management, to African-American studies, anthropology, sociology, psychology and Government and Latin American studies.

Program staff members are responsible for:

- Communicating with the multiple external constituents that exalt interfaces and partners with from referral partners, to internship providers, families, judges and other organizations that may be serving our participants in capacities beyond Exalt's scope.

- Conducting assessment interviews of program candidates to gauge their interests, as well as educational, criminal justice and living status.

- Facilitating the pre and post pre-internship training components of our model, following a proprietary curriculum.

- Developing internships and determining appropriate matches for each individual participant.

- Reaching out to program graduates on a regular basis to encourage their connection to Exalt's support services.

The second example is from WINGS to The William Bingham Foundation.

DESCRIPTION OF STAFF

(A) Key staff members and their qualifications

Bridget Laird - Chief Executive Officer
Bridget has worked on the WINGS staff since 1998. Former Program Director at Memminger Elementary School, she develops programming, provides staff training and oversees reporting and evaluation activities. In 2008 she was recognized as a promising leader on the "Forty under 40" list in the Charleston Regional Business Journal. Bridget has an undergraduate degree in parks and recreation from North Carolina State University and a masters degree in education, with a concentration in school-age development from Concordia University in St. Paul, MN

Adam Pomerantz - Director of Business Affairs
Adam joined WINGS in 2009. Prior to doing so, Adam worked in commercial real estate development and received his MBA from The University of North Carolina's Kenan-Flagler Business School. He also taught sixth grade and coached the school's cross country team. Outside of work, Adam enjoys spending time with his wife, eating good food, and running and riding his bike.

Nicole Lovecchio - Chief Program Officer
Nicole joined the WINGS staff in 2002 and worked as Program Director at Memminger Elementary School for four years before successfully implementing a new program at Chicora Elementary in 2008 and then North Charleston Elementary in 2009. She has a degree in Criminal/Juvenile Justice from Shippensburg University, and spent two years at the South Carolina Department of Mental Health working with youth and their families. At WINGS Nicole designs and manages the implementation of our social and emotional curriculum at each of our programs. She is also responsible for the training of and performance of the staff within the programs, including the Program Directors.

Liz Mester - Director of Development
Liz has worked for WINGS in our corporate office since 2007, when she began as a part-time Administrative Assistant. She graduated from the College of Charleston in 2004 with a degree in Arts Management. Liz is responsible for raising money to meet organizational fundraising goals, which she achieves by writing grants and cultivating relationships with individuals who care about kids. Liz is also responsible for leveraging partnerships with individuals and corporations that exist in Charleston and out.

(B) Paid staff and volunteers

Full-time staff = 12
Part-time staff = 53
Volunteers = 90

(C) Consultants

Outside consultants are to be used for program evaluation purposes. A Blue Ribbon Panel of evaluation experts will be formed during the upcoming fiscal year to establish the guidelines for the formative and summative evaluations planned in fiscal years 2012–2014. The panel will be selected based on experience with program evaluations similar to WINGS and their influence with national foundations where future funds may be accessed.

Finally, here is a simple, straightforward staffing section from a proposal from the Claremont Neighborhood Centers, Inc.

STAFFING

Abraham Jones assumed the duties of Executive Director in 2006. Mr. Jones is responsible for overall program guidance and development including curriculum development; coordination of on-going staff training; and evaluation design for the program participants, staff, and overall program.

Claremont's Director of Children's Services, Nicole Coleman, is responsible for the ASEP's supervision and partial training of staff in addition to handling the day-to-day operations.

Carl Johnson is our Associate Executive Director who plays an active role in the After School Education Program. Mr. Johnson is responsible for the collection of fees, facilities management, center upgrade, parent relations, and staff supervision.

Our staff also includes paid instructors who work with the children and allow us to maintain a low adult to student ratio; this is critical in that individualized tutoring sessions often act as informal counseling sessions, allowing staff to better pinpoint areas of trouble for our students both in and out of the school environment.

Describe for the reader your plans for administering the project. This is especially important in a large operation, if more than one agency is collaborating on the project, or if you are using a fiscal agent. It needs to be crystal clear who is responsible for financial management, project outcomes, and reporting.

Evaluation

A key aspect of most project descriptions is the evaluation component of the grant proposal. This section of your proposal describes how you and the funder will know if the proposed project succeeds or not. In recent years this component of the proposal has become important enough to warrant a separate discussion in this *Guide* (see Chapter 6).

Sustainability

A clear message from grantmakers today is that grantseekers will be expected to demonstrate in very concrete ways the long-term financial viability of the project to be funded and of the nonprofit organization itself. Most of the grantmakers we interviewed indicate that they look for lists of current and prospective donors among the attachments to a proposal. This is high on the list of items they expect grantseekers to provide.

It stands to reason that most grantmakers will not want to take on a permanent funding commitment to a particular agency. David Egner of Hudson Webber Foundation previously identified this as a "risk area" for his foundation when delineating a list of items he looks for during the grant review process: "Is there an exit strategy for the foundation? Since we can't fund anything in perpetuity is there an immediate way out or one that we know is going to take a decade?"

Funders will want you to prove either that your project is finite (with start-up and ending dates); or that it is capacity-building (that it will contribute to the future self-sufficiency of your agency and/or enable it to expand services that might be revenue generating); or that it will make your organization attractive to other funders in the future. With the trend toward adopting some of the investment principles of venture capital groups to the practice of philanthropy, evidence of fiscal sustainability becomes a highly sought-after characteristic of the successful grant proposal. Think of what you are presenting as the plan to make your project sustainable. The details will fall into place as the project and your fundraising efforts unfold. Should your project be one-time, a pilot, or one that will soon be self-sustaining, hence not requiring future support, be sure to explain that to the funder.

Three examples of a sustainability section follow. The first is from the Lincoln Symphony Orchestra to Cooper Foundation.

LSO was well-prepared to continue our goal of sustainable growth during and after the recent nationwide economic downturn. We made relatively small expense-side reductions while continuing to expand our audience and donor bases. We are fortunate to have a committed group of consistent corporate supporters and granting organizations who value LSO's place in the community.

In June 2008, Barbara Zach attended the Orchestra Leadership Academy seminar on Annual Fund given by Paul Hogle, Development Director for the Atlanta Symphony. The seminar set forth many strategies for running an annual fund campaign, including an excellent model for board involvement and leadership. As part of Barbara's involvement in the Executive Leadership Program with the League of American Orchestras, she was given a grant of $7,500 to be used to further the work of LSO. The grant was used to bring in Paul Hogle in October 2008 to work with our board on strengthening and institutionalizing our fundraising plans. As a result, the board segmented our Annual Fund Campaign into three sub-committees: individual giving, corporate giving, and board giving. Each sub-committee has a chairperson that oversees giving within that category. We continue to explore the possibility of LSO board involvement in solicitation of planned giving through meetings with LSO Foundation president.

Next is from a proposal submitted to The Community Foundation for Greater Atlanta by Youth Ensemble Atlanta.

This grant will enable Youth Ensemble Atlanta to expand our community programming and productions, while increasing the opportunities for YEA to support itself through ticket sales and rental income for years to come. In fact, following this initial campaign for our original expenses, we expect the space to be able to pay for itself without further support from the funding community. Over the past four years, YEA has made huge strides in becoming financially stable and preparing to occupy a space of our own. We have operated with a surplus since our founding and have been able to increase earned and contributed revenue by more than 20 percent a year for the past five years.

We are projecting an annual operating expense increase of $60,000–90,000 including increased program, production, staff and facility expenses. These expenses will easily be covered by the estimated annual addition of $100,000 in ticket sales. We currently average $10,000–15,000 a week in sales in a 200-seat venue. We will be adding at least 10 more weeks of performances in a 600-seat venue, which will comfortably meet these initial projections. Surpluses will be set aside as cash reserves to help us purchase a space of our own in the future.

And the last example was submitted to Blue Ridge Foundation New York by Green City Force.

We aim to raise significant private funds to launch the organization in its first three years. The service and green jobs movements are attracting considerable attention, and based on initial conversations, we believe there are a good number of foundations and individuals who will be ready to contribute to the start-up phase.

In addition, we are exploring possibilities to access stimulus money related to weatherization, green jobs training and national service. Our initial partners are established organizations that have deep connections to the state energy and labor authorities, and are willing to work with us to joint fundraise and identify pots of money at the state level. There is a possibility that we might access $1 million to demonstrate projects related to greening the transportation system in NYC.

In the long run, we expect to sustain our work through: 1) contracts with city and state partners in areas such as auditing and weatherization, transportation, parks and recycling; 2) the Clean Energy Service Corps, expected to be created as part of the ServeAmerica and GIVE Acts and also proposed as a stand-alone by Representatives Inslee and Sarbanes. The CESC has been written to target disadvantaged youth, with a higher cost-per member allowance and higher level of funding from the federal government (over 70 percent of per-member costs); 3) training dollars, such as Green Jobs Act funds, for which youth corps are eligible; and 4) private contributions.

It behooves you to be very specific about current and projected funding streams, both earned income and fundraised, and about the base of financial support for your nonprofit. Here is an area where it is important to have backup figures and prognostications at the ready, in case a prospective funder asks for these. Some grantmakers, of course, will want to know who else will be receiving a copy of this same proposal. You should not be shy about sharing this information with the funder.

6

Developing the Proposal: The Evaluation

Evaluation of the effectiveness of programs and strategies is a growing trend among today's foundations and other nonprofit organizations, and one to which the proposal writer should pay special attention. The well-constructed evaluation component of a grant proposal is an increasingly important vehicle for describing how both the grant applicant and the potential funder will be able to tell how well the organization succeeds at what it proposes to do.

Viewed in this context, evaluation is far more than accountability for how grant funds will be used. Rather, it is a mechanism for organizational capacity building that will enable your nonprofit to excel at whatever it sets out to do. For this reason evaluation is most effective when it is conducted as a partnership between the funder and the nonprofit, with all stakeholders, including board members and those who will benefit from the grant project, engaged in its design. The best evaluation plans entail gathering both objective and subjective data that will contribute to learning by everyone involved with the grant project. As expressed by Phillip Henderson of Surdna Foundation, Inc., "The learning from individual grants is an important part of getting smarter." Evaluation as an activity should be ongoing, not something you think about once and then never revisit.

Evaluation in the context of grantmaking derives from the social sciences. As such, it has a specific vocabulary associated with it. Nonprofit grantseekers applying to U.S. foundations in the 21st century, especially the larger ones and those with staff, will encounter a variety of terminology related to evaluation in guidelines these funders set forth for their grant applicants. For complete definitions and an in-depth discussion of these various terms as they are commonly used by grantmakers, refer to *A Funder's Guide to Evaluation* by Peter York (2006).

The Evaluation Plan

Grantmakers are in agreement that it is essential for the nonprofit grantseeker to have a plan to evaluate its programs and strategies, and that a succinct description of that evaluation plan is a necessary ingredient of the successful proposal. Evaluation is not something that can be treated as an "add-on" at the end of the process of constructing the grant proposal. It needs to be built into the conceptual design of the grant project from the outset. To quote Laura H. Gilbertson of The William Bingham Foundation: "We want to see that an organization has internal mechanisms in place to evaluate programs. How do they decide if the program was a success? They need to learn to keep track for their own use."

Grantmakers indicate that they expect to see at least one or two paragraphs describing a well-thought-out evaluation plan and some projected indicators of success, either qualitative, quantitative, or both, laid out in the body of the proposal. In point of fact, more and more grantmakers, specifically prescribe what the evaluation component of your proposal should contain, and they will not consider applications that are missing this key element. For a number of the larger foundations whose leadership advocates for more rigorous evaluation on the part of nonprofits, the instructions for composing this section of the grant proposal can be quite extensive. Although *W.K. Kellogg Foundation Evaluation Handbook* is written primarily for the foundation's own project directors who have direct responsibility for the ongoing evaluation of the foundation-funded projects, it is a rich resource for grantseekers as it provides grantseekers with a framework for thinking about evaluation as a relevant and useful program tool. The publication is downloadable from the foundation's web site.

Typically the evaluation component of your proposal will be part of the project description. Depending on the nature of the project, the evaluation component of your proposal might be one or two paragraphs or one or more pages. It makes sense to match the scope and complexity of the evaluation component to that of the project. For example, if you are asking for funds to buy an additional computer for your agency, it is probably not necessary to develop an elaborate plan to assess its impact on your operations. On the other hand, if you are requesting a significant amount of funds to conduct a scientific experiment involving multiple researchers utilizing sophisticated equipment, you should provide details on specific mechanisms to determine whether the methodology described in your proposal will have achieved your goals and objectives and will have had the desired results.

Keep in mind that not all funders require a formal evaluation; some want monitoring reports only. In this case, it is up to you to first find out what is needed and then decide whether a formal evaluation plan is an essential aspect of the project or not.

Many of the grantmakers interviewed for this book, however, told us that a sound evaluation component based on measurable outcomes, is the hallmark of a proposal they are likely to fund. You will want to remain flexible about precisely how you will evaluate your project, because in discussions about the proposal, some funding representatives may want to further help you shape the evaluation. In the words of Bruce H. Esterline of The Meadows Foundation, Inc.: "We ask the applicant to tell us how they will measure their own effectiveness. Sometimes we have to prod them to be more deliberate and precise about what they are going to evaluate."

The Evaluation Plan and the Grant Report

Several funders, when asked about evaluation, referred immediately to grantee reports as the primary mechanisms for determining success. Indeed the "evaluative report" seems to be on many funders' minds. It stands to reason that having a solid evaluation plan in place will greatly facilitate the report on the use of funds that you will need to compile at the end of the grant project and may well lay the groundwork for future funding.

The form the actual evaluation plan takes will be different in each case, but is obviously closely tied to the initial objectives for the grant project and is designed with measurable outcomes in mind, so that the grantee will be able to report back about its accomplishments to the funder at the end of the grant period. As Richard M. Krasno of The William R. Kenan, Jr. Fund notes: "The report is our 'return-on-investment.' It does matter to us. We especially pay attention to the budget and to the progress with the project. Where are you with the project?"

To quote Victoria Kovar of Cooper Foundation: "I quite often go back to the original application when I am reviewing grant reports. Especially if I have a question about something. I will go back to the application and see what the organization said they would do. If the report does not follow the application, it is a problem. Especially in reporting about the financial outcomes, I really want to be able to compare the project budget as it was in the application with the final income and expense in a similar format so I can really make an apples-to-apples comparison. That is probably where reporting breaks down the most." Andrew Lark of The Frances L. & Edwin L. Cummings Memorial Fund describes the grantmaker's communications about reports: "We make it clear in our grant materials that there are reporting requirements—progress reports at the six-month mark and at the end of the year. Hopefully they have seen that before they approach us for the grant. The grant letter clearly reflects the expectations with regard to progress reports and the timing of them. We even send along the form to use so there are no surprises."

Beyond the very practical concerns of increasing one's chances at being funded, the well-conceived grant project quite simply requires some evaluative aspect to enable both grantee and funder to ultimately determine if it succeeds or not.

Types of Evaluation

Some evaluation plans measure the product; that is, the end result. Others assess the process; that is, the ongoing activities. You may find that either or both will be appropriate for evaluating your particular project, depending on the nature of your operations and the project's objectives. No matter which type of evaluation you choose, you will want to describe how you will collect the information you need, how data will be analyzed, and by whom.

Whether you are measuring the process, the product, or both, there are two types of data to gather: qualitative and quantitative. Most sound evaluation plans include both types.

Qualitative evaluation methods include interviews, focus groups, questionnaires, notes compiled by objective observers, and/or surveys. A picture of the whole that reflects multiple perspectives should emerge from these methods. For example, an evaluation of a swimming program for toddlers might include a formal observation and written notes regarding the instructional activities that comprise the swimming lessons and a parent questionnaire in order to understand how the techniques used affected the child's learning experience.

Quantitative evaluation methods are more formal in their execution and numerical in their output. Quantitative means are used to generate statistics that demonstrate the program's effectiveness, via such metrics as test scores or numbers of participants. For example, an evaluation of the same swimming program for toddlers might include the age and number of children participating and how many reached certain milestones and passed the swimming test.

Crafting the Evaluation Component

It is essential to describe your plans to evaluate your project in such a way as to clearly indicate that you are serious about honestly assessing its potential for success. If done well, evaluation answers the following questions: Did the desired outcomes occur? Did they result from the organization's intervention? Were the strategies adopted the correct ones, or were there approaches that would have been more effective? Is the impact on the nonprofit's audience discernible and will it last? The evaluation component you construct as part of the project description for your proposal should respond to as many of these questions as possible.

Putting together a solid evaluation module for your grant proposal is a skill that most grantseekers will want to develop. Today's grant decision-makers may well assume that a well-crafted evaluation plan is an indication of a well-run organization, one they can have confidence in and one that is worthy of their investment of funds. It instills confidence in the funder.

We already mentioned that it is critical to match the evaluation to the project. A key point to keep in mind also when writing the evaluation section of your proposal is that it should proceed in a linear fashion, from the objectives and activities of your project description to the anticipated outcomes and then to the ultimate impact on the audience you serve. This is sometimes referred to as "theory of change."

It is helpful to think of this linear progression in reverse chronological order as well. Start by envisioning the anticipated impact of your grant project, then list the outcomes, then the activities you will engage in to achieve these outcomes. This approach will help make your evaluation section compelling as it projects a vision of future accomplishments. Your evaluation should be the primary vehicle for assessing the degree to which the activities successfully meet the stated outcomes. It entails very specific indicators of success. This means you will need to have a vision for success (ideally a vision that the funder shares) when you set out to construct your evaluation component. And you will want to review and refer back to your objectives and activities to ensure that you can point to a causal relationship between the procedures you're adopting, the strategies behind them, and the outcomes of the project.

To help construct a solid evaluation component, ask yourself the following questions:

- What do you consider success to be? *engagement/growth*

- What do you suppose the funder considers success to be?

- Are you using qualitative or quantitative measures, or both?

- What specific evaluative mechanisms do you plan to utilize, e.g., observation, surveys, interviews, tests, etc.?

- What format will you use in the body of your proposal to depict the various stages of the evaluation, e.g., descriptive text, tables, charts, diagrams, etc.?

- Will the evaluation be performed by in-house staff or by an outside consultant? *evaluation will be performed by in-house staff*

What follows are several examples of evaluation components from grant proposals that funders shared with us. They are notable for their variety in content and format and tend to focus for the most part on assessment of the processes entailed in each grant project.

The first example is from a proposal that Project H Design submitted to Adobe Foundation. It lists specific tools to measure the two major objectives of the project.

For Studio H, we measure progress quantitatively and qualitatively inside and outside of the classroom. For our students, we measure their engagement and growth using metrics such as attendance, grade increase, overall participation, quality of work, communication skills, and improved design and production skills. Because the program lives within the public high school, we can also measure related successes in core subject classes, and standardized test scores. By June 2012, we will be able to measure the rate of college acceptance and enrollment by our current class of junior-year students, and connect such data to Studio H-specific factors.

Beyond the classroom, our Studio H projects for the community (i.e. the chicken coops and farmers market) can also be measured in the short and long-term. Metrics for the community are based on initial needs assessments we conducted before beginning Studio H (including, for example, poverty levels, average number of miles driven to purchase food and produce, community attendance to town functions, health and well-being, etc). Once our projects are completed, we can measure against these same metrics (which we will do in particular once the farmers market is built this summer), along with attendance and capacity metrics such as people visiting the farmers market, vendor sales, increase in average household income, diversity of products sold, demographic breakdown of usage, etc.

The next example was submitted by the Lincoln Symphony Orchestra to Cooper Foundation.

With help from the *Center for What Works* in Chicago and a team of board and staff members, LSO developed a dashboard reporting structure to enable the board to more efficiently track progress toward our long-range goals. The dashboard included metrics from all aspects of our strategic plan and goals. We found that the most useful information contained in the dashboard report was annual fund progress, so we have since modified our dashboard reports to focus on that key piece of our income.

A detailed bi-weekly update on progress toward annual fund goals is emailed to every board member. This report includes both income received and pledges in order to give a more accurate picture of our financial position. The update also includes the names of donors from that two-week period and their contributions compared to the previous year.

General concert evaluation is done through our staff meetings. Additionally, each staff member privately meets with the LSO executive director twice a month to discuss goals, work in progress, and to evaluate performance.

And here is the evaluation section of the Green City Force proposal to Blue Ridge Foundation of New York.

We will know we have been successful if:

- We recruit high-potential 17–25 year olds with barriers to employment (living in poverty, court-involved, aging out of foster care, …) (at least 75 percent of the corps), retain them, and connect them to career-track employment, further education, or entrepreneurship opportunities after graduating from the corps

- We have a measurable impact on reducing green-house gas emissions, increasing sustainability and otherwise contributing to meeting the goals of the city's climate action plan

- Employer partners are happy with our graduates and with the skills acquired by them through our program, and community based partners are happy with the service work provided by the corps members

- Graduate corps members perceive themselves as advocates for action on climate change, environmental justice and sustainability

- Green City Corps has helped to stimulate demand for green job creation
- Green City Corps has helped support passage and implementation of state and national legislation related to the Clean Energy Corps, expanding opportunities for youth, and there is interest in replicating Green City Corps in other cities.

Next is an example of the evaluation section from a proposal submitted by the Center for the Visually Impaired to The Community Foundation for Greater Atlanta.

CVI measures its effectiveness and efficiency in many ways. Every five years, CVI participates in a comprehensive evaluation of programs, practices and policies as part of our national accreditation process. With input from volunteers, staff, and clients, we conduct a self-study to assess CVI's effectiveness in meeting standards in 25 categories of education, services, and management. We are in the process of completing this evaluation at this time. In addition, we evaluate our effectiveness through quantitative outcome reporting of marketing, VisAbility store sales, and number of clients served in each program area. Our annual United Way evaluation uses a logic model for each funded program to measure success. Overall, the effectiveness of our work is evidenced by the success of our clients as they pursue their goals for independence.

There are many opportunities for qualitative evaluation, as well. A client advisory committee meets weekly with the rehabilitation services director to discuss concerns and plans for improving services. The president meets monthly with clients to discuss concerns or issues such as curriculum, community resources, personnel, safety, diversity or transportation. These assessment methods help us plan for future programming. Program and administrative directors conduct an annual cultural competency review to identify areas of progress and needs for improvement.

Organization wide, CVI measures the effectiveness of staff members and organizational productivity by setting and evaluating annual objectives that align with strategic plan initiatives. In August 2010, we completed a Trustee Engagement Survey to evaluate the engagement and satisfaction of CVI's Board members.

Finally, here is an example from the WINGS proposal to The William Bingham Foundation.

Above we have described how we measure success in terms of implementing our Flight Plan and our program; this work is done internally. On a day-to-day basis we use Efforts to Outcomes to evaluate our program, staff and kids.

Each WINGS site uses the Efforts to Outcomes, or ETO, success management system to track the progress that kids are making toward the desired outcomes. This work on the program model will pave the way for a formative evaluation to be conducted in the 2011/12 school year by an external evaluator. The purpose of the formative evaluation is to validate that the SEL learning objectives are being taught through the WINGS program model. During the 2012/13 school year, another external evaluator will conduct a summative evaluation using scientifically rigorous research methods to analyze the impact of the WINGS program on participants, and the extent to which the outcomes can be attributed to the program, as opposed to other factors.

In preparation for the formative and summative evaluation, WINGS will be creating an Evaluation Advisory Group. The 8–10 members will consist of nationally prominent direct service program evaluators, performance management experts and child development experts (with an understanding of social and emotional learning). This group will advise WINGS as we carefully shape the formative and summative evaluations. Oftentimes, programs who have little experience and expertise with research and evaluation are "taken by" evaluators and end up creating a study that addresses their interests, not in the interest of the program. The Advisory Group will be sure that does not happen. They will help create the RFP for outside evaluators and be involved in the selection process. This is just another example of WINGS going the extra mile to get it right.

Who Will Conduct the Evaluation?

Determining who will conduct the evaluation is often a challenge for the nonprofit grantseeker, but an essential aspect of the evaluation component of your proposal. Many grantseekers find evaluation quite intimidating, not only because of the potential costs of such an effort, but because they have little experience with it. The fact is that funders usually leave it up to the nonprofit to determine who will conduct the evaluation. And the vast majority of evaluations of most foundation grant projects are conducted by in-house program staff. When the nonprofit's own staff or volunteers engage in evaluative activities, therefore, it is important that they go beyond simply tracking program outputs to determining the actual outcomes of the grant project and the ultimate impact on the project's beneficiaries.

Outside evaluators employ their technical and professional skills in the application of rigorous design grounded in the social sciences to the evaluation plan and its implementation. These experts bring credibility, objectivity, research and analytical skills, and expertise that most nonprofits simply lack. They can also provide confidentiality in data gathering where needed. The types of evaluation that outside consultants typically conduct include formal needs assessments, environmental scans, financial analyses, focus groups, and interviews. Funders that require outside evaluators tend to be among the larger ones, and typically this requirement applies to complex, relatively expensive grant projects only.

Costs for evaluation is often a controversial issue, especially in a time when grant dollars are increasingly competitive to secure and funding preference is for direct service provision as opposed to administrative efforts. The good news for grantseekers is that often when an outside evaluator is required, the funder will either permit the nonprofit to include the cost of such an evaluation as a separate line item in the project budget or will provide its own evaluator.

Conclusion

Evaluation of a grant project is not something that the grantseeker should treat lightly. This outcomes-based means of measuring success is becoming as important in grantmaking as it is in business or government. When approaching what is still a daunting task for many proposal writers, the very first thing you should do is to find out exactly what the prospective funder's requirements are regarding evaluation of its grants. This information will help shape the construction of a useful evaluation plan and an effective evaluation component as part of the project description of your grant proposal. But evaluation is more than just what the funder wants. It is a guiding principle and an important mechanism for the nonprofit to ensure that it accomplishes what it sets out to do. It is evident that evaluation is fast becoming an important aspect of the grant proposal, and while not as significant as the statement of need or the budget, careful consideration and skill are required in putting it together.

7

Developing the Proposal: The Budget

The project description provides the picture of your proposal in words. The budget further refines that picture with numbers. A well-crafted budget adds greatly to the proposal reviewer's understanding of your project. Darin McKeever of The Bill & Melinda Gates Foundation says: "The budget is a very important document. In some ways it is a better statement of what is truly important in the sets of activities that are envisioned. It also gives me a sense of what level of sophistication that organization might have around its finance function, and that might give me additional assurance about the degree to which they operate efficiently and with accountability and what kind of help they might need to strengthen their finance function."

The budget for your proposal may be as simple as a one-page statement of projected expenses. Or your proposal may require a more complex presentation, perhaps a spreadsheet including projected support and revenue and notes explaining various items of expense or revenue. The most important point is also the most obvious. Phillip Henderson of Surdna Foundation, Inc. adds: "The only other thing I would say is really how critically important a good budget is because it really does tell the story and often, the difference between what is written in prose and what appears in the budget is a place where the conversation gets stuck. It needs to represent the true picture of what is going to happen. It is about being realistic about the costs. It requires real attention."

Expense Budget

As you prepare to assemble the budget, go back through the proposal narrative and make a list of all personnel and nonpersonnel items related to the operation of the project. Be sure that you list not only new costs that will be incurred if the project is funded but also any ongoing expenses for items that will be allocated to the project. Then get the relevant numbers from the person in your agency who is responsible for keeping the books. You may need to estimate the proportions of your agency's ongoing expenses that should be charged to the project and any new costs, such as salaries for project personnel not yet hired. Put the costs you have identified next to each item on your list.

It is accepted practice to include as line items in your project budget any operating costs of the agency that will be specifically devoted to running the project. Most commonly, these are the costs of supervision and of occupancy. If the project is large relative to the organization as a whole, these line items might also include telephone, utilities, office supplies, and computer-related expenses. For instance, if one of three office phone lines will be devoted to the project, one-third of the monthly cost of maintaining phone service could legitimately be listed as a project cost.

There are other costs incurred by your organization that benefit your project indirectly. These can be called overhead costs, administrative costs, supporting services, or shared costs. They are the costs of running your organization: rent, utilities, maintenance, general liability insurance, and staff to perform administrative duties, such as payroll or accounting functions. These items support all programs within your organization, and you would incur these costs whether or not you operated the particular project you are budgeting for. They are often referred to as the "indirect costs" of your project.

Examples of typical costs that might be considered indirect include:

- Administrative staff

- Equipment rental

- Insurance

- Legal fees

- Audit fees

- Meetings of the board of directors

- Occupancy (rent and maintenance)

- Utilities

Since some foundations will not award grants for general operating support, it is in your organization's best interest to try to recover a portion of these costs with each project grant you prepare. After all, your project could not exist if these overhead items were not available to support its activities. To accurately depict the full costs of your project, you need to allocate some of these costs to your project.

There are two methods commonly used to add indirect costs to a project budget. The first, which is by far the most common, entails adding a percentage for indirect costs. Some funders have an allowable percentage of your project's direct costs that you can add for indirect costs. A second method is a line item by line item allocation. In this method you identify specific overhead expenses that you will add to your project budget based on certain formulas. Both methods require consultation with your organization's financial officer, bookkeeper, or other accounting professional.

It is important to include indirect costs in your project budgets because programs do not exist in isolation. You need funding from some source to cover these costs—to pay for your organization's support services (such as the bookkeeper, fundraiser, or your human resources department) and to pay for other overhead items, such as rent and telephone expenses.

Funders may have policies regarding the percentage of overhead that they will allow in a project budget. Some do not allow any overhead at all to be included. If possible, you should find out about the overhead policy before submitting your proposal to a particular foundation, because you may need to explain to that funder how you will cover overhead costs from other sources.

Your list of budget items and the calculations you have done to arrive at a dollar figure for each item should be summarized on worksheets. You should keep these to remind yourself how the numbers were developed. These worksheets can be useful as you continue to develop the proposal and discuss it with funders. They are also a valuable tool for monitoring the project once it is under way and for reporting after completion of the grant.

A portion of a worksheet for a year-long project might look like this:

Item	Description	Cost
Executive director	Supervision	10% of salary = $10,000 Benefits at 25% = $2,500
Project director	Hired in month one	11 months full time at $45,000 = $41,250
Tutors	12 working 10 hours per week for 13 weeks	12 x 10 x 13 x $10.00 = $15,600
Office space	Requires 25% of current space	25% x $20,000 = $5,000
Overhead	20% of project cost	20% x $74,350 = $14,870

With your worksheets in hand, you are ready to prepare the expense budget to accompany your grant proposal. For most projects, costs should be grouped into subcategories, selected to reflect the critical areas of expense. All significant costs should be broken out within the subcategories, but small ones can be combined on one line. It is common practice to divide your expense budget into personnel and nonpersonnel costs. Personnel subcategories might include salaries, benefits, and consultants. Subcategories under nonpersonnel costs might include travel, equipment, and printing— just to name a few items—with a dollar figure attached to each line.

Three expense budgets follow. The first example is from New York Cares, submitted to The Frances L. & Edwin L. Cummings Memorial Fund.

New York Cares
Sophomore Skills, SAT Prep, College Prep and FAFSA
FY12 Program Budgets

FY12 Expenses	% FTE	
Children's Education		
Manager, Children's Education	85	$ 31,450.00
Manager, Children's Education	85	$ 30,600.00
Director, Education Programs	20	$ 10,800.00
Seasonal Staffer from July–Oct. @ $18/hr for 40 hrs/wk		$ 11,520.00
Volunteer Recruitment and Training		
Director, Volunteer Relations	6	$ 3,276.00
Partner Relations Manager	10	$ 4,200.00
Volunteer Relations Manager	10	$ 3,700.00
Volunteer Relations Manager	10	$ 3,500.00
Leadership Development Officer	13	$ 6,305.00
Leadership Development Manager	13	$ 5,680.61
Communications		
Manager, Publications and Productions	4	$ 1,520.00
Online Marketing Manager	7	$ 3,255.35
Technology		
Business Applications Development Officer	4	$ 2,040.00
Technology Manager	4	$ 2,200.00
Director of Technology	4	$ 3,677.12
Senior Director of Programs	6	$ 5,280.00
Benefits (22%)		$ 28,380.90
Subtotal Personnel		**$157,384.98**
Direct OTPS		
Extra Material Costs ($1,200/Soph Skills site, $215/SAT site, and $80/College Prep site)		$ 23,400.00
Printing/Copying		$ 5,500.00
Supply/Delivery (storage, delivery of Kaplan materials)		$ 3,100.00
Volunteer/Student Recognition		$ 2,500.00
Occupancy 2.30 FTE x $4,857 per FTE		$ 11,171.00
Subtotal Direct OTPS		**$ 45,671.00**
Indirect Expenses (10% for insurance, phones, etc.)		**$ 7,405.19**
Project Total		**$210,461.17**

The second example is from the Goddard Riverside Community Center proposal to The Frances L. & Edwin L. Cummings Memorial Fund.

VI. Expense Budget

Expenses

Director of Training	$68,000
Fringe Benefits	$23,800
Total Expenses	$91,800

The final example is from Exalt Youth to the Brooklyn Community Foundation.

Annual Cost

The total annual cost of Exalt's Internship Program is $599,000. The main budget categories are as follows:

Personnel - $385,000
Participant Stipends - $90,000
Participant Travel - $17,000
Program Activities - $12,000
Rent/Utilities - $37,000
Insurance - $16,000
Telecom/IT - $15,000
F&E - $8,000
Supplies/postage/copying - $8,000
Professional Fees - $7,000
Miscellaneous Expenses - $4,000

Support and Revenue Statement

For the typical project, no support and revenue statement is necessary. The expense budget represents the amount of grant support required. But if grant support has already been awarded to the project, or if you expect project activities to generate income, a support and revenue statement is the place to provide this information.

In itemizing grant support, make note of any earmarked grants; this will suggest how new grants may be allocated. The total grant support already committed should then be deducted from the "Total Expenses" line on the expense budget to give you the "Amount to Be Raised" or the "Balance Requested."

Any earned income anticipated should be estimated on the support and revenue statement. For instance, if you expect 50 people to attend your performance on each of the four nights it is given at $10 a ticket, and if you expect that 20 of them will buy the $5 souvenir book each night, you would show two lines of income, "Ticket Sales" at $2,000 and "Souvenir Book Sales" at $400. As with the expense budget, you should keep backup worksheets for the support and revenue statement to remind yourself of the assumptions you have made.

Because an earned income statement deals with anticipated revenues, rather than grant commitments in hand, the difference between expenses and revenues is usually labeled "Balance Requested," rather than "Amount to Be Raised." The funder will appreciate your recognition that the project will earn even a small amount of money—and might well raise questions about this if you do not include it in your budget.

Now that your budget is complete, take the time to analyze it objectively. Be certain that the expense estimates are neither too lean nor on the high side. If you estimate too closely, you may not be able to operate within the budget. You will have to go back to funders already supporting the project for additional assistance, seek new donors, or underwrite part of the cost out of general operating funds. None of these alternatives is attractive.

Consistently overestimating costs can lead to other problems. The donor awards a grant expecting that all of the funds will support the project, and most will instruct you to return any funds remaining at the end. If you have a lot of money left over, it will reflect badly on your budgeting ability.

This will affect the funder's receptiveness toward any future budgets you might present.

Finally, be realistic about the size of your project and its budget. You will probably be including a copy of the organization's financial statements in the appendix to your proposal. A red flag will be raised for the proposal reviewer if the budget for a new project rivals the size of the rest of your operation.

If you are inexperienced in developing proposal budgets, you should ask your treasurer or someone who has successfully managed grant funds to review it for you. This can help you spot obvious problems that need to be fixed, and it can prepare you to answer questions that proposal reviewers might raise, even if you decide not to change the budget.

Budget Narrative

A budget narrative portion is used to explain any unusual line items in the budget and is not always needed. If costs are straightforward and the numbers tell the story clearly, explanations are redundant.

If you decide a budget narrative is needed, you can structure it in one of two ways. You can create "Notes to the Budget," with footnote-style numbers on the line items in the budget keyed to numbered explanations. Or, if an extensive or more general explanation is required, you can structure the budget narrative as straight text. Remember, though, that the basic narrative about the project and your organization belong elsewhere in the proposal, not in the budget narrative.

The following is an example of a budget with an accompanying footnoted narrative from a proposal of Canal Community Alliance.

Canal Community Alliance
Radio Canal Remote Studio Project Budget

Project Expenses	CCA	Amount Requested				Project Budget	Notes
		Milagro Foundation	Marin Arts Council	The Bothin Foundation			
Construction of office and studio space	$8,250					$ 8,250	a
Mixing Board				$ 4,000		4,000	b
MAC I Book				1,800		1,800	c
Pro-Tools Music Editing Software				1,500		1,500	d
Microphones		$ 250				250	e
Microphone stands		100	$150			250	f
Headphones			270			270	g
Speakers			80	20		100	h
1 Dual CD player		500				500	i
2 CART machines		1,200		1,750		2,950	j
Dedicated telephone line				550		550	k
Internet services for a year				200		200	l
Furniture				1,400		1,400	m
Carpet				1,500		1,500	n
Cables and wire adapters				400		400	o

Project Expenses	CCA	Milagro Foundation	Marin Arts Council	The Bothin Foundation	Project Budget	Notes
2 Wood doors with small window				650	650	p
Sound proofing material and installation		700		800	1,500	q
Curtains/drapes for windows				400	400	r
Radio Engineer @ $50/hr x 50 hours				2,500	2,500	s
Total Expenses	**$8,250**	**$2,750**	**$500**	**$17,470**	**$28,970**	

a. Remodeling and construction of office and studio space at CCA Teen Center.

b. Mixing board will be used to produce interviews and radio segments.

c. Laptop computer will be used in the production room which is a former closet and has no room for a desktop computer.

d. Music editing software for 3 computers @ $500 each

e. 5 mikes x $50 each

f. 5 mike stands x $50 each

g. 6 headphones @ $45 each

h. 4 speakers @ $25 each

i. CD player will be used to play music on the air.

j. Radio cart machines will be used to record and play PSAs, radio segments, and interviews. This includes one DLPS Cart-play @ $1,150 and one DLRS Cart-record @ $1,800.

k. Installation of a phone line for transmitting radio signal to and from San Rafael High School's transmitter.

l. Cost for DSL internet service for one year.

m. Furniture for meetings and production use. This includes a round table with chairs, 3 desk chairs, & a table for the mixing board.

n. The teen center does not have any carpet. Carpet is needed for Radio Canal's office and studio space.

o. Cables and wiring for installing equipment.

p. 2 solid wood doors with a small window for production rooms; includes installation.

q. Sound proofing material and installation.

r. Curtains will be used as part of soundproofing on a wall with windows.

s. Technical consultant to select, wire and install all radio equipment.

The budget, whether one page or several, is now ready to be included in the proposal document. Keep a copy of it with your backup worksheets in a special folder. The materials in this folder will assist you in tracking actual expenses as the project unfolds. They will enable you to anticipate lines that are in danger of going over budget or areas where you might have extra funds to spend, so that you can manage effectively the grant funds that you receive. These materials will also be extremely helpful when it comes time to write the grant report. An example of a program budget can be found in the sample proposal in Appendix A.

8

Developing the Proposal: Organization Information and Conclusion

Organization Information

Normally the résumé of your nonprofit organization should come at the end of your proposal. Your natural inclination may be to put this information up front in the document, but it is usually better first to sell the need for your project and then to sell your agency's ability to carry it out.

It is not necessary to overwhelm the reader with facts about your organization. This information can be conveyed easily by attaching a brochure or other prepared statement or by providing brief information and then referring the funder to your organization's web site, if you have one. In one page, tell the reader when your nonprofit came into existence; state its mission, being certain to demonstrate how the subject of the proposal fits within or extends that mission; and describe the organization's structure, programs, and special staff expertise. Here is an example from the WINGS proposal to The William Bingham Foundation.

ORGANIZATION INFORMATION

History
Since 1996, WINGS has been running innovative, results-driven programs in public elementary schools serving Charleston's most impoverished neighborhoods. Today we serve more than 435 kids at four elementary schools every day.

Milestones in History

1996–97   WINGS founded and Summer camp model developed

2000–01   Afterschool program model developed at Memminger Elementary School

2003–05   Middle School and Summer Day Camp model developed

2006–07   Decision made to focus on further development of afterschool program model using Memminger as a lab school

2006–07   Field-tests conducted with eight programs NOT run by WINGS

2007–08   Making use of field tests model further refined; performance management system designed and implemented at Memminger

2008–09   WINGS replicates program at Chicora Elementary; continues Memminger Elementary; serves total of 265 kids

2009–10   WINGS replicates program at North Charleston Elementary; continues Memminger Elementary and Chicora Elementary programs; serves total of 375 kids

2010–11 WINGS Founder takes flight; New CEO, Bridget Laird inducted; WINGS replicates program at James Simons Elementary; continues Memminger Elementary, Chicora Elementary, and North Charleston Elementary programs; serves a total of 435 kids

Mission

WINGS is an education program that teaches kids how to behave well, make good decisions, and build healthy relationships. We do this by weaving a comprehensive social and emotional learning curriculum into a fresh and fun after school program. Kids get the life lessons they need to succeed and be happy and they get a safe place to call home after school.

Discuss the size of the board, how board members are recruited, and their level of participation. Give the reader a feel for the makeup of the board. (You should include the full board list in the appendix.) If your agency is composed of volunteers or has an active volunteer group, describe the functions that the volunteers fill. Provide details on the staff, including numbers of full- and part-time staff and their levels of expertise.

Describe the kinds of activities in which your staff engage. Explain briefly the assistance you provide. Describe the audiences you serve, any special or unusual needs they face, and why they rely on your agency. Cite the number of people who are reached through your programs.

Tying all of the information about your nonprofit together, cite your agency's expertise, especially as it relates to the subject of your proposal.

This information, coupled with the attachments you will supply in the appendix, is all the funder will require at this stage. Keep in mind that funders may wish to check with other sources to learn more about your organization and its performance. These sources might include experts in the field, contacts established at organizations similar to your own, other funders, or even oversight organizations, which issue reports on aspects of nonprofit management and fundraising.

In the next example, East Side House briefly describes its history to The Frances L. & Edwin L. Cummings Memorial Fund.

History and Mission

Founded in 1891, East Side House Settlement is one of New York City's oldest not-for-profit community service organizations. Supported by a dedicated Board of Managers and a creative professional staff team, East Side House has the experience and stability to develop, implement, evaluate and sustain innovative programs that are based on the unique needs of the South Bronx. East Side House has always been committed to improving quality of life for constituents, rooting our efforts in educational attainment in accordance with our mission statement:

> *"East Side House is a community resource in the South Bronx. We believe education is the key that enables all people to create economic and civic opportunities for themselves, their families and their communities. Our focus is on critical developmental periods—early childhood and adolescence—and critical junctures—points at which people are determined to become economically independent. We enrich, supplement and enhance the public school system and place college within reach of motivated students. We provide services to families in order that other family members may pursue their educational goals. We provide technology and career readiness training to enable students to improve their economic status and lead more fulfilling lives."*

East Side House serves over 8,000 children, teens, adults and seniors each year from 16 program sites. Maintaining its focus on education and building character, the agency offers a comprehensive network of services which range from educational programs and emergency assistance to casework and counseling.

Current Programs

In the face of the severe demographics of our community, East Side House is committed to helping the people of the South Bronx develop their educational and employment skills and thus break-away from the destructive cycle of their environment. By designing services that are tailored to the social, cultural and economic fabric of South Bronx, East Side House is able to attract thousands of children and adults to come together to share, learn and better themselves and their community. Through innovative and comprehensive programming, East Side House has helped thousands of children and teens take important steps for their future through access to higher education or meaningful employment. As a result, East Side House has built a strong reputation in the South Bronx as a trusted community resource. Our core programs and services include:

- Early Childhood Program—offers educational and health services to children in preschool through 1st grade.

- After School Programming—provides critical academic/ cultural enrichment in a nurturing environment to elementary school age children in grades K to 8.

- Summer Programming—provides academic reinforcement for youth during the critical summer months.

- College Preparatory and Leadership Program at the Mott Haven Village Preparatory High School—a local college preparatory high school in which East Side House is the founding partner; students are provided a wide range of college preparation/access support services.

- Bronx Haven High School—a newly opened school for students who are over-age and under-credited and would be unable to graduate from a traditional high school.

- Youth & Adult Education Services—provides pre-GED/GED educational services, technology training, career services, college preparation, and counseling.

- Social Services Program—social workers help families remove obstacles to education and career development.
- Community Technology Services—state-of-the-art computer labs which provides Internet access to the community along with various technology classes. These services are critical to our various youth/educational/employment initiatives.

Conclusion

Every proposal should have a concluding paragraph or two. This is a good place to call attention to the future, after the grant is completed. If appropriate, you should outline some of the follow-up activities that might be undertaken, to begin to prepare your funders for your next funding request.

This section is also the place to make a final appeal for your project. Briefly reiterate what your nonprofit wants to do and why it is important. Underscore why your agency needs funding to accomplish it. Don't be afraid at this stage to use a bit of emotion to solidify your case.

The first example is excerpted from a CityKids proposal.

CONCLUSION

During the past 20 years CityKids engaged over 20,000 disadvantaged young people through our free, after-school, in-school, weekend, and summer arts-based leadership development programs. We bring together young people from different racial, cultural, and socioeconomic backgrounds in a safe environment; challenge them to better themselves and their communities; support them in developing the skills to succeed; and partner with them to produce positive solutions. A $10,000 grant from the Early Riser Fund will allow CityKids to continue to provide high-quality Support Services to New York City's at-risk youth. We hope you will join us as we lay the groundwork for a more hopeful future.

The second example is from the New York Cares proposal to The Frances L. & Edwin L. Cummings Memorial Fund.

CONCLUSION

The New York Cares model of service meets critical needs of hundreds of agencies and the people they serve. While we have several supporters for our college preparation programming, more are needed to further develop these critical services. A $50,000 grant from the Frances L. and Edwin L. Cummings Memorial Fund would enable New York Cares to expand our Sophomore Skills, SAT Prep, College Prep and FAFSA programs—helping more than 1,400 disadvantaged high school students citywide to attend college and, ultimately, break the cycle of poverty.

9

Variations on the Project Proposal Format

In the preceding chapters we presented the recommended format for components of the standard proposal. In reality, however, not every proposal will slavishly adhere to these guidelines. This should not be surprising. Sometimes the scale of the project might suggest a letter format proposal, or the type of request might not require all of the proposal components or the components in the sequence recommended here. The guidelines and policies of individual funders will be your ultimate guide. In any case, you will want to refer to the basic proposal components (see Chapter 2) to be sure that you have not omitted an element that will support your case.

What follows is a description of a letter proposal and of other format variations.

A Letter Proposal

The scale of the project will often determine whether it requires a letter or the longer proposal format. For example, a request to purchase a $300 fax machine for your agency simply does not lend itself to a lengthy narrative. A small contribution to your agency's annual operating budget, particularly if it is a renewal of past support, might also warrant a letter rather than a full-scale proposal.

What are the elements of a letter request? For the most part, they should follow the format of a full proposal, except with regard to length. The letter should be no more than three pages. You will need to call upon your writing skills because it can be very hard to get all of the necessary details into a concise, well-articulated letter.

As to the flow of information, follow these steps while keeping in mind that you are writing a letter to an individual funding representative. It should not be as formal in style as a longer proposal would be. It may be necessary to change the sequence of the text to achieve the correct tone and the right flow of information.

Here are the components of a good letter proposal from Operation Exodus Inner City.

Ask for the gift: The letter should state why you are writing and how much funding is required from the particular foundation.

Dear Donor:

I am pleased to be in touch with The Susan A. and Donald P. Babson Charitable Foundation on behalf of Operation Exodus Inner City (Exodus). I write today to request your consideration of a $5,000 grant for our **After School Program**, which provides approximately 300 children with educationally enriching activities and instruction five days a week. As budget cuts have struck nearly every school in the nation, academic enrichment programs such as ours are more important than ever.

Describe the need: In a compelling manner, tell the funder why there is a need for this project, piece of equipment, etc.

Exodus was founded in 1988 to respond to the needs of the Washington Heights community. Ninety-nine percent of Exodus' students are Latino, and many families served are recent immigrants to the United States. In a community where over half of the Latino students drop out of school, Exodus is proud to report that, for the last nine years, we have **maintained a 100 percent graduation rate**. This is particularly impressive given that many of our graduating students were the first in their families to earn a high school diploma.

Based on our reputation as a trusted resource in the Washington Heights community, Exodus expanded our programming to a second site last year, so that we can take in students enrolled in other local youth programming on the verge of shutting down. This expansion more than doubles the number of students Exodus serves with minimal increase to our operating costs. We are proud to have been selected for this ambitious project, and look forward to supporting additional youth through our uniquely tailored educational activities.

Explain what you will do: Just as you would in a fuller proposal, provide enough detail to pique the funder's interest. Describe precisely what will take place as a result of the grant.

After School Program

Founded in 1998, our **After School Program** serves approximately 300 students and operates five days per week from 3:00–7:00pm September through June. Our program maintains a 10:1 student to teacher ratio which allows students to receive the individualized attention they are not given during the school day, focusing on building critical thinking skills in the key areas of literacy and mathematics. The purpose of the After School Program is fourfold:

1) Compensate for the lack of quality public school education in the Washington Heights community;

2) Equip our students with grade level reading, math, comprehension and writing skills, including building students' fluency in English;

3) Inspire a love of learning in our students; and

4) Provide a safe, nurturing environment where students can be themselves and steer away from potentially dangerous behavior.

Our After School Program is the only comprehensive program of its kind in the entire Washington Heights neighborhood. Every child is admitted into the program, regardless of age or ability.

Thus, our program is more accommodating of the varying types of students we serve. Further, Exodus understands the difficult circumstances facing many of our families. Oftentimes, parents work until late at night and cannot pick their children up from school. Therefore, we provide a "pick up" service as well as an extended day program.

Each day, Exodus provides at least one hour of **Instructional Time**, drawing from the following academic curricula:

- *Kidzlit*, designed by the Developmental Studies Center, includes age appropriate books and instructional material and focuses on building students' vocabularies, and improving reading comprehension and critical thinking skills.

- **The 100 Book Challenge**, an American Reading Company curriculum created by teachers, curriculum specialists, and literacy activists, is an incentive based program that employs a color coding/leveling system which helps participants to find and self-select books at their independent reading level.

- ***Kidzmath***, designed by the Developmental Studies Center, includes game kits and book and story guide kits for children in two age groups, K–2, and 3–6.
- **Box Cars and One-Eyed Jacks**, a new curriculum which Exodus will pilot this year which uses cards, dice, and special multi-sided dice to teach math.

Projected Annual Outcomes

The following outlines Exodus' specific annual targets:

Outcome 1: Students develop grade level reading, math, comprehension and writing skills.
Outcome 2: Students achieve annual grade promotion.
Outcome 3: Students successfully graduate from high school.

Include appropriate budget data: Even a letter request may have a budget that is a half-page long. Decide if this information should be incorporated into the letter or in a separate attachment. Whichever course you choose, be sure to indicate the total cost of the project. Discuss future funding only if the absence of this information will raise questions.

Close: As with the longer proposal, a letter proposal needs a strong concluding statement. But it can be short and concise.

<u>**Conclusion**</u>

Since our beginning, Operation Exodus Inner City has been deeply committed to improving the lives of the children and families of Washington Heights. Our programs work consistently to fulfill that commitment, helping to inspire a love of learning and equip young people with the skills they need to realize their dreams and goals. It is our hope that The Susan A. and Donald P. Babson Charitable Foundation will partner with us and support our **After School Program** in the upcoming year.

If you should have any questions or require any additional information, please do not hesitate to contact me. I can be reached by phone at (212) 543-3305 or by email at Matt@OperationExodus.org. Thank you for your consideration of this request; I look forward to hearing from you.

Attach any additional information required: The funder may need much of the same information to back up a small request as a large one: a board list, a copy of your IRS determination letter, financial documentation, and brief résumés of key staff. Rather than preparing a separate appendix, you should list the attachments at the end of a letter proposal, following the signature.

It may take as much thought and data gathering to write a good letter request as it does to prepare a full proposal (and sometimes even more). Don't assume that because it is only a letter, it isn't a time-consuming and challenging task. Every document you put in front of a funder says something about your agency. Each step you take with a funder should build a relationship for the future.

Other Variations in Format

Just as the scale of the project will dictate whether a letter or a full proposal is indicated, so the type of request will be the determining factor as to whether all of the components of a full proposal are required.

The following section will explore the information that should appear in the proposal application for five different types of requests: special project, general purpose, capital, endowment, and purchase of equipment.

SPECIAL PROJECT

The basic proposal format presented in earlier chapters uses the special project proposal as the prototype, because this is the type of proposal that you will most often be required to design. As stated previously, foundations tend to prefer to make grants for specific projects because such projects are finite and tangible, and their results are measurable.

GENERAL PURPOSE

A general purpose proposal requests operating support for your agency. Therefore, it focuses more broadly on your organization, rather than on a specific project. All of the information in the standard proposal should be present, but there will not be a separate component describing your organization. That information will be the main thrust of the entire proposal. Also, your proposal budget will be the budget for the entire organization, so it need not be duplicated in the appendix.

Two components of the general purpose proposal deserve special attention. They are the need statement and program information, which replaces the "project description" component. The need section is especially important. You must make the case for your nonprofit organization itself, and you must do it succinctly. What are the circumstances that led to the creation of your agency? Are those circumstances still urgent today? Use language that involves the reader, but be logical in the presentation of supporting data. For example, a local organization should cite local statistics, not national ones.

The following is an example of a need statement from a general purpose proposal submitted by The Frazer Center to The Community Foundation for Greater Atlanta.

We are an inclusive community-enabling people with disabilities to be a part of what everyone else is and to be embraced as a member who belongs. According to U.S. Census data, 12 percent of metro Atlanta's population has an intellectual disability. Our goal is to provide the best model for including all people together in productive educational, volunteer and work experiences. Our Children's Program brings kids of all abilities in the same class to learn from each other, and our Adult Program helps the clients become more independent. But there is more we will do. Our strategic plan calls for us to partner with universities and similar organizations to explore how we can advocate for and implement best inclusive practices. To help us expand and enhance our programs, we are seeking operational support. A Common Good grant will allow us to meet our infrastructure costs, such as utilities which increased 27 percent in FY2010. While we are improving our programs, we also want to ensure that our participants stay enrolled. The majority of our adults rely on Medicaid waivers to attend the Center. We spend $25,000 annually to guarantee that our Medicaid submissions are accurate or we risk a client losing coverage. Because we serve children with high medical and therapy bills and from low-income families, 20 percent receive financial aid that totals $130,000 a year. With your investment, we will be able to meet our strategic plan initiatives and ultimately provide a model inclusive community.

Studies show the fastest growing population of nursing home residents is adults 31–64 years old with disabilities. Many families feel their only choice is to place their loved one with special needs in a traditionally geriatric facility—or quit their jobs to care for them. We are one of the few day programs offering an alternative for adults with mild to severe disabilities. We provide educational programs and a community where the participants interact with their peers—and can continue living with their families. For those adults seeking greater independence, we help them identify appropriate jobs, train them, and then support them working at area businesses. We are also one of the few childcare programs that accommodates children with a wide variety of special

needs. We adjust our curriculum to ensure everyone is fully
included in activities, and consult with families to monitor
their child's development and navigate the extensive network
of available resources. Our inclusive program also helps
typically developing children learn that kids who are different
can be friends. Thanks to our early intervention and engaging
curriculum, children leave our program ready to succeed—and
to be fully included with peers—in area schools.

Consider including details on recent accomplishments and future directions,
as seen in this additional excerpt from The Frazer Center proposal.

After finishing our 2005–2010 plan, we embarked on a year-
long internal and external analysis. Our new strategic plan,
approved in November 2010, describes who we are, what we
stand for, and where we are going. Our new mission statement
reaffirms our historical commitments while articulating our
vision for our next 60 years: the inclusive community. Our
guiding principles state what is most important to us. Our five
strategies outline our direction and priorities. The detailed
action plan is a pragmatic, executable map that will enable
us meet our goals over the next 60 months. It is also a
management tool that frames accountability and resource
allocation. We will calibrate decisions and direction against
our plan to ensure they are consistent with our goals. The six
board committees meet regularly and are responsible for their
specific goals. The Strategic Planning Committee will review
our progress every six months and recommend to the Board
any necessary adjustments.

Notably, our first strategic goal is to establish best practice
standards for every level of our work. After completing a year-
long strategic planning process, we hired a new Executive
Director, rewrote our governance policies, restructured our

board committees and added a new Governance Committee. We understand that to offer strong programs, we must operate optimally. Quality of service is central to our operations and we were honored that both our Children and Adult programs were recently reaccredited by their respective monitoring agencies. These successful reaccreditations—along with the annual survey results of our program participants, stakeholders and staff—speak to the effectiveness of our management and operations. Our annual independent audit reports have also shown marked improvement since the hiring of our Director of Finance in 2008. To maintain disciplined fiscal control, our management team reviews financial statements monthly and Board reviews them bimonthly. Finally, we provide ongoing professional development for staff and encourage board members to take classes through the Community Foundation and Georgia Center for Nonprofits. We will increasingly utilize these opportunities to help meet our strategic goals.

With our new Executive Director, engaged Board Members and an exciting strategic plan, we are poised to do even more for people with disabilities in Atlanta. We rely on donations from foundations, individuals and other organizations to provide 20 percent ($726,595) of our annual revenue. Support from the Common Good Fund at $75,000 a year for two years will cover 10 percent of that goal. Receiving this grant will be vital to helping us achieve our goals, especially in this very challenging economy.

CAPITAL

A capital proposal requests funds for facility purchase, construction, or renovation, or possibly land purchase or long-term physical plant improvements. Today many institutions include other items in a capital campaign, such as endowment funds, program expansion, and salaries for professors. But, for our purposes, we will discuss the more traditional definition of capital, that is, "bricks and mortar."

All of the components of a proposal will be included in a capital request. Differences in content will be found mainly in the need statement, the project description, the budget, and the appendix.

The need section in a capital proposal should focus on why the construction or renovation is required. The challenge is to make the programs that will use the facility come alive to the reader. For example, your agency may need to expand its day care program because of the tremendous need in your community among working parents for such support, the long waiting list you have, and the potential educational value to the children. Your proposal will be less compelling if the focus of the need statement is purely related to space considerations or to meeting building code requirements.

Following is an excerpt from a capital proposal for Lollypop Farm, the Humane Society of Greater Rochester.

NEED STATEMENT

Lollypop Farm has been pushing the boundaries of what a shelter can do for 135 years. Our tireless dedication to helping animals is bringing a new face to animal shelters and is an inspiration to countless other shelters across the country.

We are committed to building lifelong bonds between people and animals through education, community outreach programs and the prevention of cruelty. Over 70 staff members and more than 800 volunteers enable Lollypop Farm to provide food and shelter for homeless animals, adoption services, Pet Assisted Therapy, pet loss support, dog obedience training, veterinary pet assistance, a spay/neuter incentive program for low income individuals, no cost adoption services for senior citizens, summer farm camp, humane education and animal cruelty investigations. It is fortunate to be acknowledged for doing some of the best project-based work in the field and having the most pet-friendly shelter facilities in upstate New York.

We at Lollypop Farm, the Humane Society of Greater Rochester, envision a time when our community celebrates the human/animal bond; embraces the mutual benefits therein; and treats all fellow beings with care, compassion and respect. Day in and day out, we use every resource available to us to save the lives of animals and get them to a new "forever" home. But now we are out of space as services, staff and volunteers have increased dramatically since our "Shelter of Hope" was built in 1999. The following table documents the dramatic increase in demand for services and a growing organization committed to meeting these growing needs:

Services	1999	2010
Admissions	8,200	11,370
Adoptions	4,024	6,584
Surgeries	2,255	7,856
Staff	39	82
Volunteers	368	878

To continue to serve the communities of the Greater Rochester Area, Lollypop Farm must raise $4 million to expand its facility.

The project description component of a capital proposal includes two elements. The first is the description of how your programs will be enhanced or altered as a result of the physical work. Then should come a description of the physical work itself. The funder is being asked to pay for the latter and should have a complete narrative on the work to be undertaken. You might supplement that description with drawings, if available. These could be external views of the facility, as well as interior sketches showing people using the facility. Floor plans might help as well. These need not be formal renderings by an artist or an architect; a well-drawn diagram will often make the case. Photos showing "before" and drawings indicating what the "after" will be like are also dramatic adjuncts to the capital proposal.

The budget for a capital proposal will be a very detailed delineation of all costs related to the construction, renovation, etc. It should include the following:

- *Actual brick-and-mortar expenses:* These should be presented in some logical sequence related to the work being undertaken. For example, a renovation project might follow an area-by-area description, or a construction project might be presented chronologically. Don't forget to include expenses for such items as construction permits in this section.

- *Other costs:* Salaries, fees, and related expenses required to undertake the capital improvements should be included. Be certain to include in your budget the projected costs of architects, lawyers, and public relations and fundraising professionals. Many capital proposal writers fail to adequately anticipate such "soft" costs.

- *Contingency:* Estimates for actual construction costs often change during the fundraising and preconstruction periods. It is therefore a good idea to build a contingency into the budget in case costs exceed the budgeted amounts. A contingency of 10 to 20 percent is the norm; more than that tends to raise a proposal reviewer's eyebrows.

Here is the budget for Lollypop Farm's construction project.

CAPITAL EXPANSION DETAILED BUDGET

Expense	Amount
New Cat Holding and Vet Clinic	840,000
New Training Center	726,920
New Offices above training	490,000
Renovated Cat Room	252,000
Adoption Center Area	121,800
Converted Get Acquainted Room	13,920
Converted Small Animal	20,250

Intake Office	17,280
Intake Waiting	22,400
Convert to Office and Storage	51,200
Convert to Behavior	14,400
Cage wash	5,568
Miscellaneous Site Work	40,000
Fixtures, Furniture, Equipment	250,000
Farmyard area improvements	250,000
Professional Fees	280,000
Campaign Costs (additional staffing, consultant, supplies, etc.)	300,000
Maintenance Reserve	304,262
Total Expense	**$4,000,000**

The appendix to a capital proposal may be expanded to include floor plans and renderings if they do not appear within the proposal text. If a brochure has been developed in conjunction with the capital campaign, this could be sent along as part of the appendix package.

ENDOWMENT

An endowment is used by a nonprofit to provide financial stability and to supplement grant and earned income. Often campaigns, designed like capital drives, are mounted to attract endowment dollars. A proposal specifically requesting funding for endowment may resemble either a special project or a general operating application, depending on whether the endowment is for a special purpose, such as scholarships or faculty salaries, or for the organization's general operations. Your focus will be on the following components: the need statement, the program description, and the budget.

The need statement for an endowment proposal will highlight why the organization must establish or add to its endowment. Points to raise might include:

- the importance of having available the interest from the endowment's corpus as an adjunct to the operating budget;

- the desire to stabilize annual income, which is currently subject to the vagaries of government or other grants;

- the value of endowing a particular activity of your organization that lacks the capacity to earn income or attract gift support.

The project description will cover the impact of endowment dollars on the programs of your nonprofit. Provide as many details as possible in explaining the direct consequences of these dollars. Indicate if there are naming or memorial opportunities as part of the endowment fund.

The budget will round out all of these data by indicating how much you are trying to raise and in what categories. For example, there might be a need to endow 75 scholarships at $10,000 each for a total of $750,000.

EQUIPMENT

Frequently, organizations have a need to develop a free-standing proposal for purchase of a piece of equipment, be it MRI equipment for a hospital or a personal computer for program staff. Purchasing a piece of equipment might require only a brief letter proposal, but the scale or significance of the purchase may dictate a full proposal. Again, the need statement, the project description, and the budget will be primary.

In the need statement, explain why the organization must have this equipment. For example, "This hospital has no MRI equipment, and people in the community have to travel great distances when an MRI test is required."

Then in the project description, explain how the equipment will alter the way services are delivered. For example: "The new MRI equipment will serve some 500 people annually. It will assist in diagnoses ranging from structural problems in the foot to tracking the development of a lung tumor. The cost per procedure will be $1,000, but it will save millions in unnecessary surgical procedures."

This budget may be the easiest you will ever have to prepare. Indicate the purchase cost for the equipment, plus transportation and installation charges. Consider whether staff training to utilize the equipment properly and the added expenses of maintenance contracts should be included in your budget with the cost of its purchase.

10

Packaging the Proposal

Writing a well-articulated proposal represents the bulk of the effort in preparing a solid proposal package. The remaining work is to package the document for the particular funder to whom it is being sent, based on your research and your contact with that funder to date (as described in Chapters 11 and 12).

Be sure to check the foundation's instructions for how and when to apply. Some foundations will accept proposals at any time. Others have specific deadlines. Foundations will also differ in the materials they want a grant applicant to submit. Some will list the specific information they want and the format you should adopt. Others will have an application form. Some are posting these on their web sites. Whatever the foundation's guidelines, pay careful attention to them and follow them.

Grantmakers are extremely frustrated with applicants who do not take the time to find out what is in their application guidelines. It is in the grantseeker's best interest to follow the grantmaker's advice. Otherwise there are delays in reviewing the application while the grantmaker waits for the missing items.

Of equal concern to grantmakers is the submission of attachments that are not required by the guidelines. Nonprofit applicants would be well advised to refrain from adding any unnecessary attachments—ever! Rather, interesting items not included in the proposal package might be sent to the prospect as part of good cultivation later on.

In the following pages we will discuss the packaging of the document, including:

- cover letter;

- cover and title pages;

- table of contents; and

- appendix.

The Cover Letter

Often the cover letter is the basis for either consideration or rejection. As Hildy Simmons, formerly of J. P. Morgan Private Bank, told us in the past, "The cover letter is key. It should be clear and concise and make me want to turn the page. Here are a few dos and don'ts:

- Do make a specific request. It's inconvenient if we have to dig for it.

- Do include a couple of paragraphs about why you are applying to us. But don't quote back to us our own contribution report.

- Do note references but don't name drop."

Danielle M. Reyes of Eugene and Agnes E. Meyer Foundation suggests: "This is a place to get a little more animated and personal. It is a great opportunity to emphasize something that may not jump out in the proposal." Jane G. Hardesty of John H. and Wilhelmina D. Harland Charitable Foundation, Inc. notes: "We are very interested in hearing what your needs are. But we also need to marry your needs with ours as the grantmaker." Andrew Lark of The Frances L. & Edwin L. Cummings Memorial Fund adds: "If you have more than one project idea, sketch out the other idea here."

What a waste of your agency's resources to invest time, energy, and money developing a proposal around a terrific project and then not have it read! To avoid this happening, be clear, be succinct, and state immediately why the project fits within the funder's guidelines. For example, you might state, "Our funding research indicates that the XYZ Foundation has a special interest in the needs of children in foster care, which is the focus of this proposal." If the proposal does not fit the foundation's guidelines, this should be acknowledged immediately in the cover letter. You will then need to provide an explanation for why you are approaching this foundation.

If you had a conversation with someone in the funder's office prior to submitting the proposal, the cover letter should refer to it. For example, you might say, "I appreciate the time Jane Doe of your staff took to speak with me on December 1 about the Foundation." But do not imply that a proposal was requested if in fact it was not.

Sometimes in a discussion with a funder you will be told, "I can't encourage you to submit because... However, if you want, you can go ahead and submit anyway." In this case, you should still refer to the conversation, but your letter should demonstrate that you heard what the funder said.

The cover letter should also indicate what the reader will find in the proposal package. For example: "You will find enclosed two documents for your review. The first is a concise description of our project. The second is an appendix with the documents required by the Foundation for further review of our request."

Cite the name of the project, a précis of what it will accomplish, and the dollar amount of the request. For example: "Our After School Recreational Program will meet the educational and recreational needs of 50 disadvantaged Harlem children. We are seeking a grant of $25,000 from the Foundation to launch this project."

In the concluding paragraph of the cover letter, you should request a meeting with the funder. This can take place at the funder's office or on site at your agency. Also indicate your willingness to answer any questions that might arise or to provide additional information as required by the funder.

In summary, the cover letter should:

- indicate the size of the request;

- state why you are approaching this funder;

- mention any prior discussion of the proposal;

- describe the contents of the proposal package;

- briefly explain the project; and

- offer to set up a meeting and to provide additional information.

Who should sign the letter? Either the chairman of the board or the chief executive officer of your agency should be the spokesperson for all proposal submissions. Some funders insist on signature by the chairman of the board, indicating that the proposal has the support and endorsement of the board. However, signature by the executive director may allow for a sense of continuity that a rotating board chair cannot provide. If your group has no full-time staff, then the issue is resolved for you, and the board chairman should sign all requests. This would hold true also if your agency is in the process of searching for a new chief executive.

The proposal cover letter should never be signed by a member of the development staff. These individuals do the research, develop the proposals, and communicate with the funder, but generally they stay in the background when it comes to the submission of the proposal and any meetings with the funder. The individual who signs the cover letter should be the same person who signs subsequent correspondence, so that the organization has one spokesperson.

Variations may occur under special circumstances. For example, if a board member other than the chairperson is directly soliciting a peer, the cover letter should come from him or her. Alternatives would be for the letter to be signed by the chairman of the board and then for the board member to write a personal note on the original letter, or to send along a separate letter endorsing the proposal.

Here is an example of a cover letter from Goddard Riverside Community Center to the Cummings Memorial Fund. It includes:

- a specific request;

- a description of broader impact; and

- an offer to meet.

October 7, 2010

Ms. Elizabeth Costas
Executive Director
The Frances L. & Edwin L. Cummings Memorial Fund
501 5th Avenue, Suite 708
New York, New York 10017-6103

Dear Libby:

It is my pleasure to submit to The Frances L. & Edwin L. Cummings Memorial Fund the enclosed proposal requesting support for a new Director of Training position for the Options Center. The Options Center (formerly known as the OPTIONS Center for Educational and Career Choice) is Goddard Riverside Community Center's successful college access program. We appreciate your providing the extra time we requested to complete our proposal package.

The Options Center provides both direct service to help underrepresented young people gain admission to college and professional development and training to professionals who work with this population. The Options Center has experienced tremendous success and growth over its 25 year history. In light of this, and the increasing national attention to the urgent need for greater college access and success, Goddard Riverside embarked on a strategic planning process for the Options Center.

Over the next five years we are committed to expanding professional development and training activities, improving data collection and assessment, broadly disseminating evidence-based practices, and taking a larger role in advocacy, policy, and research. We ask that The Frances L. & Edwin L. Cummings Memorial Fund make a grant of $50,000 to enable us to create the position of Director of Training.

The enclosed proposal, copy of the Options Strategic Plan, and proposed staffing structure for Options provide additional information about our plans. If you have any questions or would like to discuss our request further, please feel free to call me.

> Thank you again for the Fund's previous support of Goddard
> Riverside Community Center and for your consideration of
> our request.
>
> Sincerely,
>
> Stephan Russo
> Executive Director
>
> Encl.

Here is another example of a cover letter. This is from WINGS to The
William Bingham Foundation. It conveys:

- excitement;

- updated information; and

- a sense of commitment.

> May 13, 2011
>
> Ms. Laura Gilbertson
> The William Bingham Foundation
> 20325 Center Ridge Road, Suite 629
> Rocky River, OH 44116
>
> Dear Laura,
>
> WINGS is having a watershed year; our Founder took-flight, and
> after 12 years with WINGS, I moved into the Chief Executive
> Officer position. In addition, The University of Virginia just
> received a $2.8 million grant to conduct research on WINGS.
> The evaluation will consist of a randomized control trial—the
> gold standard of evaluations—and will be conducted over a

four-year period at WINGS, beginning in 2012. We could not be more excited—and we hope you're proud of the hatchling you invested in that is now soaring.

WINGS is moving into our 4th year of implementing our 5-year Flight Plan (strategic plan). Our Board is determined to continue it's commitment to patience and diligence even though the economic conditions and pressure to grow fast make it much more difficult to stay on the flight path.

It is our hope that the William Bingham Foundation will make a gift so that we will have you by our side as we take final steps to assure that WINGS will benefit thousands of children every year. With WBF's support, we will continue to fly high!

With tremendous respect,

Bridget Laird
Chief Executive Officer

Cover Page and Title

The cover page has three functions:

1. to convey specific information to the reader;

2. to protect the proposal; and

3. to reflect the professionalism of the preparer.

You should personalize the information on the cover page by including the name of the funder. You might present the information as follows:

> **A PROPOSAL TO THE XYZ FOUNDATION**

or

> **A REQUEST DEVELOPED FOR THE XYZ FOUNDATION**

Then note the title of the project:

> **A CAMPAIGN FOR STABILITY**

Provide key information that the funder might need to contact your agency:

Submitted by:
The Nonprofit Organization
40 Canal Street
New York, NY 10013
url: nonprofit.org
phone: 212-935-5300

Mary Smith	Susan Jones
Executive Director	Director of Development
212-935-5323	212-935-5321
212-935-9660 (fax)	212-935-9660 (fax)
e-mail: msmith@aol.com	e-mail: SJones@aol.com

It is possible that your cover letter will be separated from the rest of the proposal once it arrives at its destination. Without key information on the cover page, the funder could fail to follow up with your agency. You are being kind to your prospective funder when you remember to add the following:

- phone extension or direct telephone line for both the person who signed the letter and a primary staff contact;

- fax number for your organization; and

- e-mail addresses for both the signer and staff contact, if available, since it is becoming increasingly common for funding representatives to contact the grantseeker via e-mail with questions and requests for additional documentation.

The cover page from the East Side House proposal serves as an example.

EAST SIDE HOUSE

**A Request for Funding to
The Seth Sprague Educational and Charitable Foundation for
East Side House Settlement's
College Preparatory and Leadership Program**

Submitted by:
John A. Sanchez
Executive Director
East Side House, Inc.
337 Alexander Avenue
Bronx, NY 10454
Tel 718.665.5250
Fax 718.585.1433
jsanchez@eastsidehouse.org

The title you assign to your proposal can have a surprisingly significant impact on the reader. It should reflect what your project is all about. "A CAMPAIGN FOR STABILITY" tells the reader that there is a formal effort taking place and that the result will be to bring stability to the nonprofit organization. It is short and to the point, while being descriptive.

There are a few suggestions for developing the title for a proposal:

• Don't try to be cute. Fundraising is a serious matter. A cute title implies that the proposal is not a serious attempt to solve a real problem.

• Do not duplicate the title of another project in your agency or one of another nonprofit that might be well known to the funder. It can cause confusion.

• Be sure the title means something. If it is just words, try again, or don't use any title at all.

Coming up with the title can be a tricky part of proposal writing. If you are stuck, try these suggestions:

- Seek the advice of the executive director, the project director, or a creative person in the organization or outside.

- Hold an informal competition among staff and/or volunteers to see who can come up with the best title.

- Go to the board with a few ideas and ask board members to select the one that makes the most sense.

- Jot down a list of key words from the proposal. Add a verb or two and experiment with the word order.

Let's take a look at a few actual titles and evaluate their effectiveness.

Title	Effectiveness
Forward Face	Arouses interest but does not tell you anything about the project. This is a proposal that seeks funds for facial reconstruction for disfigured children. With the help of the nonprofit group involved, the children will have a new image with which to face the future. The title is a pun, which is cute but not very effective.
Vocational, Educational Employment Project	This title tells us that three types of services will be offered. The project serves disadvantaged youth, which is not mentioned. The effectiveness of this title could be improved if the population served were somehow alluded to.

Title	Effectiveness
Building a Healthier Tomorrow	This title implies that construction will occur, and indeed it is the title for a capital campaign. It also suggests that the construction is for some kind of health facility. This proposal is for a YMCA to improve its health-wellness facilities. Thus, the title is very effective in conveying the purpose of the proposal.

You should evaluate any titles you come up with by anticipating the reaction of the uninitiated funding representative who will be reading this proposal.

Table of Contents

Obviously, for letter or formal proposals of just a few pages, a table of contents is not required. For proposals of five pages or more, a table of contents is essential.

Simply put, the table of contents tells the reader what information will be found in the proposal. The various sections should be listed in the order in which they appear, with page numbers indicating where in the document they can be located. The table should be laid out in such a way that it takes up one full page.

Following the proposal format we have recommended, a table of contents would look like this:

TABLE OF CONTENTS	PAGE
Executive Summary	1
Statement of Need	2
Project Description	4
Budget	7
Organization Information	9
Conclusion	10

By stating where to find specific pieces of information, you are being considerate of the proposal reader, who might want an overview of what information is included and also might want to be selective in the initial review.

A sample follows. It is from a proposal for the Rochester Area Crime Stoppers.

TABLE OF CONTENTS	
Executive Summary	1
Need for Crime Stoppers	2
Project Description	3
Core Budget	6
Organizational Background	7
Conclusion	6

The Appendix

The appendix is a reference tool for the funder. Include in it any information not included elsewhere that the foundation or corporate grantmaker indicates is required for review of your request. Not every proposal requires an appendix.

The appendix should be stapled together or bound separately from the proposal narrative. Because it usually contains information that the funder has specifically requested, keeping it separate makes it easy for the funder to find those items. The appendix may have its own table of contents indicating to the reader what follows and where to find it.

A sample table of contents to a proposal appendix, taken from the Operation Exodus Inner City proposal, follows:

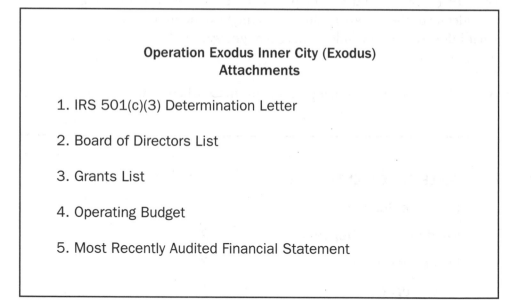

Operation Exodus Inner City (Exodus)
Attachments

1. IRS 501(c)(3) Determination Letter

2. Board of Directors List

3. Grants List

4. Operating Budget

5. Most Recently Audited Financial Statement

You may wish to include any or all of the following items in the appendix:

1. *A board list.* This should contain the name of each board member and that person's business or other affiliation, along with the person's title. The reader will use this to identify people he or she knows or whose names are familiar. It is helpful to indicate the officers of the Board.

An excerpt from the board list of King Manor Museum serves as an example:

2. *Your nonprofit's IRS Letter of Determination.* This document, issued by the IRS, indicates that your agency has been granted 501(c)(3) status and is "not a private foundation." Gifts made to your organization are deductible for tax purposes. This letter is usually requested by funders. Foundations can give most easily to publicly supported organizations,

and corporations want their gifts to be tax deductible. If your organization is religiously affiliated or a government entity, you might not have such a letter, and you should explain that fact to the funder.

3. *Financial information.* The operating budget for the current fiscal year and the latest audited financial statement or balance sheet are often appropriate to include. Some funders request your latest 990 in order to assess the financial stability of your organization. If your agency is religiously affiliated, or if for some other reason you do not file a 990, you will need to explain this fact to a funder that requests it. You may want to include a list of donors for the past fiscal year by name and size of gift. Grantmakers also want to know which foundations and corporations currently are being approached to help with the project under review, as well as who has already funded the project. An excerpt from Operation Exodus Inner City's support list follows.

Operation Exodus Inner City
List of Supporters*

FUNDING SOURCES	2010–2011
American Chai Trust	$1,000
American Eagle Outfitters Foundation	$5,000
Assurant Foundation	$2,500
Lily Auchincloss Foundation	
The Rose M. Badgeley Charitable Trust	$5,000
Banco Popular	
Barker Welfare Foundation	$10,000
Edith C. Blum Foundation	$1,000
Booth Ferris	$65,000
Robert Bowne Foundation	
Collegiate Reformed Church	$5,000
Colgate Palmolive	
ACF Compassion Capital Fund	
Con Edison	$2,000
Daniels Foundation	
The Max and Victoria Dreyfus Foundation	$5,000
Fifth Avenue Presbyterian Church	$2,500

The Glickenhaus Foundation	$2,500
William T. Grant Foundation	
The Heckscher Foundation for Children	
Hope for New York	$75,000
Hyde & Watson Foundation	$10,000
JPMorgan Chase Foundation	
Marble Collegiate Church	
Marsicano Foundation	$1,750
Medical Center Neighborhood Fund	$1,000
Metzger-Price Fund, Inc.	$1,000
Newman's Own	
New York Mercantile Exchange Foundation	
Partnership for Parks	
Pinkerton Foundation	$60,000
Rite Aid Foundation	
Ronald McDonald House Charities	$5,000
Edith Glick Shoolman Children's Foundation	$15,000
TJX Foundation	$5,000
Ushers New Look Foundation	
U.S. Airways Education Foundation	
Valentine Perry Snyder Fund	
Varnum De Rose Trust	
Verizon Foundation	
Washington Square Fund	$20,000
Laura B. Vogler Foundation	$3,000
Zale Foundation, M.B. & Edna	
TOTAL	**$303,250**

*Note: OEIC's fiscal year begins September 1st and ends August 31st.

4. *Resumés of key staff.* If the background information on key staff members is not included as part of the project statement of the proposal, it should be included in the appendix.

5. *Organizational chart.* Include this if you feel it would be helpful.

Do not include in the appendix anything that is not required by the funder or deemed essential to making your case. The key is to give the funder what is needed for review of your proposal without making the package look overwhelming. For example, many nonprofits like to add press clippings to the appendix. If they make the package appear unnecessarily bulky and are tangential to the grant review, they should be sent to the funder at another time when they will receive more attention. However, should these clippings be essential to the review of the request, then by all means include them.

At this stage of assembling the proposal, you have a cover letter and two additional separately packaged components: the proposal narrative and the appendix. If each is clearly identifiable, you will save the funder time and energy in the initial review of your proposal.

Packaging

Packaging refers to both the physical preparation of the documents and their assembly.

PHYSICAL PREPARATION

Every proposal package should be individually prepared for each funder. This permits you to customize the submission in order to reflect the interests of a specific funder and to show them that you've done your homework. This is the point at which you need to double-check the guidelines for a funder's specific requirements for the proposal package. David D. Weitnauer of R. Howard Dobbs, Jr. Foundation, Inc. warns: "We are looking for complete information. We want every question answered on the application and we want every item on the attachment list included." Paula Boyce, Grants Administrator for McInerny Foundation (Bank of Hawaii, trustee) underscores: "Even with specific guidelines, I can take two proposals and put them side by side and one will be easier to read than the other because one will have followed the guidelines explicitly."

With computerization, it is relatively easy to customize the cover letter, title page, and other components of the package that have variables in them. For those components that are photocopied, be sure that the originals you are working from are crisp and legible. For example, if your IRS Letter of Determination is in poor condition, write to the Internal Revenue Service at

I.R.S., Exempt Organizations Determinations, P.O. Box 2508, Cincinnati, OH 45201, and ask for a fresh copy of the letter. The request must be on your organization's official letterhead. The letter should contain your organization's name, address, taxpayer ID number, and a daytime telephone number, and it must be signed by an officer with that person's title. For the other documents, copy from originals whenever possible.

ASSEMBLY

When a proposal arrives in a funder's office, any binding is usually removed before the proposal is reviewed. Therefore, do not waste money on binding for the proposal and the appendix. Simply staple each document, or use a binder clip to hold together each document.

You have three documents: the cover letter, the proposal, and the appendix. The latter two are separately stapled. In all likelihood, these documents will require a manila envelope. Be certain that the addressee and return address information are printed clearly on the envelope. You might want to put a piece of cardboard in the envelope to protect the documents. Then insert the three documents with the cover letter on top, followed by the proposal and the appendix.

With regard to the funder's address, if you are following the procedure recommended in Chapter 12 for submitting the request, you will have had a conversation with the funder's office prior to submitting the proposal. Use that opportunity to verify the address and the name of the person to whom the package is to be sent.

11

Researching Potential Funders

Early on in the proposal process it is essential that you identify the foundations and corporations you will be asking to support your organization. With this list of potential supporters in hand, you will be able to tailor your proposal to the unique funding interests of each grantmaker.

In this chapter we review the principles of effective research and the factors to consider in shaping your list of prospective funding sources. Then we describe the types and uses of resources available to create your prospect list, and the steps to take in assessing the best prospects for your organization.

The Importance of Doing Your Homework

The key to success is doing your homework. Identifying potential funders requires serious, time-consuming research, but most grantseekers determine that it is well worth the effort. The foundation and corporate executives we interviewed for this *Guide* consistently advise grantseekers to pay special attention to the research effort. Amy Scop of The California Wellness Foundation cautions: "Know who it is that you are applying to and do the research." Andrew Lark of The Frances L. & Edwin L. Cumminigs Memorial Fund, Inc. adds: "If you do not do your research it will backfire because it will be pretty evident. The worst thing you can do is call a foundation office and ask questions that are easily solved by just reading materials on the foundation's web site."

The objective of your funding research is to find funders who have the same interests and values as your organization. Foundation trustees and staff generally care deeply about the problems of society and struggle to determine the most effective strategies they can use to produce the greatest impact with their funding dollars. When they describe their programs on their web site or in their printed literature, or when they announce new areas of interest, these are the result of careful planning and strategy. As a grantseeker it is your responsibility to thoroughly review all the available information about a funder to determine if your organization's programs are a potential match with the funder's stated interests. William V. Engel of The Hyde and Watson Foundation notes: "Grantseekers are reviewing our guidelines and looking at our web site. They are drilling down into the data. This makes our work easier."

As you conduct your research, be realistic in your expectations. Foundations and corporations cannot meet all, or even most, of your needs. The vast majority of the money given to nonprofits is actually donated by individuals. As already noted, foundations and corporations currently provide less than 20 percent of all philanthropic dollars, but their grants can make up an important part of your support.

Before You Begin

Successful fundraising depends on making the right match between your organization and appropriate funders. And, as in most relationships, both parties must have common interests and motivations for that relationship to work. Determining your options for funding from foundations and corporations requires a thorough examination of where these common interests converge. Before you begin the research process it is a good idea to review your organization's attributes and clearly define its program and financial needs so that you can match those requirements to funders' potential interest and capacity to give. Your objective here is to think of your organization's work in ways funders will connect to it. Ask yourself the following questions:

- *Do you have a clear picture of the purpose of the program or project for which you are seeking support?* It is generally a good idea to have at least a detailed outline of your project or a preliminary proposal in hand before you begin your foundation and corporate funding research. What you have written about your organization's unique characteristics, and the specific details of your project, will equip you with the facts and terminology you need to find funders with similar interests.

- *What is your organization's mission?* Know your organization's guiding principles and fundamental goals. For example, let's assume you represent an organization whose mission is "to strengthen the lives of diverse communities by assisting individuals in attaining their goals for self-sufficiency." Think about the important concepts here—"strengthen the lives of diverse communities" and "attaining their goals for self-sufficiency"—and how these key phrases might connect to funders with similar missions or stated programmatic interests.

- *Can you describe the audiences served by your organization's programs?* Does your organization serve the general population, or does it address the needs of one or more specific racial, ethnic, age, gender, or other group, such as Asians, Latinos, immigrants, people with disabilities, women, or youth?

- *Where does your organization operate its programs?* You should be able to describe the geographic scope of your organization's programs. Do the programs have a national or international focus, or are there specific countries in which your organization operates?

- *What are the distinctive features of your project/organization?* Are you collaborating with, or do you have an affiliation with another organization? Do your services generate income? Are you creating a model program that other organizations can replicate? Does your organization provide direct services, or are you an advocacy or research group? Your organization or project may have other features that distinguish its activities. In each example here, there are some funders that may look more favorably on an organization that meets one or more of these criteria.

- *Do you know the total dollar amount needed from foundations for your organization or project?* When you create an outline for your proposal, you will be deciding whether you are seeking general support for your organization or support for a specific project. If you are seeking project support, you must create a budget to determine the amount of money you will need for a specific time frame (see Chapter 7). Then, you will determine how much of the funding you need is likely to come from one or more foundations and corporations versus other sources.

- *What is the grant amount you are seeking?* Before you start your research it can be helpful to consider the general size of the grants you are seeking. This, in turn, will help you gauge the number of funders you will need to fully fund your project. For example, if your project budget is $80,000, are you seeking four grants of $20,000 each, or two grants of $40,000 each? Your organization's annual budget and the size of the project budget, as well as the giving capacity of various funders and their typical grant range, will help determine the answer to this question.

The Research Process

Once you have taken a careful look at your organization's program, its specific assets, and the ways it can connect to funder interests, you are ready to create your prospect list. Researching potential sources of grants is a two-step process. First, you compile a list of prospects that is as comprehensive as possible. Second, you refine your list by researching all the available information on each funder. And that step will help you to evaluate each prospect to ensure that there is a good "fit." At the same time, you will prioritize the top prospects among your potential supporters.

Step 1: Creating Your Preliminary Prospect List

In this first step of the research process, you are looking for funders who meet, at least, these two important criteria:

- Program interests that match your organization's needs or have a demonstrated pattern of giving in your area of interest; and

- Giving in the geographic area in which your organization operates, or no stated restrictions as to where they give.

Like the individuals and corporations who established them, foundations and corporate giving programs differ dramatically from each other in their giving interests. A number of key resources will help you focus on those funders whose priorities most closely match your organization's interests. Try to be inclusive at this first stage for your research. If preliminary investigation makes you think that a specific foundation or corporate donor should be on the list, go ahead and include it. Let further research you conduct on that funder tell you otherwise.

These resources will help you compile your prospect list:

- Foundation and corporate databases and directories

- News sources

- Grantmaker web sites and publications

- IRS Form 990-PF

AVAILABILITY OF RESOURCES

In accordance with its mission of strengthening the social sector by advancing knowledge about philanthropy in the U.S. and around the world, the Foundation Center provides free public access to funding resources at five library/learning centers (in New York, Atlanta, Cleveland, San Francisco, and Washington, DC) and more than 450 funding information centers located in public libraries, community foundations, and educational institutions nationwide and around the world. Visitors to the five Center-operated sites have access to the Center's databases, its content-rich web sites (including grantspace.org, the Center's learning community for the social sector), and a vast collection of fundraising and philanthropic materials. The Center-affiliated funding information centers also provide free access to the Center's databases, the Center's web sites, and a core group of other Center publications. The balance of the fundraising materials available are unique to each site and often reflect the regional focus of the collection. The Center provides free and fee-based training in the grantseeking and proposal writing process at its library/learning centers and beyond, as well as online learning opportunities.

FOUNDATION AND CORPORATE DATABASES

Because of its broad coverage of the grantmaking universe and its ability to search for multiple funder characteristics, many grantseekers start their research with the Foundation Center's highly regarded *Foundation Directory Online*. The *Foundation Directory Online* is available at several subscription levels, each providing access to additional information. These examples assume you are using the highest subscription level, the *Foundation Directory Online Professional*, which contains more than 100,000 foundations, corporate donors, and grantmaking public charities, and over 2.8 million recent grants. You can find potential funders by using four separate databases devoted to Grantmakers, Companies, Grants, and 990s, or by using Power Search, which allows you to type in your own search terms to search across nine Foundation Center databases—in addition to the four databases, news, jobs, RFPs, nonprofit literature, and PubHub reports.

FOUNDATIONS

Grantmakers database. A good initial strategy is to begin your search for funders in the *Foundation Directory Online*'s Grantmakers database where you will be searching funder profiles. For example, let's assume you represent a nonprofit in Chicago that is seeking funding for a theater program. Using the *Foundation Directory Online*'s predetermined index terms you can create a few simple searches that combine subject interests with geographic criteria:

- *Search 1:*
  Geographic Preference: Illinois
  Field of Interest: Arts

- *Search 2:*
  Foundation City: Chicago
  Field of Interest: Performing arts, theater

Both Searches 1 and 2 use appropriate beginning strategies. Search 1 uses broad terms to retrieve a potentially larger list of prospective funders, while Search 2 is more targeted to the organization's exact funding interests and geographic location. Whether you start with a broad or a narrower search strategy is partially determined by the number of funders you think you might retrieve and your personal preferences.

A successful search result will include a list of foundations and/or corporations that have a demonstrated interest in your subject area and your geographic location.

You can then research each funder on the list by first reviewing its profile.

Here is a partial view of a foundation's profile in the *Foundation Directory Online.*

It is always a good strategy to assume that you will conduct several different searches. While initially you may have the inclination to locate just those funders that match your exact interests, this is not always the best approach because you may be excluding other funders that have not supported the precise program you are seeking to fund, but that may be interested in your organization anyhow.

Other funding criteria can also be added to your search strategies, such as the audience that benefits from your program. In our example the intended population group is African Americans.

- *Search 3:*
  Geographic Focus: Illinois
  Field of Interest: Arts and African Americans/Blacks

- *Search 4:*
  Grantmaker City: Chicago
  Field of Interest: Performing arts, theater, and African Americans/Blacks

The *Foundation Directory Online*'s Grantmakers database allows you to select from 11 different criteria to create other variations in your search strategies, such as adding the type of support you are seeking (seed money, capital support, etc.) or searching for something very specific using the keyword search feature to find terms that might appear in a foundation's profile.

CORPORATE GRANTMAKERS

The fundraising strategies of many nonprofit organizations include seeking support from corporations. Corporations may provide support to nonprofits in a variety of ways. Some corporations give only through a private foundation, while others give only through direct corporate giving programs. Still others use both vehicles to support nonprofits in their communities. If a corporation has a foundation, then a 990-PF will be available for that funder, just as with other private foundations. If the corporation has a direct giving program, it is not required to file a publicly available report on gifts awarded under that program. This can make it difficult to unearth information on a corporation's non-foundation giving. However, some corporations have special sections of their web sites devoted to their philanthropy, and others issue guidelines on their giving.

In seeking grants from corporations it is important to consider their motivations for funding nonprofit organizations. Unlike foundations, corporations do not exist to give money away. Their allegiance, instead, is to their customers, shareholders, employees, and—most of all—to the bottom line. It is fair to assume that although many corporations award grants out of a combination of altruism and self-interest, most corporations will seek some benefit from their charitable activities. As a grantseeker, it is up to you to determine which attributes of your organization will be attractive to each corporation on your prospect list. For example, a local orchestra or a community center may receive funding because it serves the interests of corporate employees and the larger community, while a clinic providing health services to Latinos may be funded in part because the corporation wants to enhance its image among members of that population.

A good place to start your search for potential corporate donors is the *Foundation Directory Online*.

Companies database. The *Foundation Directory Online* contains information on nearly 5,000 company-sponsored foundations and other corporate giving programs. These corporate givers are also available in the Grantmakers database, but selecting the Companies database allows you to search corporate-specific data. For example, since corporations generally contribute in the geographic areas in which the company operates, you can search to find corporations that have headquarters, subsidiaries, or plants in your local area or that have international operations in countries in which your organization operates programs.

- *Search 5:*
  Subsidiary City: San Diego

- *Search 6:*
  Subsidiary State/Country: Brazil

The Companies database can also be searched by a corporation's business type to find corporations that might have an affinity with your organization. For example, in addition to cash grants, you may uncover a potential funder in your state whose product donations would benefit your work, as in the sample search below.

- *Search 7:*
  Business Type: Computer and office equipment
  Company State: Connecticut

Here is the company profile of the Xerox Corporation that resulted from the above search.

FOUNDATION DIRECTORY ONLINE
PROFESSIONAL

Xerox Corporation

Close Window

Copyright © 2012 Foundation Center

| Company Profile | People | 10-K | Grantmaker |

Company Profile

Jump To
Business Activities
Financial Data
Corporate Officers
Board of Directors
Plants and/or Offices
International Operations
Additional Location Information

At A Glance
Xerox Corporation
45 Glover Ave.
P.O. Box 4505
Norwalk, CT 06856-4505
Telephone: (203) 968-3000
URL: www.xerox.com

Establishment Information
Established in 1906.

Company Type
Public company

Ticker Symbol and Exchange
XRX/NYSE

Business Type (SIC)
Computer and office equipment
Photographic equipment and supplies

EIN
160468020

Tools
✉ E-mail
🖨 Print/Save

In addition to searching for corporate attributes that match your organization's goals, you should also search grantmaker records in the *Foundation Directory Online*'s Grantmakers database for stated philanthropic programs and the Grants database described below for demonstrated funding patterns.

Corporate databases such as *Corporate Affiliations* or the Foundation Center's *Corporate Giving Online* can also be helpful in identifying potential corporate support. Other research tools include print sources such as *National Directory of Corporate Public Affairs*, published by Columbia Books; the *National Directory of Corporate Giving*, published by the Foundation Center; and resources on foundation and corporate giving published by various regional associations of grantmakers.

Grants database. Another research strategy is to search the actual grants awarded by funders that share your organization's interests. To quote Andrew Lark of The Frances L. & Edwin L. Cummings Memorial Fund: "Look at our past grants. This will often help to indicate the likelihood of your grant application's future success." The *Foundation Directory Online*'s Grants database contains more than 2.8 million grants awarded by the nation's largest foundations. Examining a foundation's grants history helps illustrate how it has translated its mission and program interests into the actual funding of specific organizations and projects. It also can help reveal recent funding patterns.

A beginning approach is to search for grants to organizations in your city or state for purposes similar to your project. Using the same theater program example as we did for our grantmakers search, we can perform the following searches:

- *Search 8:*
  Recipient State: Illinois
  Subject: Arts

- *Search 9:*
  Recipient City: Chicago
  Subject: Performing arts, theater

Here again you will notice that we can search broadly—looking for organizations within a state and a broad subject category—and also by using more specific criteria.

Another research strategy using the Grants database is to find out which foundations are funding other agencies with similar interests operating in your community. These foundations may be likely sources of support for your own organization as well. For example, we can look for donors to an organization we know runs a program similar to our own in the Chicago area by searching on that organization's name.

- *Search 10:*
  Recipient Name: Black Ensemble Theater Corporation

A successful search result will include a list of recently awarded grants to this organization; a sample grant record is shown here.

FOUNDATION DIRECTORY ONLINE
PROFESSIONAL

Copyright © 2012 Foundation Center   Close Window

Grant Details   Grantmaker

Grant Details

Recipient

Name	Black Ensemble Theater Corporation
Location	Chicago, IL
ZIP Code	60640-5519
Recipient URL	www.blackensembletheater.org...
Type of Recipient	Performing arts, theater
Additional Location Information	County: Cook; Metropolitan area: Chicago-Naperville-Joliet, IL-IN-WI
EIN	362852762
Recipient 990	2010 2009 2008 2007 2006 2005 2004 2003 2002 The IRS has announced processing errors on electronically filed Forms 990 for filing years 2007-2009. Learn More»

Grant

Amount	$15,000
Year Authorized	2010
Description	For general operating support
Type(s) of Support	General/operating support
Subject(s)	African Americans/Blacks; Performing arts, theater

Tools

✉ E-mail
🖨 Print/Save

Similar to the Grantmakers database, the Grants database can also help you find funders that have awarded grants for specific types of support, or by keyword to find something very specific, such as funding for a "mime troupe."

990 database. Also in the *Foundation Directory Online*, the 990 database can be helpful in uncovering smaller grants and/or grants awarded by smaller foundations that are not covered in the Grants database. All foundations regardless of size are required to file a 990-PF information return with the

IRS each year, and all public foundations file Form 990. Among other data, a foundation's 990-PF contains a list of grants for each year. The 990 database works by searching every word in its database of more than 730,000 990-PFs and 990s. This database can be searched using keywords that might be in the description of a grant, such as "arts" or "theater," or by searching by an organization's name to find grants to organizations similar to yours.

The 990 database, of course, can also be used to find a specific 990-PF for a foundation that you want to learn more about. You can also locate 990-PFs using Foundation Finder, a free search tool accessed through the Foundation Center's web site, and they are also available on other sites like Guidestar.org and the web sites of certain state attorneys general. While the 990-PF will not give you as much information about a foundation as its web site, annual report, or printed guidelines, it is the only source of information for the majority of small and medium-sized foundations that do not issue these other information sources. Among other useful data on a 990-PF, reviewing two or three years' worth of a foundation's grants can uncover patterns in giving to certain organizations and projects similar to your own.

DONOR LISTS

In addition to the databases in the *Foundation Directory Online* and the 990-PFs filed by private foundations, sometimes lists of a nonprofit's donors, which may also be prospects for your organization, will be found on its web site or in its annual report. Other nonprofits may occasionally thank funders in a local newspaper, and arts organizations often list their donors in event programs.

NEWS SOURCES

News sources that cover philanthropy can also be helpful in creating and refining your prospect list. One such source is *The Chronicle of Philanthropy*, a biweekly news source covering philanthropy and the nonprofit world, including articles on foundations and other grantmakers, coverage of recently issued annual reports, and announcements of recently awarded grants. In addition to using it as a source to keep current on the foundation field, subscribers to the print version can acquire a password to search back issues by keywords. This can be helpful, for example, in uncovering a recent article on a specific foundation, or a list of recent grants in a specific subject area.

The Foundation Center's *Philanthropy News Digest* (PND) is another resource you can use to help you create your prospect list. PND is a daily online news service providing abstracts of philanthropy-related articles covering the major media, funder press releases, and other news sources. It also provides interviews, commentary, and profiles of foundation and nonprofit leaders and the organizations they represent. Because PND's archives can be searched using any words in its text, it can be useful in uncovering recent articles in your subject area or information about a specific grantmaker. Another source that can be searched by subject area is the Center's *RFP Bulletin*, a compilation of recently released requests for proposals issued by foundations. You can sign up for free e-mail versions of these resources. By scanning these news sources regularly, plus the local newspapers and journals in your community, and any newsletters produced by local grantmakers or grantmaker associations, you can add potential funders to your prospect list.

GRANTMAKER WEB SITES

While the majority of grantmakers do not have web sites (only about 6,300 foundations do), those foundation web sites that do exist provide information that can help you determine if your nonprofit's programs are a good fit with a funder's priorities. Typical web site contents can include a brief history of the foundation, program descriptions, recent grants lists, and application guidelines. Some also contain electronic versions of the foundation's annual reports. The breadth of information on grantmaker web sites can vary significantly from one foundation to another. Although the quantity of information available often correlates with a funder's size, sometimes you will come across a small foundation with a very comprehensive web site, and the reverse may be true as well.

Since the information on a foundation's web site is likely to be the most current data available, it is important that you review all the information that is relevant to your organization's potential solicitation of that funder. Remember, this is one of the few primary sources of data available for a foundation, other than its 990-PF or annual report. And it is often the best place to read about a foundation's interests in its own words. Robert B. Jaquay of The George Gund Foundation indicates: "I like to think that our electronic presence is sufficiently descriptive to actually say that we receive fewer cold calls than we did at one time."

The Foundation Center helps grantseekers to identify which foundations and corporate giving programs have web sites. At the Center's own web site you can search via Foundation Finder, which has links to the home pages of funders that have web sites. Also, the *Foundation Directory Online* allow you to visit a grantmaker's web site by clicking a link in its profile.

GRANTMAKER GUIDELINES

A foundation or a corporate giver's application guidelines provide critical information for the grantseeker. Guidelines generally provide a description of the types of programs and organizations grantmakers will and will not fund, as well as other restrictions on their giving. Some contain detailed program descriptions, while others only briefly mention the funder's main areas of interest. In addition, they usually indicate any specific application procedures and deadlines for submitting proposals.

If a grantmaker does not have this type of information on its web site, check the funder databases or directories you are using to see if the funder indicates that it has published guidelines. Even if you have a copy of a funder's guidelines, it is always a good idea to check to make sure you have the most recent version. Although foundations tend to "stay the course" for several years, it is not unheard of for a grantmaker to make a major change to its program focus or revise its applications procedures.

FOUNDATION ANNUAL REPORTS

If a foundation publishes an annual report, it can be a valuable asset in researching that funder. It is important not only for determining current giving patterns but also for anticipating future trends. The annual report reflects the personality, style, and interests of a foundation. More than 3,500 foundations currently publish annual reports. These documents can often be found at a foundation's web site and in PubHub at the Foundation Center's web site. Many can still be requested in print format directly from the foundation, although some funders are now issuing them only online.

In reading an annual report, you should look most closely at two sections. First, read the statement by the chairman, president, or chief executive. Look for clues that reveal the foundation's underlying philosophy. What are the problems in society that the foundation wants to address? What kind of impact does its leadership hope to make with the foundation's funds? This section will also reveal any new or changed program areas. Such shifts in direction can present you with a significant window of opportunity, if your project happens to fit within new areas the foundation intends to explore.

Another section to examine carefully is the list of grantees for the past year or years. Check the grants list against what the foundation says it wants to fund. You are looking for clues that will illustrate specific areas of interest and how the foundation implements its stated priorities in the grants it awards.

Step 2: Evaluating Your Prospect List

In this next stage of your research you will be evaluating the funders on your prospect list by gathering important information on those funders whose guidelines or funding patterns most closely match your organization's funding needs. As you research the funders on your initial list of prospects, you will be looking for answers to the following questions:

- *Does the funder accept applications?* You may find it surprising that some do not. You'll want to find this out early in the research process so you don't waste your time. However, even when the funder says it does not accept applications and/or gives only to preselected organizations, you should not completely disregard it as a prospect, if your research shows that it has the potential to be a very good fit. Check to see if anyone on your board of directors, staff, or volunteers knows someone connected to the foundation and/or begin to cultivate the prospective funder by sending a letter introducing your organization.

- *Has the funder demonstrated a real commitment to funding in your subject field?* Check to see that the funder's stated mission, program descriptions, and/or recently awarded grants indicate that there is a match with your organization's funding needs. Sometimes you may come across one or more grants by a particular foundation in your subject area, but they may be the exception to the rule. They may be grants awarded for reasons other than a specific commitment to that field, such as a special relationship between a board member and the recipient. Other foundations have historic and continuing relationships with particular organizations, perhaps due to a specified interest of the donor, which may cause them to fund activities outside of their current giving guidelines.

- *Does it seem likely that the funder will make grants to organizations in your geographic location?* Most foundations and corporations have stated geographic limitations. Although it isn't necessary for a funder to have awarded grants in your state or city, prior giving in your geographic area is a good indication that a funder may be interested in your project. Check the funder's guidelines for specific geographic limitations, and be on the lookout for local or regional giving patterns, or concentrated giving in rural or urban areas that might exclude your project.

- *What are the financial conditions that may affect the foundation's ability to give?* In general, a foundation's prior level of giving is a good indication of its capacity to give in the future, since foundations must pay out five percent of their assets each year. However, this amount can increase if the funder has recently received a large contribution, possibly from the donor. Also, foundations are affected by economic conditions. In a strong economic environment a foundation's assets will often increase, and in a slow economy assets will often decline, reducing the amount of funding that is available to nonprofit grantseekers.

- *Does the funder give to the same nonprofit groups every year, or has the funder committed its resources many years into the future?* Some foundations fund the same organizations each year and have few grant dollars left to support a new grantee's projects. Check a funder's list of grants for the past two to three years to discern patterns like this that would limit your chances of funding. Other funders make multiyear grant commitments that can limit the amount of funds they have available for new projects. Grants lists should indicate such long-term funding commitments as well.

- *Does the amount of money you are requesting fit within the funder's typical grant range?* You are looking for patterns in the foundation's past giving. If your research shows that a grantmaker's largest grant over the past few years is $25,000, you should not ask for $40,000. At the same time you should be looking for more subtle distinctions, such as the giving range in the particular subject area for which you seek funding. Also remember that some funders may give first-time grantees smaller grants until they have an established relationship with that organization.

- *Does the funder have a policy prohibiting grants for the type(s) of support you are requesting?* Some foundations will not make grants for the general support of your organization. Others will not provide funds for endowments, building projects, or equipment. Determine whether the funder is willing to consider the type of support you need.

- *Does the funder usually make grants to cover the full cost of a project or does it favor projects where other funders will participate?* Unless you are seeking funding for a very small project, it is unlikely that a first-time donor will fund an entire project. Most funders assume that grantseekers will be approaching multiple funders for their project, asking each to contribute a portion of the needed funds.

- *Does the funder put limits on the length of time it is willing to support a project?* Some foundations favor one-time grants, while others will continue their support over a number of years. However, it is rare to find a grantmaker that will commit funding to an organization for an indefinite period of time.

- *What types of organizations does the funder tend to support?* As part of your research, check to see if the funder favors large, well-established groups such as universities and museums, or supports smaller, community-based groups. Some funders will support a wide range of organizational types, while others will not. Lists of past recipients can provide good insight into this matter, whereas it may not be stated in a funder's printed guidelines.

- *Does the funder have application deadlines?* Note carefully any information you uncover regarding deadlines and board meeting dates so that you can submit your proposal at the appropriate time. Some funders have application deadlines, while others review proposals on a continuing basis.

- *Do you or does anyone on your board or staff know someone connected with the funder?* You will want to gather background information on the funder's current trustees and staff. In doing so you may find some connections between your organization and a potential funder that will make it easier to approach the funder. While knowing someone who is affiliated with a prospective funder usually is not enough to secure a grant, it does tend to facilitate the process (see Chapter 12 for more on donor cultivation).

Refining Your Prospect List

The importance of answering all of the above questions to the best of your ability and doing a thorough job in your research cannot be overstated.

As you winnow and prioritize your list you may be tempted to focus all your efforts on one or two "ideal" funders. You should resist this temptation. As long as the funder's guidelines and the other information you uncover do not rule out your organization as a potential grantee, you should keep it on your list. A funder may not have stated the exact specifications of your program as a particular area of interest, but your program may still fit within its broader funding goals.

For those funders that remain on your list, those that match your organization's interests most closely and have the ability to provide the greatest financial support will rise to the top of your list. But don't forget about the others that have made it through your preliminary screening. For example, smaller funders can play a significant role in your overall funding strategies. Remember, this year's small grants may turn into future years' larger grants, and both large and small funders have the ability to become long-term supporters. Also, funders that may turn you down this year because your project is not an exact fit with their interests, may be impressed by your organization's work and may look favorably at your next request. And Roxanne Ford of W. M. Keck Foundation sums up on a positive note: "Institutions are getting much better at all of this!"

12

Contacting and Cultivating Potential Funders

Making the Initial Contact

Once you have determined that a foundation is a likely funder, then you must initiate contact. Some, not all, foundations prefer that you call first to see if your project fits their specific guidelines. If you decide to call first, be sure you don't appear to be going on a fishing expedition. Your conversation needs to make it clear that you have read the guidelines and want further clarification on whether your particular project would fit. You are not making a solicitation by telephone.

Matthew Klein of Blue Ridge Foundation New York comments: "Calls are helpful from the grantseeker perspective in the sense that you do put your organization on the radar. So even if a funder tells you 'do not do a phone call,' it cannot help but make them remember your proposal once it comes in. And if there are specific things to emphasize, you can do that directly. The key is to be brief." Kathleen Cerveny of The Cleveland Foundation notes: "If the foundation's web site does not provide the information, the grantee should call and ask: 'What is your process? We want to submit a proposal. Can you tell me about the timeframe and process?' Stay informed. I think that would be a very smart thing to do. Make contact up front rather than bugging the funder after the proposal has been submitted. But check the web site first." Darin McKeever of The Bill & Melinda Gates Foundation adds: "Most often a conversation comes about because a grantseeker takes the initiative to reach out to find out about our grantmaking; what our interests are. I should say most of the successful ones take the time to reach out." Curtland E. Fields of Turrell Fund points out: "Many of the best applicants tend to call. The ones who seem to be good at everything else avail themselves of our advice and guidance. They are not afraid to call. They are not afraid to ask a question. They are not afraid to ask for advice on how to position something." Matt Carpenter of El Pomar Foundation summarizes: "Calling can open up the door for a couple of reasons. First, just trying to share what can be miscommunicated or read incorrectly. So the ability to start off that relationship, to share some ideas and answer some questions is extremely helpful. Ten or fifteen minutes of a phone call can save you some time preparing a proposal, and it is a valuable investment for anybody writing a grant proposal."

Funders caution that, if you do call, you should listen carefully to what is being said. Equally important: listen for the "no."

There are three objectives to the initial call:

- It promotes name recognition of your group.

- It tests the possible compatibility between the potential funder and your agency.

- It permits you to gather additional information about the funder and about possible reaction to your project before you actually submit your proposal.

How should you proceed? First, develop a script for what you will say about your organization. You may be given just a few minutes by the foundation or corporate representative. Also, have on hand the background information you have compiled about the potential funder, what you would like them to fund, and the size of the potential request. Danielle M. Reyes of Eugene and Agnes E. Meyer Foundation reminds us: "The challenge is that so many groups are trying to remember the specifics of what one funder wants versus what another funder wants. In some cases, even just reviewing the web site before the conversation would help them be more prepared for which funder they are talking to."

Second, make the call. It would be great if you could speak directly with the president of the foundation or senior vice president in charge of corporate contributions. But this will not often happen. Be satisfied with anyone who can respond to your questions. In the process, don't underestimate the importance of support staff. They can be very helpful. They can provide you with key information and ensure that your proposal is processed promptly.

Be sure to obtain the name of the person you do speak with so that reference to this conversation can be made when you submit your formal request. This may be your contact person for future calls and letters.

What should you say? Be prepared to:

- Introduce your agency: Give the name, location, purpose, and goals.

- State up front why you are calling: You have done your homework. You believe there is a fit between the grantmaker and your organization.

- Inquire if you can submit a proposal: Be specific about which one and the hoped-for level of support.

- Request an appointment: Few funders are willing to grant the request for a meeting without at least an initial proposal on the table, but it's always worth inquiring about this. As a matter of fact, each time you speak with a funder, you should ask if a face-to-face conversation would be appropriate.

Variations will emerge in each call, so you must be sharp, alert, and ready to respond. At the same time, try to seem relaxed and confident as the discussion proceeds. Remember that you are a potential partner for the prospective funder.

Many foundations have no staff or limited office support. Some corporations assign their philanthropic activities to executives with very heavy workloads. The point is, repeated calls may go unanswered. Above all, be persistent. Persistence will set your agency apart from many nonprofits whose leaders initiate fundraising with determination but quickly lose heart. If you cannot get through to a potential funder on the telephone, send a letter of inquiry designed to gain the same information as the call. If your letter goes unanswered, then be prepared to submit a request anyway.

The message here is that, like people, every foundation is different. Foundations, in fact, are made up of people. It is important to listen to and to respect what the funding representative is telling you about preferred styles of approach.

The Letter of Inquiry

Many grantmakers today are requesting that applicants provide a brief letter of inquiry (or intent) about their project before submitting a complete proposal. Just like the introductory phone call, this letter, often referred to by the acronym LOI, is used by funders as a simple screening device, enabling the grantmaker to preclude submission of an inappropriate application and to encourage the submission of proposals with funding potential. It also enables those grant decision-makers who prefer to be involved in the shaping of a proposal at the very earliest stages to do so. The letter of inquiry can be useful to the grantseeker, since it saves time compiling lengthy documents and attachments for proposals that are unlikely to be favorably received.

The requirement to submit a preliminary letter of inquiry is not always a plus for the grantseeker. In the first place, it is an extra step, requiring that additional time be factored into the application cycle. Second, some view this procedure as a way for the funder to cut off an application before the grantseeker has had the opportunity to fully portray the benefits of the project. And finally, you need to have the full proposal, at least in draft form, before you can submit a letter of intent, which in a sense is a highly compacted proposal with most of the components covered, albeit briefly. Jacob Harold of The William and Flora Hewlett Foundation points out: "Letters of Inquiry for me are most important because I need something to show to other people in the foundation. They are a tool that an applicant is giving me to advocate for them internally."

A talent for précis writing is definitely required to get the letter of inquiry just right. It should not be longer than two to three pages.

What follows is excerpted from a letter of inquiry from the Ingenuity Festival of Art + Technology to The Cleveland Foundation.

Ingenuity, The Cleveland Festival of Art and Technology, plans to use the requested $10,000 for an extension of our Ingenuity 2020 educational programming, through an exciting outreach project called the Science (Fiction) Fair. It's designed for teenaged students from the Cleveland Metropolitan School District's STEM (Science, Technology, Engineering and Math) schools to participate in as a special project activity during the 2011–12 school year. The Ingenuity Science (Fiction) Fair offers promising young people an opportunity to imagine the creative breakthroughs of the future and develop their ideas in collaboration with Northeast Ohio leaders in science, technology, engineering, and math, as well as the arts and education fields.

Ingenuity plans to group students with science and technology experts to explore a specific scientific principle of their choosing and blue-sky its potential application to an innovative product or process. The students and mentors will then team with Ingenuity artists, selected through an application process juried by Ingenuity and CMSD staff, to create displays and presentations of their ideas. The program outline includes these steps: initial meeting to explore student interests and mentor expertise; mini-brainstorming sessions to imagine futuristic ideas; idea presentation from students to mentors; consulting with creative professionals on presenting ideas; workshop student presentation to the mentor group for development and critique; and completion of project displays and video presentations to be posted on Ingenuity's website. This year-long effort will culminate in a showcase at the Rock Your World with STEAM Family Festival at the Rock Hall and Great Lakes Science Center in May 2012, and in an exhibition at the 2012 Ingenuity Festival in September. STEAM refers to adding the Arts to STEM (as described above)

Anticipated outcomes for the students include focused learning about a scientific or technical subject of personal interest; deepened general knowledge of scientific principles and their applications; increased confidence and ability to think creatively; helpful connections to the professional NEO science and arts communities; increased proficiency in working as part of a cross-functional team; and improved project-based learning skills involved in designing and presenting their ideas.

Ingenuity will undertake the fair as a collaborative project. Several Ingenuity artists, NASA, Hyland Software, Ursuline College, and Rogers Displays have already expressed interest in working with us on this project, as has the CMSD through Director of Arts Education, Tony Sias. We're also looking for additional partners from the nonprofit and corporate sectors. Ingenuity is involved in the programming of the Rock Your World with STEAM Family Festival this year (2011) in an attempt to build synergies with CMSD, the Rock Hall, the Science Center and other supporters of this annual family event.

While the letter of inquiry has its pluses and minuses from the grantseeker's perspective, this is still required by many funders as a preliminary step in the process. And writing such a letter is a skill that proposal writers need to develop.

Submitting the Proposal

Actually submitting the proposal may seem anticlimactic considering the amount of preparation that has gone into identifying and researching the prospective funders and putting together the various components. But eventually there comes the time to submit the full proposal to the funders on your list.

Checklists may prove useful at this point. You may wish to check and double-check one last time to ensure that all requirements of the funder have been met and that all of the pieces of the proposal package are there in the proper sequence. Above all, you will want to be sure that you submit the proposal in accordance with the funder's deadline. If possible, whether you use regular mail, e-mail, or are applying online, send in your proposal at least two weeks in advance of the deadline. This enables the funder to request additional information, if needed.

Grantseekers often wonder whether they should mail in their proposals, send by overnight mail or messenger, or hand-deliver them. By far the best choice is the least expensive one. Use regular mail unless there is a very good reason to do otherwise.

Cultivating the Potential Funder

Don't forget to continue to communicate once you have submitted your proposal. Cultivation of the funding prospect can make the critical difference between getting a grant and getting lost in the shuffle.

Knowledge of the funder's situation, and of that particular grantmaker's procedures for processing proposals, can be extremely helpful in developing your cultivation strategy.

Funders are flooded with proposals. Even if they turn down all that are clearly outside their guidelines, they still get many more than their budgets will allow them to fund.

Foundations frequently work closely with the grantseeker in developing the request. Peter F. Bird, Jr. of The Frist Foundation suggests: "We have a very relational kind of grantmaking approach. It is not our thing to build a bunch of walls between ourselves and grantseekers. A very important part of grantmaking is for the foundation to be accessible. And being accessible does not end with a web site. It may start with a web site. It really means being available by phone and e-mail and showing up at events within the community where you will see a lot of nonprofit organizations and board members. It is all about staying in touch with the community." Julie Brooks of John S. and James L. Knight Foundation adds: "The proposal stage is a relationship-building stage. Once you submit a proposal it is not the end of it." Bruce H. Esterline of The Meadows Foundation, Inc. describes a very interactive process: "During the early stages of the program officer's review, there probably have been a few e-mail exchanges, a few calls, probably a site visit. Then there is a lull. The month before the program officer is ready to take it to the board meeting, there is a flurry of communication of all types to pull things together, to complete the profile—very high-impact conversations."

Several forms of cultivation may be particularly valuable after the proposal is submitted:

- Communication by phone or e-mail;

- Face-to-face meetings;

- Using board contacts; and

- Written updates and progress reports.

Follow-up by Phone or E-mail

Normally you should plan to call or send an e-mail about two weeks after the proposal package is mailed. The primary purpose of this communication is to make sure that the proposal has been received. You have requested a meeting in the cover letter and offered to supply any additional information required to help the funder consider your request. You should therefore ask if it is appropriate to schedule a meeting at the foundation or corporate office or a site visit at your agency. Be sure to ask about the process and timing for the review of your proposal. This will guide you as to when you might call back or send updated information.

Call periodically thereafter to check on the status of your proposal. If you have had no response in the expected time frame, call to find out if there has been a change in the schedule. Ask the same types of questions as you did previously: Is additional information required? When will the proposal be reviewed? Would the foundation or corporate representative like to meet? Be brief. There is a fine line between being helpful and being too pushy.

Each time you call, be prepared to answer the program officer's detailed questions about any aspect of the proposal or of your agency's work. You should also expect to receive calls or e-mails from your program officer during the course of the proposal review.

Jane G. Hardesty of John H. and Wilhelmina D. Harland Charitable Foundation, Inc. notes: "We encourage organizations to be back in touch with us and to provide updates. We will call them if they indicated that something might be in flux or to see if something has changed, as their priorities may have shifted based on developments during the course of the application process."

It helps to stay in touch by phone or e-mail. This gives you a chance to find out what is happening with your proposal and to share information with the foundation or corporate funder.

When appropriate, follow up the phone conversation with a note or e-mail message about the next step you plan to take or confirming any new information you provided over the phone. While phone communication is often the most convenient way to keep in touch, you need to be sure that any agreement or information that is critical to a successful outcome of the review process is put in writing.

Using Board Contacts

A contact from one of your board members with a peer affiliated with the foundation or corporate funder you are approaching will usually reinforce the relationship you are building.

How do you discover if your board members have contacts that can help with raising funds? First, circulate to all of the members of your board the names of the officers and directors of the foundations and corporations you plan to approach. Ask your board members to respond to you by a certain date about those whom they know. Then work one-on-one with individual board members, developing a strategy for them to utilize their contacts. Another approach is to meet with the board members to talk about individuals with whom they can be helpful. You may find contacts with funders that you had not intended to approach, where having an entrée will make a difference.

Knowing that you have board-to-board contact is not enough. You must assist your board member in capitalizing on this relationship on behalf of your nonprofit group. First, develop a scenario with the board member focusing on how to approach the contact. The more personal the approach, the better it is. Second, assist your board member with understanding why this funder would want to help your organization, finding the right language to discuss your agency and your funding needs, and drafting correspondence as needed. Then make sure that the board member makes the promised contact after the proposal has been submitted. Periodically remind this individual of the next step to be taken. The groundwork you have done is wasted if the board member never follows through.

The staff of foundations and corporate grantmakers may be concerned about your board members contacting their board members. They may consider it inappropriate or may view it as interference. Some funders feel strongly that an agency should not use a board contact, even if they have one.

Still others report that their trustees are encouraged to indicate their interest in a project. At a minimum, staff want to know in advance that a board contact will be used. To quote Rober B. Jaquay of The George Gund Foundation: "If it is not done to excess. If it is done in a way that is not overly pressuring. If it just comes up naturally in conversation, I don't think anybody really takes offense." Phillip Henderson of Surdna Foundation, Inc. adds: "We have to say no 90 percent of the time, so having some entrée actually allows you to cut through the noise." William V. Engel of The Hyde and Watson Foundation notes: "The proposal is going to stand and fall on its merits and how it fits our guidelines and how it fits with the other proposals we are considering. If we know good people are involved in the organization, that is a plus, but that is not going to get them a grant necessarily." Bruce H. Esterline of The Meadows Foundation, Inc. summarizes: "If your board members know our board members, by all means they can say whatever they want. I have been doing this for 20 years and at no time have I been pressured by a board member to put forward a proposal that would not have met the general standards for a project to be considered. Our board members like it that they can explain to all the people that do approach them by saying: 'Hey, we have a process and we ask you to follow it. You can trust our system.' And I think it speaks to the fact that they trust us and the processes that they have put forward."

Where you already are in contact with the foundation staff, it is critical to discuss a board contact with them. Finally, keep in mind that relying on board contacts can backfire. At some foundations, if a board member has had contact with an agency, he or she is expected to disqualify himself or herself from discussion about the specific proposal.

Written Updates

Written communication helps a foundation or corporate donor learn more about your group and reminds them that you need their support. You should plan to send materials selectively while your proposal is under review. Here are some ideas for what you might send:

- summary reports on what is going on in your organization;

- financial information, such as a new audit;

- newsletters, bulletins, brochures, or other frequently issued information;

- updates/reports on specific projects; and

- newspaper or magazine articles on the project for which you have requested support, the work of your nonprofit, or closely related issues.

It is usually not necessary to customize the materials, but a brief accompanying note always helps to reinforce your relationship with the funder.

Listservs and E-newsletters

Don't overlook the possibility of selective e-mail contact with prospective funders, if they have communicated with you that way in the past or have indicated a preference for this vehicle for providing updates. A concise e-mail message with, perhaps, a link to an appropriate area of your web site or other coverage of your activities, can have a significant impact. Repeated or unnecessary e-mail messages directed at funding program officers can prove annoying, however.

Some agencies have developed listservs or broadcast e-mail services to keep various constituents apprised of recent developments. It would be wise not to add a funder's e-mail address to your listserv without prior permission to do so. On the other hand, this is a very convenient way to keep donors and prospective funders aware of your agency's accomplishments if they agree to it. In general, such cultivation is welcomed by today's grantmaker.

Even after your project has concluded, don't forget to continue to cultivate your donors. Fundraising is all about relationship building. Kathleen Ceverny of The Cleveland Foundation put it very succinctly in the past: "Communication is important and a challenge."

13

Online Applications

A major force in our professional and social lives, the Internet and its impact interest foundations for many reasons. This is especially true among our grantmaker interviewees, who have recently given much thought to the impact of online innovations on the grantmaking process. Grantmakers and grantseekers are going to have split views on this issue for quite some time to come. Only a relatively small group across the entire potential universe of grantmakers has web sites and allows electronic submissions of one kind or other. This means that the grantseeker will be working with some grantmakers online and with others via the more traditional media of phone, fax, and snail mail. Speaking of web sites and the electronic world, Jacob Harold of The William and Flora Hewlett Foundation reminds us that online innovations are "...the tool that enables the conversation," but cannot take the place of building a rapport with a grantmaker through phone and face-to-face conversations.

Because the use of technology is so new with grantmakers and of keen interest to grantseekers, you will be well served to think about the following points as you develop the strategy of approach to a specific grantmaker.

Web Sites

Grantmaker web sites provide incredible insight into the interests and inner workings of the foundation. They outdo all other research tools, often succinctly describing the history, areas of interest, guidelines, reporting requirements, and grantees of the grantmaker.

From the grantmaker perspective the web site provides transparency. Edmund J. Cain of Conrad N. Hilton Foundation notes: "Technology makes it less of a mystery. Who is this Conrad N. Hilton Foundation? What are they all about? I will have encounters with potential grantees at various meetings or gatherings, and my first suggestion is to look at our web site." Also, according to Laura H. Gilbertson of The William Bingham Foundation and many of the other interviewees, foundation web sites reduce the number of inappropriate requests because of the clarity of the information. Karen Kinney of The Morris & Gwendolyn Cafritz Foundation suggests web sites enable grantseekers to easily answer questions they may have. On the other hand, Maria Mottola of New York Foundation worries that the "…web site can be viewed as a gatekeeper impeding the development of a relationship with the nonprofit."

Ironically, many foundations that have established a prominent online presence do not accept proposals electronically. For example, The Hyde and Watson Foundation, Inc. has a web site with terrific and thoughtful information. Its Executive Director William V. Engel indicates: "Hard copies of proposals are requested. It is the nature of how we review. We would probably print everything out anyway, so we can write notes on it or highlight what we want someone to look at." At the New York Foundation, which also has an outstanding web site, Maria Mottola notes: "Our potential grantees don't want to submit applications electronically, so we don't ask for them." She went on to say that objections include the character/word count limitations and lack of a dialogue. Amy Scop of The California Wellness Foundation adds another dimension, noting that "some nonprofits may have internal policies that prohibit them from submitting online," or as Karen Kinney of The Morris & Gwendolyn Cafritz Foundation adds, "antiquated equipment may put nonprofits at a disadvantage when applying online." While much of its work with awardees is electronic, The Clark Foundation in New York City does not have a web site. As Executive Director Doug Bauer explains the decision against creating a site: "It really springs from a long-held family value that you let the work speak for itself. They've not been ones to seek a lot of attention for what they do philanthropically."

Just like their grantees, most grantmakers are not satisfied with their sites and expect the next iteration to be easier to navigate, more user-friendly, and more informative. As David D. Weitnauer of R. Howard Dobbs, Jr. Foundation, Inc. says of his foundation's site: "It is not a fancy web site. It is not very interactive. But it serves its purpose. We update the site when experience tells us that something is not working."

E-mail Communication

Regardless of whether the proposal is submitted electronically or in hard copy, grantmakers and grantseekers alike love the ease of e-mail communication. If information is missing from an application, foundation staff can inform nonprofits quickly, and nonprofit staff can often send the missing item electronically. Program officers are able to ask questions raised in their review of a request and obtain a fast response. Jane G. Hardesty of John H. and Wilhelmina D. Harland Charitable Foundation, Inc. notes that "We rely heavily on e-mail communications to collect all necessary information and to clarify any questions." Bob Wittig of Jovid Foundation adds: "I try to do as much electronically as I can." Laura H. Gilbertson of The William Bingham Foundation concurs, pointing out: "We've really gone electronic. Whatever can possibly be e-mailed to me, I want e-mailed." Robert B. Jaquay of The George Gund Foundation reminds us how liberating e-communication can be: "Increasingly we're communicating with our grantees electronically. We're less anchored to our desks and still communicate on a regular basis with our laptops and blackberries."

Online Applications

We covered in Chapter 12 that some foundations use the letter of inquiry as a preliminary step in the proposal process. Online applications often follow this two-step process as well.

Some grantmakers have online application forms that function as letters of inquiry. What follows is the online Inquiry Form from John S. and James L. Knight Foundation's web site.

Inquiry Form

Please fill in or correct the contact information for your organization.
Fields marked with an asterisk (*) are required. Please do not use all caps.

Organization Name	_____ *
Legal Name (as noted on your 501(c)(3) letter)	_____ *
Also Known As	_____
Tax ID Number	_____
Mailing Address	_____ *
City	_____ *
State	_____ * **Zip** _____ *
Country	United States
Phone	_____ *
Fax	_____
Website	_____

To whom should Knight Foundation respond? Please provide your contact information below. Fields marked with an asterisk (*) are required.

Prefix	[▼] *
First Name	_____ *
Last Name	_____ *
Middle Name or Initial	_____
Suffix	[▼]
E-mail Address	_____ *
Confirm E-mail	_____ *

Is your mailing address the same as your organization's mailing address? ○ Yes ◉ No

Mailing Address (if different from organization)	_____
City	_____
State	_____ **Zip** _____
Country	United States
Phone	_____ *
Fax	_____

Project Title
In 200 characters or less, please provide a title that describes your project.
Character count: 0

Project Purpose
Please describe the proposed project and include the following information:
- Tell us about the opportunity presented by your idea/project, what it will transform.
- How will it create lasting, visible change?
- Tell us how you identified this opportunity and why the time is right for it.
- What other partners or funders are involved in your idea/project?
- How will you measure success?
- How are you uniquely qualified to implement your idea/project?
- Please describe organizational and financial capacity to implement your idea/project.
- How will your idea/project be sustained beyond Knight Foundation's funding?

> Please note that you will not be able to save your work. We recommend that you edit your inquiry offline, then paste the information into the box below.

(5,000 characters max. = approximately two pages)
Character count: 0

Amount Requested from Knight Foundation
What is the total amount of money you wish to request, and over what time period?
We are requesting $ [   ]
(Example: 500,000)
over [   ] **year(s)**
(whole years only. Example: 2)

What is the total project cost?
Total Project Cost $ [   ]

ⓘ You will have a chance to review the information you are submitting when you click on the **Submit** button.

[Submit]

Submitting an online application often involves creating an account using an e-mail address and password. Using the login information, the grantseekers can start an application and access their in-process applications and online application history.

Online Applications: The Grantmakers' Perspective

Grantmakers have a number of players to think about when evaluating the costs and benefits of incorporating electronic submissions. Most certainly there are the grantseekers, but also different levels of foundation staff who must interact with the document and the members of the board who provide some level of review. Most adopters of electronic submissions aim for a seamless process and a paperless office. Edmund J. Cain of Conrad N. Hilton Foundation notes: "We are trying to become a paperless office. We have started a pilot program now with staff having iPads so they do not have reams of paper at program meetings."

Online applications make for increasingly seamless review by moving the electronic document directly into the program officer's computer. From this point the data can be exported and formatted appropriately for the staff's and then Board's review and discussion. As Phillip Henderson of Surdna Foundation, Inc. indicates: "Content gets dropped into the online application. But then it lives in that world, not in paper files. We have everything from contact information and executive summaries to proposal narrative to delineation of the set of activities the organization is going to undertake, the outcomes they hope to achieve. It is the place where reporting happens as the grant period comes to a close." And Elizabeth B. Smith, Executive Director of The Hyams Foundations, Inc., adds: "Funders spend a fair amount of time summarizing a docket. I think one of the reasons we wanted to go to an online system is so that the summary data are online and can be analyzed and reported on more easily."

Program officers may or may not review the document online. Many grantmakers admit that staff will print the application to read and make notes! Finally in some form the information goes to the Board. Again foundations vary widely in what the Boards request—from a segregated place on the web site, to thumb drives, CDs, and hard copies, with some grantmakers working in all of the above simultaneously.

Clearly, grantmakers think about the grantseeker when an online application is involved. Marilyn Gelber of Brooklyn Community Foundation points out: "There is a lot of handholding that goes with it." Matt Carpenter of El Pomar Foundation adds: "Our goal is to be helpful to the nonprofit. We want to create a database online, so when they need to create a new proposal they can easily repopulate those key fields and they are finished!" And Julie Brooks of John S. and James L. Knight Foundation reports: "There is a lot of resistance from grantees regarding online applications. We're going through this soul searching through interviews and nonprofit feedback to learn what the issue is and how we can respond."

Online Applications: The Grantseeker Issues

There are five very real challenges for nonprofits in dealing with online applications. First, there is the complication of a lack of standardization among the applications. Darin McKeever of The Bill & Melinda Gates Foundation notes: "When applications are submitted electronically, often you need to submit something that is different from one foundation to another, and that is different from a third. So the electronic aspects do not always improve the efficiency. In fact it sometimes creates further aggravation."

Secondly, information is expected in an abbreviated style. Grantmakers place word or character limits in each text field. These limits allow no leeway for grantseekers, who are forced to take information about which they are very passionate and streamline the data to meet those limits. Working within strict word or character constraints is not necessarily a bad thing, though. As Phillip Henderson of Surdna Foundation, Inc. points out: "Character limits force grantseekers to embrace two important characteristics of an outstanding proposal: clarity and brevity."

Next, often the applications are in English only. Jessamine Chin of Adobe Foundation points out: "A challenge for us is that the application is in English and we work with international grantseekers." Not only is this a problem for international grantseekers but also for U.S. organizations working with non-English-speaking populations.

Additionally, as mentioned earlier, some nonprofits may not have computers or may have old equipment or outdated software or limited bandwidth, which compromises their ability to apply.

Finally, most nonprofits are frustrated by the ways in which technological innovation has limited communication with the grantmaker before applying. Grantmakers are aware of this issue and try to mitigate it, but as Marilyn Gelber of Brooklyn Community Foundation suggests, online applications "are not nearly as friendly a process." She goes on to say that, while the efficiencies of online applications are wonderful, they "are no substitute for the relationship building that is absolutely necessary in a healthy relationship between a foundation and its grantee partners." While we cannot make these issues disappear, perhaps the grantmaker's tips with regard to electronic applications will help.

Online Application Tips

Online applications are here to stay. No one is especially pleased with them as they currently exist. The nonprofits are unhappy with online applications because they do not save time and are hard to fill out. Grantmakers feel they do not get enough information. Grantseekers may also take solace in the fact that foundations are aware of the problems inherent in today's online applications and are working to make the process more efficient and user-friendly as they continue to review and refine their online application systems. So what's a proposal writer to do? Unfortunately, there is only one course of action: soldier on.

Thankfully, our interviewees have provided us with a number of tips to deal with the online application in its current state. First off, is the writing itself. David A. Odahowski of Edyth Bush Charitable Foundation, Inc. indicates that "Overall you have to be a better writer." Building on that, Phillip Henderson of Surdna Foundation, Inc. suggests that you have to explain the "essence of the project" and Elspeth A. Revere of The John D. and Catherine T. MacArthur Foundation reminds us the proposal needs to reflect a "commitment to something important." Finally, Curtland E. Fields of Turrell Fund suggests we "make every word count." As is the case with hard copy proposals, being clear, concise, and simple goes a long way. The main difference between hard copy and online proposals is that an online application's word limits leave no wiggle room: if a given text field limits you to 200 words, you had better find a way to delete that 201st word. Being concise in the online application is not only suggested but enforced without exception!

The second set of suggestions deals with answering the questions. Kathleen Cerveny of The Cleveland Foundation reminds us to answer the question directly; the lack of space does not allow for a meandering response or one that misses the point entirely. Lita Ugarte Pardi of The Community Foundation for Greater Atlanta warns that a less-than-diligent grantseeker working online may accidentally skip questions altogether. She goes on to say: "Incomplete applications are not accepted by us. So the grantseeker has to be very careful."

From a very practical perspective, Kathleen Cerveny of The Cleveland Foundation notes: "Write your responses first in Word. Then cut and paste the document [into the text field]." Always working from your master proposal makes sense in dealing with the electronic world. Jessamine Chin of Adobe Foundation points out that creating links to existing materials can be a wonderful short cut in providing information. Laura H. Gilbertson of The William Bingham Foundation warns, however, that you need to be certain that the links connect! And regarding attachments, Bob Wittig of Jovid Foundation says: "Please don't send huge attachments." These can be a burden to the grantmaker, especially if the information was not requested.

Grantmakers acknowledge that many electronic requests look awful. As Kathleen Cerveny of The Cleveland Foundation indicates: "Online applications aren't as visually friendly as a word processed narrative might be." Laura H. Gilbertson of The William Bingham Foundation suggests that you check to see "…what the final document looks like to others." And Lita Ugarte Pardi of The Community Foundation for Greater Atlanta warns: "Recheck your work. There is no margin for error." She goes on to say that typos and grammatical mistakes contribute to a negative impression and because most online text fields do not have spell- or grammar-check features, it is important to ensure your text has been proofed and re-proofed in your word processing software before pasting it into the field.

Once we have whittled our brilliant prose to fit the character count and checked and double-checked our document, Julie Brooks of John S. and James L. Knight Foundation notes: "If you cannot do it and the grantmaker needs it—you might not be a good partner to the grantmaker." And Curtland E. Fields of Turrell Fund adds: "Before pushing the 'submit' button, we suggest that it is a wise practice for applicants to ask themselves whether they have answered basic questions relative to whom they are serving, why our funding is needed and how it will be used, and how our support specifically will make a difference." So, as in the hard copy applications, no amount of craft will get our round peg into the square hole.

Finally, David A. Odahowski of Edyth Bush Charitable Foundation, Inc. suggests that even when submitting a proposal online, multiple communication streams are paramount to building a relationship with a potential funder. For those of us who fear we will never speak to a grantmaker again, take heart from the comment by Phillip Henderson of Surdna Foundation, Inc.: "At the end of the day technology does not replace face-to-face human interaction. It is about adding a level of sophistication to those interactions and allowing the relationship between the foundation and the grantee to be a little smarter and more sophisticated than it has been. The Surdna Foundation is not investing in abstractions. We are investing in the ability of people in organizations to do important stuff and that remains true whether we have technology or not."

Beyond the Request

Grantmakers are using technology in ways that go beyond the application. To mention just a few: Lita Ugarte Pardi of The Community Foundation for Greater Atlanta describes using ReadyTalk, a webinar software that allows the foundation to hold virtual orientation sessions, saving travel for the nonprofit participants. Elspeth A. Revere of The John D. and Catherine T. MacArthur Foundation uses Skype for seamless grants management.

Social media is a big issue for foundations and nonprofits alike. A few of our interviewees have ventured into it. Danielle M. Reyes of Eugene and Agnes E. Meyer Foundation notes: "The Facebook page is more about having a presence within that Facebook community. It has a different voice and tone. It gives us a chance to post certain things related to grantees that we might not otherwise share." Robert B. Jaquay of The George Gund Foundation indicates: "Like a lot of places, we've tried to think through whether or not the social media advances will work," while at foundations like Conrad N. Hilton Foundation, grantmakers are building communications strategies that will ultimately encompass social media but they are not there yet. It is a future direction.

Grantseekers not already active in online social networks should make plans to become so, if only to access direct communications from funders. For nonprofits entrenched in Facebook, Twitter, and other social media, make sure to connect to foundations as many more find it easier to communicate.

In sum, foundations are shifting toward the implementation of online applications, but many foundations continue to resist this trend. Those of us actively engaged in foundation fundraising today will find ourselves working in two modes: electronic and "old world." We need to keep in mind that all grantmakers welcome and encourage our outreach to them. Even those grantmakers deeply committed to electronic submissions acknowledge the importance and necessity of human interaction. Grantmakers, whether they request online or hard copy applications, remain committed to building relationships with like-minded nonprofits from the earliest stages of the application process. They seek highly collaborative partnerships with their nonprofit grantees, and this will continue to hold true regardless of the way in which a proposal is requested.

14

Funder Reviews of the Proposal—Due Diligence

You may wonder what actually happens to your proposal once it arrives at the offices of your prospective funder. Grantmakers call their review "due diligence," a term that has migrated to the nonprofit world from the legal and financial professions. In this context it relates to the careful scrutiny and consideration of your request for funding. Here we describe what is likely to happen to your proposal. But keep in mind, there is no "typical" situation when it comes to grants decision-making, and foundations may differ from one another in the procedures they adopt. Remember, grantmakers are very deliberate in the steps they take in this review process. Now is when they will turn to you with questions and requests for additional information. The following chart and narrative will assist you in understanding what happens next.

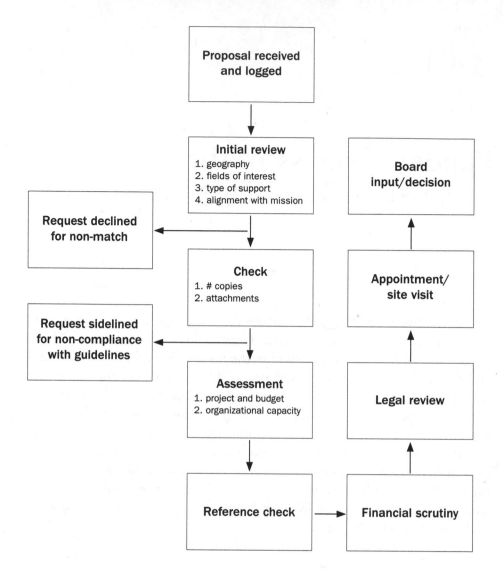

Receipt of Proposal

Not surprisingly, many grantmakers have computer systems that enable them to track the receipt and review of your funding request. A staff person enters into the system all of the pertinent information about your proposal, including organization name and contact information, the title of the project, the amount of the request, a summary of the project (ideally abstracted from your executive summary), and your recent relationship with this particular funder, if any. Of course if the application was filed electronically all of the data is automatically entered into the program officer's review system.

Often at this stage the cover letter and appendix materials are separated out and placed in a folder while the proposal narrative with its project budget are forwarded to a program officer, staff member, or trustee for initial review.

Initial Review

To save time, the program officer or another assigned staff member will scan the executive summary, budget, and other key sections of the proposal document to make certain that the project serves a geographic area and/or audience that is of interest to the grantmaker. The program officer wants to be certain that the project aligns with the grantmaker's mission and current specific interests. Does this project complement and/or enhance other projects the grantmaker may be supporting? This is particularly important if the grantmaker is in the midst of a well-publicized initiative of one kind or another. Requests that are clearly outside of the grantmaker's guidelines are likely to be sidelined at this stage. Grantmakers report that many requests are not a fit. They do not want to waste precious time on a detailed review if a project is clearly not going to be funded.

Attachment Check

At this juncture, there will be a quick review of the attachments to your proposal. If all requested documents are not included, you will receive a letter or a phone call asking for the missing elements. Most grantmakers insist that all of the required information be in place before the due diligence process proceeds. Not having everything they need to make a decision may result in a rejection of your proposal or suggestion that you withdraw it. So it goes without saying that a prompt reply to a request for additional information is essential on the grantseeker's part. The grantmaker will also check to be certain that requested copies of the narrative and/or attachments are also in place, as they are needed for multiple readers. Lack of the correct number of copies will sideline the request.

Assessment

The proposals that are now being looked at very carefully have all of their attachments and have been determined to fit the grantmaker's guidelines.

Special attention is paid to the ability of the organization to implement the project. Grant decision-makers will analyze the organization's track record, its staff and board leadership, and the reputation of the nonprofit in the community. Current interviewees underscore the importance of staff and board leadership. Matt Carpenter of El Pomar Foundation notes: "We try to ascertain if there is good leadership within the organization. Is the Executive Director doing a good job in leading the organization? Our trustees philosophically believe, if there is good leadership, then the organization will be successful through good times and bad times." And Bob Wittig of Jovid Foundation adds: "For me the character of the Executive Director and of the people running the program are important. Do I feel that they have a vision for where they are going? Does it fit their mission?"

The program officer looks at the perceived value of the grant project. Does it make sense as described? Is it likely to have the intended impact? Is there enough money in the proposed budget to operate the project? As you can see, all of the components of your grant proposal as outlined in this *Guide* will come into play in responding to the various screens the grantmaker applies to your request.

Reference Check

In considering your proposal the grant decision-maker is likely to speak with internal and external sources familiar with your organization. Grant decision-makers may also reach out to representatives of other nonprofits whom they know and trust to see if they are familiar with your organization and its work. Darin McKeever of The Bill & Melinda Gates Foundation points out: "If an organization identifies a partner or a beneficiary of their services, and I know somebody at that organization, I will call up and say: 'Can you tell me how it is going?'"

There may also be conversations with other grantmakers, especially your current and past foundation and corporate donors, to learn how your agency handles the grantee relationship and its responsibilities. Doug Bauer of The Clark Foundation states: "I have found that there has always been a pretty decent level of sharing of information and even strategy to some extent among the giving entities, which is hugely important, especially in this environment. Our dollars should be trying to complement as best we can each other's funding streams and strategies." William V. Engel of The Hyde and Watson Foundation adds a different dimension: "Smaller foundations use the other foundations as essentially adjunct staff because none of us has a lot of time to spend on a grantee. If I see that Victoria or Schumann has funded them, and we have not heard of them, I will call Irene or I will call

Barbara and say: 'You guys are listed as a funder on this, are you still funding them?' And other foundations will call us. It allows us to have more eyes and ears." Matt Carpenter of El Pomar Foundation notes: "We have no problem interacting with other donors and finding out their perspective. We want to know: Why are you not listed here? Have you seen a proposal? Did you say yes or no? Is it a fit, not a fit? What do you know about the organization?"

A few of the grantmakers we interviewed conduct Internet searches to learn more about grant applicants, along with referring to local media sources. Susan M. Carter of Georgia Power Foundation, Inc. reports: "I review their web site and research them on the Internet to see what other information is available about the organization." And Laura H. Gilbertson of The William Bingham Foundation adds: "I always look at their web site, and I Google them, too. And I use that as a way to evaluate their capacity." Finally, Danielle M. Reyes of Eugene and Agnes E. Meyer Foundation notes: "I use Google frequently. I sometimes Google an Executive Director's name. Most proposals do not include resumes and so we are left to do our own research."

Keep in mind that some grantmakers use web sites that are dedicated to analyzing information about nonprofits. It behooves you to know what is being said on those sites about your nonprofit. All of these efforts are aimed at determining the credibility and reliability of the potential grantee, to ensure that the organization will be able to deliver on the promise implied in its grant request.

Financial Scrutiny

Grantsmakers look for financial stability. Based on your operating budget, audited financial statement or balance sheet, and the most recent 990 you filed with the IRS, they conduct an analysis of the overall fiscal soundness of your agency. They look for patterns of growth. They want to know if administrative expenses seem to be in line with your operating budget and with what they know other similar organizations are spending on such items.

Current interviewees report spending a great deal of time and energy on fiscal review. Doug Bauer of The Clark Foundation asks to see the management letter to the audit: "I think it is hugely important and very telling. If your fiscal controls and your contract administration are not up to snuff and it's mentioned in the management letter, that is a huge red flag." Susan M. Carter of Georgia Power Foundation, Inc. provides a different perspective of the review: "We look at things like compensation, outstanding loans to officers/directors. We look at how much they have paid other contract vendors and who the vendors are and if they have any relationship with the organization. We typically do not fund organizations in the red unless a unique situation." Victoria Kovar of Cooper Foundation adds: "There are questions we may ask that go beyond looking at the financial reports or board lists to questions of their own internal processes. How often does your board meet? How often does your board review financial statements? Who prepares your financial statements? There is a whole list of things we go over with organizations, especially if they are new to us, to see whether what is happening on the back end of the organization seems appropriate." And Danielle M. Reyes of Eugene and Agnes E. Meyer Foundation notes: "With our financial checklist, we are looking for a few core things. One is that revenue meets or exceeds expenses and that the audit was clean. Another is that cashflow looks healthy. Who prepares financial information to be presented to the board? Who presents it? How frequently is it presented? And what sort of internal controls and procedures do they have?"

Finally comes the issue of sustainability. Grantmakers will ask themselves if it appears that your organization will be able to attract the full support it needs to operate this program. How will it sustain itself over time? Is there a possibility that it will generate enough earned income ultimately to be self-supporting, or is there a finite period for this grant project after which no additional funds will be needed? Grant decision-makers may even speak with other potential donors to assess the possibilities for joint funding or collaboration in support of your grant project.

Legal Review

Foundations face oversight of their work from the IRS. In many cases, concern about this oversight has grantmakers checking information about the nonprofit grant recipient many times over. This may include: being certain that the name of the organization is the same as that which appears on the 501(c)(3) letter of determination from the IRS; insisting that the organization sign disclaimers; and requiring that the nonprofit cash the check from the grantmaker and send a thank-you letter for audit purposes. All of these steps seem fairly reasonable to most active fundraising nonprofits. But when any of these steps is ignored, it can cause major problems for the grantmaker.

Appointment

The meeting with a grantseeker is a critical part of due diligence. For more about the meeting, please see Chapter 15.

Decision and the Board's Role in the Process

The program officer digests the information that has been accumulated on the project and the organization. At times, this person may seek input from other staff and from specialists within the foundation such as the finance officer.

Generally, a staff grants committee reviews all of the projects under serious consideration. This will be an open dialogue about the prospective grantees, their organizational abilities, and the likelihood of success with the project under consideration. Inputs and suggestions are shared and questions raised. It will be at this juncture that the program officer compiles a final document of between one and five pages for board review.

A Board Grants Committee may provide an interim review at this juncture.

Doug Bauer of The Clark Foundation provides us with a glimpse into the kind of information that will go to the board: "We take all that information—the proposal, notes and comments that we absorb from the site visit, the 990, the audits. The first section of the write-up is context and background. Next are programmatic and organizational analyses. We then make a recommendation. This final document of four to five pages in length is what the board sees."

There are three different levels of board involvement in awarding grants.

For some, the role of a board is limited strictly to governance. This means the grant decisions are made by staff. These boards deal only with the larger issues of investments and areas in which the foundation will make grants.

Secondly, some boards review staff summaries before casting a ballot that helps form the agenda for the board meeting. There will be some projects that everyone agrees should be funded or denied. The balance are then discussed in the meeting. Clearly these boards are a bit more hands-on, and a lack of consensus means that a project should be discussed.

Finally, other boards invite staff representatives from all of the applicant organizations to the board meeting. The thought behind this is that the nonprofit organization can represent itself better than any written summary. It allows the nonprofit to learn from the competition and to form networks with other recipients, as well as to bond with the board directly.

It should be noted that today boards and staff often share the grantmaking decision function, with requests above a certain level being acted on by the Board and below that level, by the staff.

As is evident, the due diligence process described here is not a "one size fits all" procedure. Each grantmaker has its own variation on the theme. But all of these efforts are aimed at developing objective ways of learning as much as possible about prospective grantees to ensure that precious grant monies are expended on the best possible applicants and on projects with a high potential for achieving success.

15

Meeting with Funders

The grantseeker process and grantmaker due diligence converge with a meeting or appointment, which may take place in the form of a site visit paid by the grantmaker to the nonprofit organization. You are anxious to meet the grantmaker to learn more about the foundation and what it is looking for. For the grantmaker, this is the final step in the due diligence process described in Chapter 14, after which staff will be ready to take your request to the Foundation's board. Each grantmaker takes a slightly different approach to these meetings, but it is fair to say that if a grantmaker contacts you to schedule a visit, staff has found promise in your proposal. Now you make the final case to an interested grantmaker that your project is worthy of funding. As Doug Bauer of The Clark Foundation notes: "It is kicking the tires. There is only so much you are going to learn by kicking the tires, but nevertheless it is important to get out there and see what is going on."

In this section we will review what the grantmaker hopes to learn, who should be present, and a few dos and don'ts.

Across the board, grantmakers concur that they want to see firsthand what an organization looks like. During a site visit, they hope to see agreement between the proposal and the reality of the nonprofit. They expect to observe a staff that effectively serves its clients and undertakes its work with passion. Doug Bauer of The Clark Foundation adds: "The meeting is a pretty thorough discussion not only of the proposal but of the current health of the organization; the issues, good and bad, they have been dealing with; and how they see the environmental context in which they are operating. Is it positive or negative? What is their competition doing that they are not doing or that they are doing better? So we really try to get a thorough understanding of what the organization is dealing with." Andrew Lark of The Frances L. & Edwin L. Cummings Memorial Fund focuses on the facility: "Is it bright and cheerful or is it just institutional gray or green with no art or posters on the walls? It reflects on the agency and what they are doing. Even the exterior of the building, is it an inviting façade? Is there broken glass in front of the building? We have seen that and that is a problem. A youth-serving agency with glass on the sidewalk? That is a problem." David D. Weitnauer of R. Howard Dobbs, Jr. Foundation, Inc. notes: "From a 30,000-foot level you are trying to get a sense of whether there is coherence between what is on paper and what your experience is during the site visit. Is there integrity about it? Are there weaknesses there we did not anticipate? What are their growing edges? What are the kinds of things that they have to pay particular attention to? And sometimes those add up to a tipping point where you draw a conclusion that this does not seem like a sustainable organization. It is really more unhealthy than we realized. And that could lead to a decline based on what the trustees do with the information."

Irene Frye of The Retirement Research Foundation is looking for a greater understanding of the project and how it relates to the foundation's key interests, while Bob Wittig of Jovid Foundation says that the visit makes an organization come alive. Darin McKeever of The Bill & Melinda Gates Foundation indicates the visit creates a deeper sense of empathy that leads to a candid, trusting relationship with the grantee. And David A. Odahowski of Edyth Bush Charitable Foundation, Inc. adds that in a meeting you see body language and there is better communication.

Clearly, grantmakers are expecting a lot to come out of a meeting with the grantseeker. This means you need to think carefully about who should participate in the meeting. There is agreement among the grantmakers that the Executive Director/CEO, project director, and a board member should be present. Dianne Yamashiro-Omi of The California Endowment notes: "The executive leadership should definitely be present. If there is a board member and Executive Director present, that is ideal. If there are program staff in place who are going to be charged with implementing a program, then they should be there. A lot of times it becomes a conversation between the Executive Director and the Program Officer. I think we look to the Executive Director as the one responsible for the implementation of the grant and the one who holds the organization accountable." Karen Kinney of The Morris & Gwendolyn Cafritz Foundation adds: "My preferred people are executive directors, program people, and participants. Sometimes I will ask for a board member to come. My biggest pet peeve is to solely meet with the development director. Having a finance person there is very helpful."

Curtland E. Fields of Turrell Fund comments: "I am interested in seeing hands-on staff to understand what their philosophy of service delivery is, to get a sense of their leadership, how well they staff, and whether they pursue certain quality initiatives." David A. Odahowski of Edyth Bush Charitable Foundation, Inc. indicates: "A board member is very very helpful because if a board member is able to articulate the constraints they are having with revenue streams or programming or other funders, you are saying to yourself: 'They are dealing with that problem. They are doing everything they can internally.' Before you ask for assistance externally you have to do all you can internally. And board members should not sit around a table for an hour or two. They need to know about revenue, expenses, programming, strategy, marketing. If a board member can articulate that, it acts as an endorsement."

Because all the participants should speak during the meeting, you might find it helpful to develop an agenda. You can assign speaking roles via the agenda to all of your team while taking into account the need of the grantmaker to ask questions. This will not only ensure balanced participation among your staff, but will also serve as a way to ensure your meeting progresses in an organized manner and covers all the points you seek to convey to the grantmaker. Be sure to include in your agenda an opportunity for grantmaker input.

The following outline might help.

- *Use an icebreaker.* The first few times you attend a meeting with a funder, it can be nerve-racking. Break the tension by telling an amusing anecdote, by relaying a true incident of interest to the group, or by commenting about the view or an object in the room where the meeting takes place.

- *Introduce all of the meeting participants by name, title, and/or role.* This way the funder will know the players and be clear to whom specific questions should be addressed.

- *Get down to business.* Once introduced, the participants should promptly move on to the real purpose of the meeting: Your group hopes the funder will become a partner with you in getting your project off the ground.

- *Remind the funder about the mission and history of your agency.* Be thorough but brief in this review.

- *Describe the programs you offer.* Again, be succinct, but be certain that the funder has a good overview of your services. This is important in case the project submitted for funding proves not to be of interest. The funder may request a proposal relating to a different aspect of your agency's work, having achieved a good grasp of the whole program.

- *Describe the project for which you are seeking support.* It is critical that you demonstrate the conviction that success is likely. Provide the necessary detail for the funder to understand the problem being addressed and your agency's proposed response to it.

- *Keep a dialogue going.* It is easy to speak at length about your organization. But it is also easy to bore the funders and, even worse, for you to come away from the meeting not having gained any relevant new information about this grantmaker. Keep funders engaged. Inquire about current programs they have funded that address similar problems. Treat grantmakers as potential partners. Remember, their dollars have significance only when combined with programs. Listen carefully to their responses, comments, and questions. This dialogue will clue you into the real interests and concerns of this potential funder, and will give you invaluable insight into the proper next steps to take in ensuring that your proposal is funded. Do not assume anything.

- *Obtain a clear understanding of the next steps.* You should determine the following: if anything more is needed for review of the request; when the proposal will come up for review; and how the agency will be notified about the outcome. If, as a result of this conversation, it is clear that the proposal is unlikely to be funded, you should ask what you might do to resubmit this or another proposal.

Finally, the grantmakers we interviewed provide some very helpful guidance about the meeting. The following should be avoided:

- The dog/pony show: Do not have a canned presentation. Think about what the grantmaker needs to discuss and to see.

- Food/lunch/coffee: Ask the grantmaker in advance if food or coffee would be appreciated. Whatever you provide, make it simple.

- Red carpet treatment: The grantmaker is trying to see the organization and your programs in a natural state. Grantmakers want to be the fly on the wall. As Ilene Mack, formerly of the Hearst Foundations, said, "Do not gussy up the place!"

There are a few things that you should do. First, be prepared. Bob Wittig of Jovid Foundation notes: "The biggest challenge for everybody is being able to explain their financials." Bruce H. Esterline of The Meadows Foundation, Inc. sums up: "Be prepared to answer a lot of questions about the project, and the way it will be financed."

Jane B. O'Connell and Karen L. Rosa of Altman Foundation indicate that you need to be yourself and be able to engage the grantmaker in conversation, as opposed to simply answering the grantmaker's questions. Maria Mottola of New York Foundation adds: "A dialogue is important." Lita Ugarte Pardi of The Community Foundation for Greater Atlanta explains: "We meet with organizations for generally two hours. We let them know up front: this is not a meeting where you will pitch your program and give us a grand tour of your organization. This is a meeting where we will talk about a number of aspects of the organization and we are very specific about who should be at the meeting."

Finally, you need to be respectful of the grantmaker's schedule. Share what is needed without going off on tangents. Grantmakers are perpetually busy people, and are likely to have other scheduled appointments on the day of your meeting. So be mindful of the time. Make sure you have touched on each point outlined in your agenda before the scheduled end of the visit, when a grantmaker is likely to depart immediately for other business. If the grantmaker wishes to stay beyond the allotted end of the meeting, all the better!

This is your opportunity to be passionate about your work and its impact.

The staff and trustees of The Frances L. & Edwin L. Cummings Memorial Fund shared the following evaluation form, detailing the questions they ask themselves as part of a site visit.

THE FRANCES L. & EDWIN L. CUMMINGS MEMORIAL FUND

TRUSTEE'S SITE VISIT EVALUATION

I. GENERAL INFORMATION

Name of Organization:

Location:

Date of site visit: Board Member:

Other Attendees:

II. PROGRAM INFORMATION

1. Rate Executive Director with respect to the following:
   (Scale: 1=Excellent, 2=Very Good, 3=Good, 4=Fair, 5=Poor)

   Understanding of his/her job

   Leadership

   Relationship to staff

   Understanding of needs of community being served

   Effective communicator of ideas

   Dedication to job

   Ability to respond under pressure—deal with critical problems

   Additional comments:

2. Is the organization overloaded with professionals, properly lean, or understaffed for program efficiency?

   _____

   _____

   _____

3. Does this organization have a proven track record in general? Specifically or as to this program(s)?

   _____

   _____

   _____

4. Does this organization have the potential to expand to meet increasing needs of the community? (If this organization is already expanding/ expanded, has it done so in a manageable fashion?)

_____

_____

_____

5. Is this organization offering innovative programs or are they replicating/ duplicating others' efforts?

_____

_____

_____

III. BOARD OF DIRECTORS

1. Is the Board of Directors an "active" or a "paper" Board? Explain.

_____

_____

_____

2. Using the same scale as above, rank the Board of Directors with respect to:

Leadership

Relationship to staff

Dedication to achieving stated objectives of the organization

Personal knowledge of organization's daily activities

Amount of time personally committed to organization

Personal financial commitment

Distribution of responsibility among Board Members

Additional comments:

IV. FACILITIES

1. Is the space effectively utilized?   Yes   No   Describe.

_____

_____

2. Is the atmosphere conducive to the programs being operated? Yes No
   If no, please explain.

   _____

   _____

   _____

V. PROPOSAL INFORMATION

1. Is there a need for this kind of service in the community? Are other agencies
   already providing the same kind of service(s)? If so, is the proposal(s)
   unique in any respect?

   _____

   _____

   _____

2. Are the goals of the proposal(s) aggressive enough? Too aggressive?

   _____

   _____

   _____

3. Is the budget for the proposal(s) realistic?

   _____

   _____

   _____

4. Is the proposal(s) cost-effective in its anticipated results?

   _____

   _____

   _____

5. Has the program(s) been well-planned?

   _____

   _____

   _____

6. Is the Board/Staff committed to undertaking the project(s) regardless of Cummings Fund support? (If so, how?)

_____

_____

_____

VI. FINANCIAL INFORMATION

1. What is the overall present financial situation of this organization?

_____

_____

_____

2. Additional comments/Summary:

_____

_____

_____

_____

_____

_____

_____

_____

After each meeting with a funder, be sure to make a checklist of any issues the funder asked you to follow up on. It is crucial that you follow up with any additional information requests from the funder in a timely fashion.

Here is an example of a letter following an appointment submitted to The Frances L. & Edwin L. Cummings Memorial Fund by New York City Outward Bound.

Dear Libby,

As promised, I am writing to send updates on two items related to our grant request in advance of your Board meeting on Wednesday.

School Designer Search

In conducting this search, we have been fortunate to secure the volunteer help of one of our Board members, who has a background in both human resources and education. With her help, we have written a job announcement and posted it on about eight different sites that are likely to be visited by candidates with the kinds of qualifications and backgrounds we are looking for. So far, we have received inquires from approximately 20 qualified candidates. We are currently in the midst of screening these candidates, and have asked six applicants to prepare for phone interviews. We expect to invite a handful more for phone interviews in the next few days. We aim to have the phone interviews completed by the end of the first week of January, followed by in-person interviews and school visits of the next round candidates to be completed by the third week in January, demo lessons by finalists by the middle of February, and an offer made by the end of February.

Other Funding Prospects

To cover the remaining cost of hiring an additional School Designer, we have approached or are planning to approach the funders below. In each case, were we to receive the grant funds we are requesting, we would apply a portion of those funds to cover costs associated with bringing on board another School Designer.

- We are currently preparing a request to Bank of America for $100k.

- We are also in conversation with the Hearst Foundations and hope to submit a request this spring for $75k to $100k.

- We will be submitting a $30k request to the Stella and Charles Guttman Foundation by the end of December

- In addition, we hope to submit requests to a few other foundations (including Booth Ferris), but the conversions are not far enough along to include them as firm prospects.

I hope this is clear and gives you the information you had requested. If it is not, please don't hesitate to contact me. And, as always, please don't hesitate to let me know if you have any further questions or would like additional information.

Best,
Richard

Richard Stopol
President
New York City Outward Bound
29-46 Northern Blvd
Long Island City, NY 11101
718-706-9900, x112
rstopol@nycoutwardbound.org
www.nycoutwardbound.org

Find us on facebook.com/nycoutwardbound
Follow "NYCOutwardBound" on twitter.com

Bringing Demanding Academics, Community & Character to New York City public schools

16

Life After the Grant— or Rejection

The Initial Follow-up to a Grant

You've just received a grant from a foundation or corporation. Congratulations! What should you do? First of all, you should celebrate. Include everyone in your agency who contributed to this wonderful outcome. Thank them for their help and remind them about what this means for your organization.

Next, send a thank-you letter to your funder. This seems so obvious that one would think it hardly worth stating. Yet a number of the grantmakers interviewed for this book responded to the question, "What is the best thing an organization can do after receiving a grant?" with the simple response: send a thank-you letter.

Here are three sample thank-you letters. The first is from The Children's Institute.

September 24, 2010

Ms. Katie Goodspeed
Executive Director
Variety, The Children's Charity
505 Eight Avenue, Suite 1800
New York, NY 10018

Dear Katie:

On behalf of The Children's Institute, I would like to thank Variety for your recent donation of $25,000 in support of our After School and Respite programs.

We are most appreciative of your caring and thought-fullness. Contributions such as yours are very meaningful to our students, since so many programs depend on the dollars that we raise from families, friends and corporations.

Your kindness will help The Children's Institute to continue to provide comprehensive educational, therapeutic and caring programs for children on the autistic spectrum and related disabilities, so that each child can reach his or her maximum potential. Our goal is to address the needs of the "whole child", so each may become an independent, productive member of the community.

Please be advised that no goods or services were provided in exchange for this gift.

Again, thank you very much.

Sincerely,

Barry Haber
Chief Development Officer
The Children's Institute

The next example from East Side House is quite brief and to the point.

June 16, 2011

Ms. Alexandra A. Herzan
President
The Lily Auchincloss Foundation, Inc.
16 East 79th Street #31
New York, NY 10075

Dear Alexandra:

What a great pleasure it was to receive your letter of June 13th
and very generous grant of $10,000 in support of our Youth
and Adult Education Services (YAES) Program! We greatly value
your foundation's prior support and we sincerely appreciate
your including us in your giving for this year.

Your grant is very timely, as demand for East Side House's
educational and supportive services continues to increase in
the face of a deepening recession.

As always, I will be pleased to update you on our work. If you
have any questions or wish to see our programs in the interim,
please do not hesitate to call me.

Again, on behalf of East Side House's Board of Managers,
staff, and—most importantly—the many young people
and families who will be working to make bright futures for
themselves through our programs, I thank you for this grant.

Sincerely,

John A. Sanchez
Executive Director

The final example is from St. John's Foundation.

St John's
Embrace Living

April 26, 2011

Mr. Verne Moore
14 Bay Park
Webster, NY 14580

Dear Mr. Moore:

Thank you so much for your grant of $100,000 in support of the St. John's Green House project. The continuing generosity of the Daisy Marquis Jones Foundation is inspiring and energizing for us as we move forward with our vision of changing the way elders experience care.

We are very excited that our Green Houses are under construction in Penfield, and look forward to taking you on a tour.

Please feel free to call if you need further information. The signed authorization is enclosed, as requested. Again, thank you for your generous support.

Sincerely,

Catherine (Kit) Pollicove
President

150 Highland Avenue   Rochester, New York   14620-3099 • 585-760-1300

The foundation representatives we interviewed expressed a concern that needs to be taken to heart. Appreciate the investment that has just been made in your agency. Recognize that it is not just an institution that is supporting you but the actual people within that institution. Remember that the grant decision-makers feel good about the commitment to invest in your organization. They may even have had to fight for you in the face of opposition by other staff and board members. Show your thanks and appreciation for this vote of confidence.

Grantmakers want to ensure effective communication after a grant is awarded. They remind us that a grant is a contract to undertake a specific set of activities, and they want and need to know what has transpired.

Remember the watchword of all fundraising: communication. A telephone call to say "thank you," an update on recent activities, or an announcement of additional funding committed or received are all ways to keep in touch after the grant is made.

Written Updates

Each grantmaker has its own means of tracking grant funds, which in most cases consists of some form of grant reports. Beyond the required reports, you should also maintain effective communication with the grantmaker. Demonstrate your ability to fulfill your obligations by keeping the grantmaker informed of your progress over the course of the grant period. Sometimes plans change, or unexpected events occur. Share both good news and obstacles you have encountered, and engage the grantmaker as your partner. Remember that the grantmaker wants you to succeed.

The first example is from Big Brothers of Nashville to The Frist Foundation.

Re: Grant from the Ansley Fund of the Frist Foundation to Big Brothers of Nashville of $25,000

I want to thank you for your generous grant to Big Brothers of Nashville. I also want to try and explain to you how much this grant means this year and at this time. On June 17, 2011, Metro Action Commission just announced that they were changing their funding year, from July 1 to October 1, so that the thousands of Davidson County residents who have received help last fiscal year, will not be able to get the expected help starting July 1. What that means is that there is no other agency that is available in Nashville to pick up the slack but Big Brothers of Nashville.

Your donation is so very timely. We anticipate being slammed during these next three months, more than we usually are, and although we will not be able to help all those that are in need, we will be able to make a significant difference in the lives of at least 25 to 35 families each month. That may not sound like many, but to each one of these families that we do help, it will mean a secure home and warm water to bathe with, it will mean they don't have to take their children and frantically seek someone who will temporarily house them, hoping to move in with a cousin, or friend and bounce from one house to another until they can afford to get their electricity turned back on. It will mean safety, security, comfort and happiness.

So, thank you for your generous donation, and our assurance to you is that we will administer these funds with great care and compassion.

Gay Levine Eisen (glevine@comcast.net)
Board Member/Compliance Officer
Big Brothers of Nashville

The example that follows is excerpted from an e-mail update from Sanctuary for Families, Inc.

I hope you're well and enjoying this unseasonably balmy "holiday weather"! I wanted to alert you to a number of recent articles, including two in the New York Times, touching on Sanctuary's work. Links to all of them are below, and please feel free to forward widely to your fellow trustees and any other colleagues as you wish.

The most recent was the story of Virna, a Sanctuary client featured in a NY Times Neediest Cases Fund stories (page A30 on Tuesday 12/20). A little background: Virna came to Sanctuary after suffering severe physical violence at the hands of her partner. Our immigration attorneys were able to assist her with obtaining her U Visa, and are now working to reunite Virna with her two other children who are still in Mexico. Legal staff referred Virna internally to Sanctuary's Economic Empowerment Program, and she has successfully completed our career readiness and job training program, graduating in June. She is actively looking for a job while juggling all of the issues with her diabetic son, as detailed in the story.

The link to that story is here: www.nytimes.com/2011/12/20/nyregion/a-boys-diabetes-his-mothers-dedication.html?_r=1&scp=2&sq=neediest%20cases%20fund&st=cse and a full copy of the story is also inline below.

The other major article appeared in the print edition of last Wednesday's (12/14) New York Times. Our client Sofia (a pseudonym), a trafficking victim, and Sanctuary's Anti-Trafficking Initiative, are the focus of the article, which describes the role that taxi and livery cab drivers play in trafficking networks in NYC, something that Sofia brought to our attention and that Sanctuary brought to the attention of the Taxi & Limousine Commission and City Council. The Council held hearings on this topic last Wednesday, where two Sanctuary trafficking attorneys testified. Sofia herself also testified, behind a screen to protect her identity, with her Sanctuary counselor by her side for support.

Many thanks for your support of Sanctuary this past year. It has been quite a year—with new and expanding programs, major accomplishments in both direct service and policy advocacy for our trafficking work, a New York Times Nonprofit Excellence Award, and many other milestones for Sanctuary. Needless to say, we couldn't do it without the Foundation's support.

With best wishes for the holiday season,

John Wyeth

John Wyeth, Jr.
Assistant Director of Development for Institutional Giving
Sanctuary for Families
PO Box 1406, Wall Street Station, New York, NY 10268
P: 212.349.6009 x 266
F: 212.349.6810
www.sanctuaryforfamilies.org

Grant Reporting

If a foundation has specific reporting requirements, you will be told what they are. Usually reporting requirements are included in the grant letter; sometimes you are asked to sign and return a copy of the grant letter or of a separate grant contract. These "conditions," which a representative of the nonprofit signs, sometimes require timely reports that are tied to payments.

Here is the Cooper Foundation Grant Agreement form.

COOPER FOUNDATION GRANT AGREEMENT

SAMPLE AGREEMENT

[GRANTEE ORGANIZATION] (Recipient) hereby accepts this grant from the Cooper Foundation (Foundation) in the amount of[GRANT AMOUNT] and agrees to comply with the following terms and conditions.

1. The grant funds will be used solely for [PROJECT TITLE OR PURPOSE]. If unable to proceed with the activities described in the proposal dated [PROPOSAL DATE], Recipient agrees to contact the Foundation in writing. Substantive changes in the program, budget or use of the grant funds must be submitted in advance, in writing, and approved by the Foundation in writing.

2. In the case of a contingent grant, Recipient agrees to provide information that the contingency has been met prior to the Foundation making payment. This grant is contingent upon [CONTINGENCY DESCRIPTION].• The deadline for this information is [DATE]. Failure to provide this information may result in the grant monies being rescinded. Any request to extend the deadline or change the nature of the contingency must be submitted an advance to the Foundation in writing.
   • *Examples: raising the full project budget; receipt of necessary information or permissions; confirmation that a particular position has been filled, etc.*

3. The grant term shall start at the date of approval and end [PROJECT END DATE].

4. If any grant funds remain unused at the end of the grant term, Recipient agrees to contact the Foundation to determine whether to return the funds or expend them for another purpose.

5. Recipient agrees to provide written reports, including program and financial information, by [REPORT DATES]. *This section used when interim reports are required for multi-year grants.*

6. Recipient agrees to provide a final report by [DATE]. The final report must include the organization's most recent audited financial statements and current financial reports.

7. Recipient may not seek additional funding from the Foundation during the grant term or for 12 months after the last payment date, whichever is later.

Recipient certifies that its 501(c)(3) status with the Internal Revenue Service remains in full force and effect, and that we are not a private foundation within the meaning of section 509(a) of the Internal Revenue Code.

For [GRANTEE ORGANIZATION}:

Board Chair or President

_____   _____   _____
Signature   Print Name   Date

Chief Executive Officer

_____   _____   _____
Signature   Print Name   Date

For the Foundation:

    Art Thompson, President   _____   _____
                                   Signature   Date

What follows are the Grant Letter and Grant Agreement used by Conrad N. Hilton Foundation.

[Date]

«Org_Primary_Contact_Name»
«Org_Primary_Contact_Title»
«Org_Name_Address»

Re: Grant «Request_ID»
        (Please refer to this number when corresponding with us.)

Dear «Org_Primary_Contact_Name»,

It is a pleasure to inform you that the Board of Directors of the Conrad N. Hilton Foundation has approved a grant payable to «Org_Legal_Name» (Grantee; EIN «Org_Tax_ID») in the amount of «Request_Recommended_Amount» over «Request_Term_ » years beginning on «Request_Project_Start_Date», «Request_Project_Title»

Within 30 days, please submit a signed copy of this grant agreement to the Foundation (GMDepartment@HiltonFoundation.org) indicating Grantee's agreement with the following terms and conditions.

1.   Purpose: This grant, and any interest income earned thereon, will be used as described in Grantee's application dated «Request_Date», as well as any approved revisions. No substantial changes will be made without prior written approval of the Foundation.

2.   Payment and Reporting Schedule: This grant is payable in "[one, two, three . . .]" installments upon the receipt of this signed grant agreement and upon the satisfactory completion by Grantee of all the terms and conditions, including any deliverables, contained in this grant agreement and in Grantee's application dated «Request_Date», as well as any approved revisions. Progress reports shall be completed using the provided format. Payment will be issued within 60 days of approval of an acceptable progress report or other listed contingency.

   Submit reports to the Foundation at GMDepartment@HiltonFoundation.org; enter grantee name, grant number, and type of report in subject line. Final report shall reference the specific activities proposed in the Grantee's application and describe the extent to which those activities have been successfully implemented. (or Final report shall reference the specific activities that have been implement as a result of this grant, including successes and challenges.)

Amount	Reporting Period	Report Due	Payment Contingent Upon
$XXX,000	N/A	N/A	Return of signed grant agreement
$XXX,000	xx/xx/xxxx-xx/xx/xxxx	xx/xx/xxxx	Acceptable progress report, including x, y, and z
$XXX,000	xx/xx/xxxx-xx/xx/xxxx	xx/xx/xxxx	Acceptable progress report
N/A	xx/xx/xxxx-xx/xx/xxxx	xx/xx/xxxx	Acceptable cumulative final report
total	confirm total equals grant amount; then delete row		

3.   Active Grant: This grant shall be considered active for a period of 12 months from the date of the Foundation's final disbursement of grant funds and until the final report has been received. The Foundation has a general policy of not considering an additional request from an organization that has an active grant.

4.   Account and Evaluation: Grantee agrees to maintain complete and accurate accounting of all expenditures made under this grant to enable the Foundation to easily determine how the grant funds, including any interest earned thereon, were spent. Grantee also agrees to retain these records during the grant period and until the final report is received and approved by the Foundation. During this time if requested, Grantee shall make records available at reasonable times to the Foundation (or its designated representative) for inspection or audit at the Foundation's expense. Further, Grantee agrees to participate in evaluation activities organized and funded by the Foundation that relate to this grant.

5.   Tax Status: Grantee warrants that it is exempt from income tax under Section 501(c)(3) of the Internal Revenue Code and is not a private foundation as described in Section 509(a). Any change in this status shall be communicated to the Foundation immediately. Grantee further warrants that this grant will not result in it becoming a private foundation under the public support test, if such test is applicable.

6.   Non-Permitted Uses: Grantee warrants that none of these funds will be used to influence legislation unless permitted by law.

7.   Anti-Terrorism and Re-Granting: Grantee agrees that these funds will be used in compliance with all applicable anti-terrorism financing and asset control laws and regulations and that none of these funds will be used to support or promote violence, terrorist activity or related training, or money laundering. Re-granting is not permitted unless specifically approved in the grant budget. Grantee is required to cross-check all sub-grantees approved for re-granting against the terrorism watch lists designated by U.S. Treasury Office of Foreign Assets Control (OFAC) and refrain from providing financial or material support to any listed individual or organization.

8.   Convening and Publicity: The Foundation may request that Grantee participate in periodic meetings convened by the Foundation that relate to this grant. Further, the Foundation requests that in any publicity given this grant, acknowledgement be made that funding was received from the Conrad N. Hilton Foundation, using its complete name. In addition, the Foundation respectfully requests that prior to its release, the proposed publicity be approved by the Foundation. Please submit the proposed press material to program staff assigned to this grant. The Foundation requests that, once available, a copy of the finalized material be furnished to the Foundation.

9.   <u>Compliance</u>: Failure to comply with any of the terms of this grant agreement, and any subsequent agreed upon modifications, may result in one or more of the following.

        (a)   Termination of the grant.
        (b)   Suspension of future grant payments until Grantee demonstrates compliance.
        (c)   Grantee's immediate reimbursement to the Foundation of the amount of any Foundation grant funds expended for purposes not previously approved by the Foundation.
        (d)   Grantee's immediate reimbursement to the Foundation of all unexpended Foundation grant funds.

10.   <u>Jurisdiction</u>: This grant agreement shall be governed and construed in accordance with the laws of the State of Nevada, U.S.A. applicable to contracts made in such State without regard to conflicts of law doctrines, and the parties agree that jurisdiction and venue for any dispute regarding this grant agreement will be in such State.

It is the policy of the Conrad N. Hilton Foundation to discourage beneficiaries of its grants from making gifts to Foundation personnel, giving honoraria in any form, or sending plaques or other memorabilia. The Foundation prefers that the cost of such items not be incurred by a recipient agency.

The Foundation appreciates your organization's cooperation in preparing for this grant and we extend our best wishes for its successful implementation.

Sincerely,

Steven M. Hilton
President & CEO

SMH:"[PO initials]" -[initials]

c: «Contact_Name_Full», «Org_Legal_Name»

Accepted:

_____   _____
«Org_Primary_Contact_Name»   Date
«Org_Primary_Contact_Title»
«Org_Legal_Name»

When a foundation provides formal reporting guidelines, in most cases there will be dates when the reports are due. If a funder has given you specific dates for reporting, develop a tickler system to keep track of them. If you can tell now that you'll have a problem meeting these deadlines (such as your auditors are scheduled for March, and the audited financial report is due in February), discuss this with the funder immediately. If the foundation staff has not heard from the grantee within a reasonable time period after the reports are due, they will call or send the grant recipient a note to follow up.

Some funders want reports at quarterly or six-month intervals, but most request an annual report and/or a final report, two to three months after the conclusion of the project. Even for grants of fairly short duration, foundations often express the desire to receive an interim report. Unless otherwise stated, an interim report can be informal.

The Cleveland Foundation issues very specific reporting instructions. Its Grant Report Preparation Guidelines provide a useful framework to guide agency staff in drafting a report to any funder. While these guidelines are designed for The Cleveland Foundation's grantees, they provide a reliable model for reports to other foundations that may not be as specific in their requirements.

The following guidelines are reprinted in their totality with permission from The Cleveland Foundation:

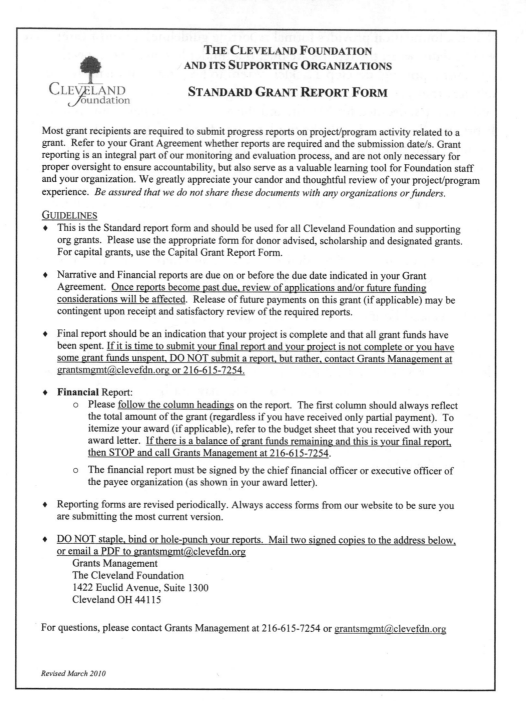

**THE CLEVELAND FOUNDATION
AND ITS SUPPORTING ORGANIZATIONS**

STANDARD GRANT REPORT FORM

Most grant recipients are required to submit progress reports on project/program activity related to a grant. Refer to your Grant Agreement whether reports are required and the submission date/s. Grant reporting is an integral part of our monitoring and evaluation process, and are not only necessary for proper oversight to ensure accountability, but also serve as a valuable learning tool for Foundation staff and your organization. We greatly appreciate your candor and thoughtful review of your project/program experience. *Be assured that we do not share these documents with any organizations or funders.*

GUIDELINES
- This is the Standard report form and should be used for all Cleveland Foundation and supporting org grants. Please use the appropriate form for donor advised, scholarship and designated grants. For capital grants, use the Capital Grant Report Form.

- Narrative and Financial reports are due on or before the due date indicated in your Grant Agreement. Once reports become past due, review of applications and/or future funding considerations will be affected. Release of future payments on this grant (if applicable) may be contingent upon receipt and satisfactory review of the required reports.

- Final report should be an indication that your project is complete and that all grant funds have been spent. If it is time to submit your final report and your project is not complete or you have some grant funds unspent, DO NOT submit a report, but rather, contact Grants Management at grantsmgmt@clevefdn.org or 216-615-7254.

- **Financial** Report:
  - Please follow the column headings on the report. The first column should always reflect the total amount of the grant (regardless if you have received only partial payment). To itemize your award (if applicable), refer to the budget sheet that you received with your award letter. If there is a balance of grant funds remaining and this is your final report, then STOP and call Grants Management at 216-615-7254.

  - The financial report must be signed by the chief financial officer or executive officer of the payee organization (as shown in your award letter).

- Reporting forms are revised periodically. Always access forms from our website to be sure you are submitting the most current version.

- DO NOT staple, bind or hole-punch your reports. Mail two signed copies to the address below, or email a PDF to grantsmgmt@clevefdn.org
  Grants Management
  The Cleveland Foundation
  1422 Euclid Avenue, Suite 1300
  Cleveland OH 44115

For questions, please contact Grants Management at 216-615-7254 or grantsmgmt@clevefdn.org

Revised March 2010

THE CLEVELAND FOUNDATION
AND ITS SUPPORTING ORGANIZATIONS

FINANCIAL
STANDARD GRANT REPORT

CLEVELAND
foundation

Check one: _____ **Interim Report**

_____ **Final Report** *(Check only if project is complete and all grant funds spent. Otherwise, STOP and contact Grants Management)*

Organization Name: _____

Grant Number: _____

Report Due Date: _____

Project Title:

	Total Grant Awarded (regardless of pmts received) **(itemized)**	**Total Grant Funds Expended to Date** **(itemized)**	**Balance of Grant Funds** (or zero $0 if final report)* **(itemized)**
Salaries & Wages			
Benefits & Payroll Taxes			
Consultants & professional services			
Travel			
Equipment			
Office Supplies/Materials			
Printing			
Utilities			
Postage/Mailing			
Rent/Occupancy			
Building maintenance			
Depreciation			
Marketing			
Indirect Expenses			
Other			
TOTAL	$	$	$

*Please contact Grants Management if other than zero ($0).

Signature: _____ **Date:** _____

Circle one: Chief Financial Officer or Executive Officer/Director

Name: (print) _____ **Title:** _____

CFO/Executive Officer/Director

Telephone: _____ **Email:** _____

Revised March 2010

THE CLEVELAND FOUNDATION
AND ITS SUPPORTING ORGANIZATIONS

NARRATIVE
STANDARD GRANT REPORT

Check one: _____ **Interim Report**

_____ **Final Report** *(Submit only if the project is complete. Include a review of performance and activities covering the entire grant period.)*

Organization Name: _____

Grant Number: _____

Project Title: _____

Reporting Dates: From: _____   To: _____

Signature: _____

Name *(please print)*: _____   **Date:** _____

Email: _____   **Telephone:** _____

I. <u>PROJECT INFORMATION</u> *(Please type directly on this form. Indicate N/A for questions not applicable. Be sure you are using the appropriate form for your grant.)*

1. Please summarize the expected outcomes for this project and to what extent they have been achieved.

2. What have been the principal accomplishments of the project to date and how have they been achieved?

3. The Foundation recognizes that circumstances can change, possibly affecting project implementation. What, if any, difficulties have you encountered; why did they occur; and what refinements or plans have been made to overcome them? Please indicate activities that are behind schedule or not yet begun, and any changes in project plans or personnel.

4. What have been the most challenging or surprising aspects of this project? Have there been any unexpected outcomes?

Revised March 2010

5. Based on your experience to date, what advice would you give to other organizations planning a similar program? What have been the strengths and limitations of the project? What would you do differently if you had the chance?

6. Please describe your post-grant plans for this project. How will it be financed?

II. ORGANIZATIONAL INFORMATION

It is very helpful to understand the organizational context in which your project is proceeding. Please take this opportunity to update us on any significant organizational changes, developments or challenges. How have these developments contributed to or impeded the success of the project? Additionally, are there any problems or issues confronting your organization that may require assistance? How might Foundation staff be helpful?

III. ATTACHMENTS (Optional)

Please include copies of any supporting materials, public recognition, awards, press releases or news articles pertinent to this project/program.

The Cleveland Foundation guidelines are particularly applicable if you have received special project support. Don't be concerned if your project does not lend itself to many of these questions. For instance, if you have received $15,000 to hire a tutor for your after-school program, some of the sections are probably not applicable. Others, like post-grant plans, should be addressed in some fashion in almost any report.

Even if you have received unrestricted, general-purpose support, funders want to know what overall goals you set for your agency for the year. Did you achieve them? What were some specific triumphs? What were some particular problems you faced, and how did you overcome them? Or, are you still dealing with the challenges? (Remember, being realistic is what counts, along with a sense of confidence that you are appropriately managing the grant.) What follows is a report to Turrell Fund from its grant recipient, the Tri-County Scholarship Fund.

Mr. Curtland E. Fields
Executive Director
Turrell Fund
21 Van Vleck Street
Montclair, New Jersey 07042-2358

Dear Mr. Fields:

Tri-County Scholarship Fund (TCSF) is extremely grateful for the continued support of the Turrell Fund. With your help over the past nine years, TCSF has been able to give greater support to children in Passaic County with a more meaningful level of financial aid. I am pleased to submit this report on the use of the June 2007 $25,000 scholarship grant from the Turrell Fund.

The Turrell Fund's grant provided 25 elementary school students with scholarships, allowing them the opportunity to obtain a quality, values-centered education in a private school. Scholarship recipients are immersed in school environments that, in addition to providing strong academic programs, strengthen student skills and values, thereby empowering them to contribute back to society. These students are given the tools they need to break the cycle of poverty.

TCSF scholarship recipients participate in Leadership Development Programs which are geared towards fostering leadership and personal growth and development. These programs provide students with a more complete picture of the larger world around them and of life's possibilities. For example, close to 1,000 elementary school students from the inner-city areas will attend a production at the Community Theatre of New Jersey. This past Fall, over 300 students traveled to a farm in Hunterdon County, NJ where they went pumpkin picking, went on pony rides and roasted marshmallows over an open fire. These are simple activities that the schools, because of their location and income, can not afford to provide to their students. TCSF and its generous donors seek to fill this void in students' life experiences.

In the 2007/2008 Academic Year, TCSF funded scholarships totaling $907,934 for 701 students. Due to limited funding, only half of those who applied for help for 2007/2008 received it. Passaic County continues to have the largest number of recipients totaling 648 or 92 percent of the total number of scholarships awarded. Of this, 489 recipients are elementary school students in Passaic. Passaic County recipients received $827,962—91 percent of the total awards. In the organization's 26 years of operation we have awarded close 26,000 scholarships and distributed close to $16 million.

Attached is a Final Report on the use of the Turrell Grant, statistics on the distribution of our scholarships in Passaic County, and an Applicant/Recipient Profile. Tri-County Scholarship Fund is committed to continuing the success we have already achieved and to strengthening and expanding opportunities responsive to the needs of the low-income families we serve. We will continue to grow our income for funding scholarships through grant writing, solicitation of private and corporate monies, and our two yearly major special events.

We thank the Turrell Fund for its continued support of our
scholarship recipients. Please know that your assistance
is greatly appreciated by the students and their families.
Only with help such as yours will TCSF be able to continue
impacting and improving the surrounding community by
providing economically disadvantaged families with
educational choice.

Sincerely,

Gregory Floyd
President

Attachments

**FINAL REPORT ON USE OF $25,000
2007 TURRELL FUND GRANT
TO TRI-COUNTY SCHOLARSHIP FUND**

- For the 2007/2008 Academic Year Tri-County
  received 1,675 applications and awarded $907,934 to
  701 students.

- Passaic County
  - Applicants: 1,376
  - Recipients: 648 (92 percent of total recipients)
  - Awarded: $827,962 (91 percent of total awards)
  - # of High Schools recipients attend: 5
  - # of Elementary Schools recipients attend: 20

- 2006–2007 Top 4 Passaic County Elementary Schools
  Receiving Awards:

  Pope John Paul II School:
  - Applicants: 287
  - Recipients: 144
  - Awarded: $131,747

  Passaic Catholic Regional School:
  - Applicants: 65
  - Recipients: 43
  - Awarded: $31,62

  Blessed Sacrament School:
  - Applicants: 65
  - Recipients: 42
  - Awarded: $41,054

  Our Lady of Mt. Carmel/St. Nicholas School:
  - Applicants: 61
  - Recipients: 42
  - Awarded: $35,062

- The grant of $25,000 received in June 2007 provided
  tuition assistance at $1,000 each for 25 children attending
  elementary schools in Passaic County.

The next example is a cover letter to a final report to Georgia Power Foundation, Inc. from the Fernbank Museum of Natural History.

FERNBANK™
MUSEUM OF NATURAL HISTORY

July 22, 2011

Ms. Susan M. Carter
Georgia Power Foundation
Bin 10130
241 Ralph McGill Boulevard, NE
Atlanta, GA 30308

Dear Susan:

On behalf of Fernbank Museum of Natural History's Board of Trustees, I wish to express, once again, our deep appreciation for Georgia Power's tremendous generosity in support of the Campaign for Fernbank, the largest project of which was *Fernbank NatureQuest*. Since opening in late March, *NatureQuest* has inspired thousands of visitors and transformed early childhood and family learning at Fernbank.

The Museum's immersive new habitat-themed exhibition addresses a critical community need--to provide engaging formative experiences in science and nature for young children. Not only are children's experiences with nature diminishing, but less than one-third of Georgia's children demonstrate science proficiency in national tests. By reaching the youngest members of our community when they are most receptive to learning about science and the natural world, we are inspiring both a greater interest in science and a stronger desire to protect the environment.

We are delighted to share with you the enclosed Final Report on *Fernbank NatureQuest*. Inside you will find a brief narrative, budget, photo gallery and donor list as well as curriculum and field guides and selected media coverage. Should you have any questions or need any further detail, please contact our Development Director, Marissa Greider at 404.929.6364 or marissa.greider@fernbankmuseum.org or me at 404.929.6311 or susan.neugent@fernbankmuseum.org.

Again, thank you for Georgia Power's longstanding support for Fernbank and generous investment in *NatureQuest*. I look forward to giving you a personal tour at your convenience.

Sincerely,

Susan E. Neugent
President
Chief Executive Officer

767 Clifton Road, N.E. • Atlanta, Georgia 30307-1221 USA • 404.929.6300 • 404.929.6405 • www.fernbankmuseum.org

These examples are presented as general models only. If a foundation supplies its own guidelines for reporting, then be sure to adhere to those instructions.

In sum, good practice when a grant has been awarded includes:

- saying thank you

- conveying excitement about your work and its success

- sending requested materials, such as a signed grant contract, to the donor

- knowing what you are obligated to do

- getting reports in on time

- communicating both positive and negative news to the grantmaker

Seeking a Renewal

In certain cases, you will want to request that the grant be renewed or that a follow-up project be supported. Some funders refuse to give renewed support because they do not want to encourage dependency or because they see their funding as providing "seed money."

Other funders require a certain period of time to elapse between the grant and the renewal request. For instance, the Hearst Foundations currently require three years between grants.

Even a grant that could be a candidate for renewal may be labeled a one-time gift. Ordinarily the phrase "one-time gift" means that the funder is making no commitment to future funding. It does not necessarily mean that no possibility for future support exists.

If you know that you will want to request renewed support, you should communicate this early on to the foundation in order to determine the best time to submit another request. Be careful not to wait too long before requesting a renewal. By the time the funder receives the request, all the foundation's funds may be committed for the following year.

You should also determine early on the format required by the funder for submitting a renewal request. Some foundations require a full proposal; others want just a letter. This is another illustration of the differences among funders. It reinforces the need to communicate with the grantmaker to determine its particular requirements.

A report on funds expended and results of the first grant is a particularly critical document if you are going to ask for renewed support. However, many funders want your request for renewal to be separate from the report on the grant. In larger foundations, the report and the request for renewal might be handled by different departments; therefore, if you submit your renewal request as part of the report on the first grant, it might not find its way into the proposal system.

Following Up on a Declination

The most important response to a rejection letter is not to take it personally. An old fundraising adage is, "Campaigns fail because people don't ask, not because they get rejected." If your proposal gets rejected, it means you are out there asking. You are doing what you should be doing. Hopefully, you have sent your proposal to a number of other appropriate funders and have not put all your eggs in one basket.

Some funders will talk with you about why the proposal was rejected, particularly if you had a meeting with the program staff. A phone call following a rejection letter can help you clarify the next step. Your request may have been of great interest to the foundation but was turned down in that funding cycle because the board had already committed all the funds set aside for projects in your subject or geographical area. For example, if your request was for an AIDS program in South Chicago, the foundation may have already committed its grants budget for that geographic area. A call to a foundation staff member might result in encouragement to reapply in a later funding cycle.

All funding representatives emphasize, however, the need to be courteous in the process of calling once you have received a rejection letter. It is never easy to say "no," and a program officer who fought hard for your proposal may feel almost as disappointed as you are that it was turned down. While foundation staff usually want to be helpful, it is important to recognize that it can often be difficult to tell someone why a proposal has been rejected.

Richard M. Krasno of The William R. Kenan, Jr. Fund sets the stage by noting: "It is tragic but grantmakers spend a lot of time saying 'no.' This cannot be helped. It is a by-product of the process." Matt Carpenter of El Pomar Foundation encourages the follow-up call: "Call and see if you can get any feedback. Ask follow-up questions. See if you can get any insight. And of course, the all-important question is when you are eligible to apply again." And Paula Boyce of McInerny Foundation (Bank of Hawaii, trustee) adds: "It is perfectly all right for a charity to call after they have received a declination letter."

It is important to take your cue from the funder, either from the rejection letter or from the follow-up call to staff. If you are not encouraged to resubmit, then you probably shouldn't.

There are times when a funder will encourage you to resubmit the same request at a particular time in the future. If you have been given this advice, then follow it. In your cover letter, be sure to refer to your conversation with the funding representative, remembering to restate, but not overstate, the earlier conversation.

Even if a foundation is not interested in funding the particular project you submitted, by keeping the lines of communication open and remaining respectful you will be nurturing the opportunity for future funding. Peter F. Bird, Jr. of The Frist Foundation notes: "In a turndown, the classiest thing you can do is give a gracious thank-you. Let the foundation know that you are not going to hold it against them or make them feel bad. Say 'We hope we can keep the lines of communication open and maybe what we do next time will merit your support and if not, maybe you can steer us to someplace else that might be able to help us.' Smart grantseekers know that you can make a sale without necessarily getting a grant by winning the goodwill of a grantmaker."

In summary, best practice, when your request has been rejected, includes:

- say thank you

- figure out with the grantmaker what your next step should be

- follow the grantmaker's suggestions

- refrain from arguing.

Here is a sample letter from Claremont Neighborhood Centers, Inc.

January 20, 2012

Ms. Phyllis Criscuoli
Executive Director
Cleveland H. Dodge Foundation, Inc.
420 Lexington Avenue, Suite 2331
New York, NY 10170

Dear Ms. Criscuoli:

Thank you for your recent letter informing us that the Cleveland H. Dodge Foundation, Inc. cannot provide support to Claremont Neighborhood Centers at this time. While we are disappointed, we understand that the Foundation receives more requests than resources available.

We appreciate your taking the time to review our request and hope that the Foundation might be in a position to assist us at some point in the future.

Sincerely,

Abraham Jones
Executive Director

Final Tips

What to do if you receive a grant:

- Send a personalized thank-you

- Keep the funder informed of your progress

- Follow the funder's reporting requirements

What to do if your request is turned down:

- Don't take it personally

- Be sure you understand why

- Find out if you can resubmit at a later date

17

What the Funders Have to Say

It is an understatement to call the last few years tumultuous for grantmakers and grantseekers alike. You are probably wondering just what the grantmakers are feeling and seeing and how that is affecting their financial support. This chapter will attempt to summarize the wide array of comments compiled over the course of interviews with forty grantmakers. First, we will look at grantmaker trends. Then we will explore trends grantmakers have observed among nonprofit organizations. Finally, we will review tips from the current interviewees related to the fundraising process.

Trends Among Grantmakers

Due to the downturn in the stock market and subsequent volatility in investments, most of our interviewees experienced a significant reduction in available resources and, therefore, in what they were able to give away in grants during the past few years. How did they deal with this? For many grantmakers there was a cutback in staff. As with nonprofits, vacant positions went unfilled. Staff were offered buy-outs. Trimming of budgets took place whenever possible.

Having less money to give away led some funders to make no new grants. Peter F. Bird, Jr. of The Frist Foundation indicates: "Our assets were down 50 percent. It dried up our ability to make new grants." Other grantmakers took this opportunity to clarify their grantmaking process, to be selective against stated goals. As Thomas Hildebrandt of The Davenport-Hatch Foundation puts it: "What you do is to align yourself more with your giving principles. You don't stray too much." Some funders limited a few categories of support in order to make more funds available to a broader audience. Matt Carpenter of El Pomar Foundation reports: "Trustees have put limits on the size of capital grants in order to provide more funding for general operating and programmatic grants. They are making smaller grants but trying to serve as many as possible and spread the wealth."

Across the board, grantmakers learned a great deal from these experiences, and their grantmaking has changed. First, they are awarding grants in categories that they haven't considered before, especially advocacy. Bruce H. Esterline of The Meadows Foundation, Inc. notes: "We are helping folks stay in business. We made emergency general operating grants and loans. All of this is quite a departure, not our normal way of doing business. And the type of requests we are now getting reflect that's what people need." Related to advocacy, Curtland E. Fields of Turrell Fund tells us: "Even the largest foundations in the country have concluded that they do not have the resources to solve the problems that they are committed to address. Many foundations are therefore investing some of their grantmaking in advocacy or policy change. So in other words, trying to bend public policy at the state level to favor conditions for the issues that you are committed to. We have begun to do some of that. It is difficult, because if you fund a charter school you can go there and visit it. If you fund advocacy for several years, you are never sure if your dollars are the ones that made the difference."

Secondly, grantmakers are being increasingly strategic in their funding. Kathleen Cerveny of The Cleveland Foundation says: "Funders are thinking more and more about how their work can have a strategic focus. Boards want to know that their dollars are making a difference in some way. So funders are operating more strategically and sometimes that means narrowing the focus of what they are interested in funding."

Further, frequently paired with the idea of a more strategic approach to grantmaking, our interviewees discuss the desire to work with other grantmakers and to leverage dollars. Robert B. Jaquay of The George Gund Foundation says very directly: "There is collaboration among many grantmakers. I see it in many communities." Julie Brooks of John S. and James L. Knight Foundation indicates: "Finding partners in our work, making sure that the dollars are being leveraged, is very important." Edmund J. Cain of Conrad N. Hilton Foundation adds: "I think this whole notion of funder groups and alliances is getting more currency." Jacob Harold of The William and Flora Hewlett Foundation adds another dimension: "Most complicated social problems require meaningful engagement from the corporate sector, government, and nonprofits. This is what has been called 'collective impact' that brings together cross-sectors in a coherent, organized way to solve complicated problems that require everyone's participation and engagement." Darin McKeever of The Bill & Melinda Gates Foundation sums this up: "On the grantmaker's side there is an increased emphasis on the word 'leverage.' I think it is a trend where donors are reaching out to potential co-funders or collaborators."

Coming out of this very difficult time, we have grantmakers looking at their work through a new lens. Andrew Lark of The Frances L. & Edwin L. Cummings Memorial Fund describes for us: "I see grantmakers being more careful and demanding accountability because accountability is being demanded of grantmakers." But they also have more empathy for the issues faced by the nonprofits. They are looking at what can be done to help, frequently without direct grant support. Grantmakers realized when there was less money to give away that they could help nonprofits in nonmonetary ways. Let's take a look at a few of them:

Blue Ridge Foundation of New York: Blue Ridge Foundation of New York may have been the earliest adopter of non-cash support. Its grantees are all start-up nonprofits. The foundation provides housing, obviously expensive in New York. The grantees form a natural network, learning and growing together with the foundation's support in such areas as training, coaching, and consulting services.

Turrell Fund: After losing significant financial resources, the Board decided to permanently reduce the level of annual giving. But to assist grantees, the foundation undertook research into alternative funding streams that could be used by all nonprofits in their geographic areas. By just accessing the foundation's web site, a nonprofit can find ideas about other private and public donors to approach. Further, the foundation is exploring fundraising training and coaching assistance.

The Frist Foundation: The staff at this foundation are engaged in the total health and success of their grantees. They point them to other donors and prospects. They assist them in figuring out their programmatic ideas and how to implement them for less cost. All spell an invaluable and objective perspective for a nonprofit from a caring external source.

The William Bingham Foundation: Its web site provides resource tools and best practice ideas to assist nonprofits in thinking creatively and outside the box.

The Retirement Research Foundation: The foundation makes coaches available for grantee executive directors. It makes grants to support fundraising assistance and also to improve technical needs such as accounting systems.

Altman Foundation: Recognizing the unusual cash flow pressure faced by nonprofits, the foundation participates with other grantmakers in a Program Related Investment pool for bridge loans to nonprofits suffering cash flow problems due to slow payments on government grants and contracts.

The Hyams Foundation, Inc.: Like Altman Foundation, The Hyams Foundation, Inc. is participating in a Catalyst Fund with other grantmakers to enable nonprofits to explore shared services, collaborations, or mergers.

Each of these represents a unique response by a grantmaker and one that assists nonprofit organizations in being better managed. Yet there is minimal cost to the grantmaker. No one saw this trend developing. It evolved out of the adversity of the stock market downturn.

Trends Among Nonprofits

Grantmakers indicate observing two interrelated trends in the nonprofit world. The first is the impact of an uncertain economy on nonprofits. The second and related trend centers around nonprofits disappearing, merging, or collaborating. There are a few tangents related to each that we will discuss.

ECONOMIC IMPACT

With the downturn in the investment world in 2008 and 2009 and the continued volatility of the financial markets, nonprofits find themselves with less foundation, corporate, and individual financial support. As Julie Brooks of John S. and James L. Knight Foundation describes it: "We saw a lot of nonprofits struggling to survive and I do not know if it was the economy or their business model. Were they just making it in a good economy but had a poor business model, so when the economy tanked their poor business model no longer supported them? If they had a good model they would have been fine regardless of the economy. It was not uncommon that we heard, 'We are down to three months operating' or 'there is a chance we may have to close our doors because government, foundation, or corporate funding has been cut.'" Andrew Lark of The Frances L. & Edwin L. Cummings Memorial Fund adds: "I have seen organizations scale down size of staff and size of offices. Any perceived excess is really frowned upon."

There is no doubt that nonprofits faced unprecedented issues and, with resiliency, worked through them. David A. Odahowski of Edyth Bush Charitable Foundation, Inc. says: "The recession has really worn the nonprofit executives. They are not as optimistic. They are not as willing to take a risk. They are not willing to expand or establish a new program. 'Let us keep our powder dry. Let us maintain these core services.' And that is not good because you need people to step up and say there is a different way of doing this and here is something we can do to make the community better." Susan M. Carter of Georgia Power Foundation, Inc. agrees: "I am surprised that more of them did not go under. They were running on adrenaline to get through because their needs were increasing so much when all this was happening that they did not really have time to react or think about things, they just had to do."

Addressing how nonprofits worked through the recent challenges with resiliency, Roxanne Ford of W. M. Keck Foundation notes: "If they did it right, they are leaner and stronger." And Matt Carpenter of El Pomar Foundation agrees: "The organizations that are going to succeed and do well are not going to go away. They are going to come out of this situation better than they ever would have been before things started to go south. So I look at it as an opportunity for organizations to help strengthen themselves and make sure that they are staying true to themselves and their mission." Danielle M. Reyes of Eugene and Agnes E. Meyer Foundation summarizes this perspective: "Far beyond the stories of tragedy are the stories of resilience and success. One thing that is inherent to nonprofit culture is survival through challenges such as government funding shortfalls, losing funding, etc."

Whether nonprofits are barely hanging on or are ready to re-stabilize, grantmakers agree that the loss of federal and state government support is devastating. The private sector cannot replace it, and it can only assist nonprofits in dealing with the fallout. So what happens to the safety net associated with government programs and support? Doug Bauer of The Clark Foundation addresses this issue: "There will be a rethinking of the social safety net. So what is the weave of that safety net? It is not going to be as tightly woven as it used to be. Are we still going to catch disconnected youth?

Are we still going to catch a single mom and her children? These are really important questions, and this is what is going on out there."

The bottom line: nonprofits are changed.

CLOSE, MERGE, COLLABORATE

A little bit of all three is happening. Elizabeth B. Smith of The Hyams Foundation, Inc. summarizes: "We are seeing a few nonprofits go out of business—it is not a lot. We are seeing a few more under what I would call financial stress. There have been a few mergers and definitely efforts to think about how we can combine back office services or programs."

At the beginning of the recession, there were dire forecasts that 100,000 nonprofits would disappear. Our interviewees did not see that happen, although virtually all grantmakers saw some nonprofits go out of business. Phillip Henderson of Surdna Foundation, Inc. notes: "Nonprofits have found a way to pare down to bare bones and stick it out. People have hunkered down in survival mode and most of the ones that are staffed and substantial are going to find a way to make it. I do not mean to be overly optimistic, but it does not feel like the tidal wave is shaping up as we had anticipated."

Some grantmakers took this opportunity to comment that perhaps there are too many nonprofits and the loss of a few is healthy. First, Kathleen Cerveny of The Cleveland Foundation explores the overall dynamic: "There is no barrier to entry into the nonprofit world and no incentive to leave it. So there is constant growth in a time of diminishing resources, and it just cannot hold." David D. Weitnauer of R. Howard Dobbs, Jr. Foundation, Inc. adds: "I do not have any hard data on this, but I have heard it observed that we have overcapacity where nonprofits are concerned—that we have more out there than the community can adequately support. So in that respect, while having an organization close is an awful thing for the people whose lives are built around it, it can actually be a healthly thing for the overall 'market.' The recession forced that issue for some." And Julie Brooks of John S. and James L. Knight Foundation agrees: "Maybe it was a good thing because sometimes it is sort of a natural survival of the fittest. So many nonprofits out there are doing similar work. Maybe the economy was a sort of natural cleaning process."

So while some nonprofits have disappeared, grantmakers were hoping to see more mergers among the remaining group. Julie Brooks of John S. and James L. Knight Foundation indicates the trend never happened: "We had conversations with some people about merging with other organizations. Not many people were interested in merging. They would rather close." Irene Frye of The Retirement Research Foundation concurs: "We have not seen the degree of mergers that I would have expected." Doug Bauer of The Clark Foundation adds that for the benefit of the sector we need to figure this out: "The mergers and acquisitions issue: there's a lot of smoke and no fire. I tend to be skeptical about the role of mergers and collaboration. There is no incentive for an executive director of a nonprofit to merge. There is no upside to it, and that is a problem and we need to figure that out. I think we are in a situation where we are going to have to look at mergers." Doug Bauer does go on to say that acquisitions of weaker nonprofits by stronger ones may actually be where the sector is going: "I am wondering less about mergers and more about absorptions—the three to four million dollar program with back office operations that are costly. Why not be absorbed by a much larger entity, which can support that backroom cost, have that infrastructure, and would have the value added of including that program in its portfolio. So it is a win for the community, it is a win for the small nonprofit that is now part of a bigger ship, and it is a win for the larger nonprofit. I am wondering if that is going to be something we will see more of."

Another hoped-for by-product of the economic stress is collaboration among nonprofits, especially with merger being so difficult. This tends to come in the form of facilities and back-office sharing. As Victoria Kovar of Cooper Foundation notes: "We have seen more facilities and management sharing. I would love to see more of that—where can we economize?" Lita Ugarte Pardi of The Community Foundation for Greater Atlanta describes what she is experiencing: "We are seeing nonprofits partner a lot more. We launched a program in 2010 called Organizational Partnerships and it focuses on helping nonprofits partner and restructure. We are having a lot of conversations with nonprofits about different types of partnerships. For example, does it make sense for a small organization to have a lot of back office staff? Can you partner with others and create a shared back office function? We are seeing people become more strategic in their operational partnerships and they are partnering more programmatically."

Overall, the trends the grantmakers describe underscore the resiliency of the nonprofit world.

Tips

As with past interviews for the *Guide*, our current grantmakers provide a number of suggestions. Take these to heart. Incorporate them. Think about them as you write your proposal and reach out to grantmakers.

LONG-LASTING PARTNERSHIP

A refrain, which appears in each edition of the *Guide* and has only grown stronger, is that the nonprofit and the grantmaker form a unique relationship or partnership that is long lasting. There is a synergy between the grantmaker, who provides the financial support, and the nonprofit, who provides the constituency, the creativity, and the services. Irene Frye of The Retirement Research Foundation summarizes this concept: "We really do look at nonprofits as our partners and try not to be the ivory tower funders. Our work is only accomplished by the work of our partners whom we happen to fund. I hope we are able to do more than be just an ATM machine. I hope that we are partners in making meaningful change. We can do that through not only financial resources but by knowing what is going on, on a state and local and national level, and how to connect people who are doing similar work. We know of projects that have worked well and how to bring them to other organizations for consideration and replication. We are in this together." Andrew Lark of The Frances L. & Edwin L. Cummings Memorial Fund adds: "Stewardship is so critically important. It is not just the grant proposal, it is what you do with it and how you monitor it and run the program and account for it that will put you in line for the next request. Transparency and clarity. That is what I am looking for. It is not just the courtship—it is the whole marriage thing." Dianne Yamashiro-Omi of The California Endowment reminds us that we need to understand each role in the partnership: grantmaker and nonprofit alike. Roxanne Ford of W. M. Keck Foundation notes: "We try constantly to be aware that we are nothing without the development people and the project leaders and the institutions that have the ideas and do all the work. We are just a facilitator of their good work. So we try to maintain our humility and help do good work the best we can do."

WRITING

Writing encompasses a number of specific items for the grantmakers. They are looking for clear, direct prose. That means:

- no jargon;

- distilling your ideas so they can be understood by an "outsider"; and,

- an appropriate story or two.

Julie Brooks of John S. and James L. Knight Foundation tells us that we "have to constantly work the writing muscle." William V. Engel of The Hyde and Watson Foundation suggests that "…the first paragraph should state what you are asking for." Curtland E. Fields of Turrell Fund adds: "Take some time. Make sure your best people are writing the application, and telling the story as well as they can and making the case for why our money should go to their organization." Jessamine Chin of Adobe Foundation connects the program to the writing: "It is great when an organization is authentic. By that I mean that they are realistic about the work that they are doing, while still maintaining their vision. If their words aren't grounded and they are making dramatic claims, then it weakens their application. For me, it is really about describing their programs in a way that an outsider can understand. It can be a challenge for grantwriters, who are surrounded by the day-to-day work of the organization, to be able to translate their programmatic language for someone who is not as familiar with it." Laura H. Gilbertson of The William Bingham Foundation summarizes: "It may not be fair to judge an organization based on the writing skills of one individual, but it happens. No fluff or unsubstantiated claims. Plain language that is clear is better than something very sophisticated and puffed up. And if there is a little story, it helps. It illustrates what you do better than trying to describe it sometimes."

RESEARCH

The key to succeeding in fundraising is to pursue the right grantmakers. That will happen through research. Identify the correct sources. Work to understand the grantmaker's niche. Investigate whom they have funded. Grantmakers are frustrated by nonprofits who do no research at all, ignore what they have found, or fail to dig deeply enough. William V. Engel of The Hyde and Watson Foundation reports: "We demystify the process. Grantmakers provide so much information about themselves. Yet nonprofits often do not take the time to learn about us." Amy Scop of The California Wellness Foundation adds: "One thing that we have on our web site is a database of what projects we have funded in the past. It is essential information for any prospective grantee to study."

David D. Weitnauer of R. Howard Dobbs, Jr. Foundation, Inc. encourages us to "Take the first learning steps. Do your homework to get to know the grantmaker." Andrew Lark of The Frances L. & Edwin L. Cummings Memorial Fund indicates that by doing so, "You learn the foundation's personality. What makes them tick. A foundation is very much like an individual. It really has likes and dislikes and if you find the right niche, you can really cultivate that relationship over a long time." Research is the tool that enables you to maximize your time, energy, and resources.

GENERAL OPERATING SUPPORT

Due to the stress on profits caused by the economy and the poor fundraising climate, a few grantmakers began making general operating support grants. It is very important that you not view this as a trend. The grantmakers themselves report making such awards in only a few cases and not expecting to continue that grantmaking into the future.

STRATEGIC PLANNING

For quite some time, grantmakers have wanted us to demonstrate a project's relationship to our strategic plan. For the first time, funders are asking that the entire plan be an attachment to a request. Further, they are looking for an indication of board participation in the planning process—not a staff-developed plan that has board approval. You need to think seriously about how your nonprofit can incorporate strong planning as part of the fundraising process and how to demonstrate that in the proposal.

DEVELOPMENT STAFF

Grantmakers express shock at the short-sightedness of some nonprofits that lay off development staff as part of budget cutting. Laura H. Gilbertson of The William Bingham Foundation aptly summarizes: "When they make budget cuts, the first person to get laid off is the development person and that is the person you need the most right now. So not only do you not have the person who is an expert at raising money, but you have also given that job to somebody who might not have any training in that area, and who will not turn out good proposals."

But there is also criticism of the development field. William V. Engel of The Hyde and Watson Foundation notes: "I am surprised to see very few outstanding development officers."

Peter F. Bird, Jr. of The Frist Foundation comments: "I see musical chairs in development jobs. The development staff should be rainmakers but they are not."

Perhaps we all have some soul searching to do here!

NUTS AND BOLTS

The pet peeves of grantmakers rise to the surface a bit in this section. They are truly trying to be direct here about what does and does not work.

First point: Get the request in ahead of the deadline. Curtland E. Fields of Turrell Fund suggests: "They may do themselves a disservice by waiting until the last minute. Staff has less time to field perfectly legitimate questions and certainly there is less time to recover from the unforeseen such as computer problems, mistakes, internal reviews, illness, and the like as the deadline draws near." William V. Engel of The Hyde and Watson Foundation adds this persuasive point: "We do a rolling review. It is important to get a proposal in early because we may have more money."

Second point: Be sure to proofread. Again William V. Engel of The Hyde and Watson Foundation notes: "Take five minutes and proof a letter. I am very big on that because I am a lawyer. I tell my staff: I am going to proof everything you give to me, because I am going to sign it." Especially make sure the name of the funder and the name of the staff person are both spelled correctly.

Third point: Send only relevant attachments. Kathleen Cerveny of The Cleveland Foundation points out: "Be judicious. Give us just what we need to understand your organization. Too much information can be a distraction and confuse the reader. Be respectful of the funder's time. We have to read a lot and don't appreciate having to read material that is not pertinent to the project."

Fourth point: Be cost efficient. Most grantmakers do not want to see glossy materials. They do not want you to over-spend by express mailing the proposal. A misstep in this direction might cause a grantmaker to wonder if you really need the financial assistance.

With open hearts, our interviewees share their concerns and hopes for all of us in the nonprofit world.

What follows are selected responses to our questions in the grantmakers' own words. Other responses to interview questions are found throughout the *Guide* as quotations we've selected to exemplify key points being made.

Do you find that most grantseekers have done their homework before contacting you?

Yes:

More and more we are seeing folks do their homework. Folks we have had a relationship with are increasingly sophisticated about working with our foundation. (Kathleen Cerveny)

The fidelity to following our guidelines is about 99.9 percent—it appears that everybody has read our grant guidelines. I could not have said that 10 years ago. To my mind it is completely about the fact that everybody is online and they are savvy enough to know to do research as a first step. (Bruce H. Esterline)

People have generally done their homework. (Matthew Klein)

More so than ever. Far less "fishing" taking place! (Maria Mottola)

Our web site has made a huge difference. Before we had a web site, we received three to five letters per week from all over the world, when we give only in NYC. Talk about not doing their homework! Today outreach to us can be selective and rooted in research, depending on how thoughtfully grantseekers review what is available on the web site. (Jane B. O'Connell and Karen L. Rosa)

Smart grantseekers don't waste their time chasing funders who aren't focused on their issues. (Christine Park)

Most grantseekers do their homework. It is best when the applicant really knows the individual funder's priorities. This is key. (Elizabeth B. Smith)

I find that those who call have looked at the web site and are more informed, more so than they might have been five or six years ago. (Bob Wittig)

Sometimes:

Many callers have not done their homework; however, I like the conversation because I can provide them with guidance if they call. (Paula Boyce)

Fifty percent are well informed; 50 percent are fishing for a match. For those that are fishing, we do invoke the principle that we do not entertain unsolicited proposals. (Edmund J. Cain)

We receive a number of cold calls that seem like they are shots in the dark, wide casting of the net for potential funders. And then again we get some very thoughtful, well-grounded calls that are obviously connected to our grantmaking interests that have been researched beforehand by the grantseeker. I like to think that our electronic presence is sufficiently descriptive that we receive less of those cold calls than we did at one time. (Robert B. Jaquay)

What is the best initial approach to your foundation?

Telephone:

It is surprising how few use phone as first mode of contact. We still get 250 to 300 unsolicited requests annually, and twenty to thirty requests from individuals. (Doug Bauer)

We discourage unsolicited proposals but sometimes receive tactful queries such as "We read your web site and learned that you are a strategic grantmaker. Would you mind if we sent you some information about our organization since we are working in the same areas?" Since this sort of "foot in the door" communication is not a proposal and carries with it no expectation of follow-up, we might nevertheless read the materials and follow up with the organization if the materials provoke our interest. (Edmund J. Cain)

We will talk to people in advance of a proposal being submitted. The process starts with the receptionist who answers the phone. She is the most important person in the whole communication chain. (Bruce H. Esterline)

Nonprofits sometimes try to stretch their missions to try to make them fit with funders' missions. I know I did when I ran programs and raised money! We encourage people to call or e-mail us and ask questions. If we are not the right fit, we will try to connect them with foundations that are the right fit for them. (Julie Farkas)

We encourage calls, but we also encourage that, prior to doing so, they take a moment and read everything that is available online. It is not a great thing when a grantseeker calls to ask a question that is answered either in the electronic application or on the web site. After a thorough review of the materials we certainly welcome calls. That is what we are here for. (Curtland E. Fields)

Lots of calls with lots of questions. Some of those questions could have been answered by reading online materials. (Marilyn Gelber)

They do call. It is fine to call with questions. (Laura H. Gilbertson)

The number of calls varies from docket to docket. (Robert B. Jaquay)

We encourage the call. We want the human touch with prospective grantees. (David A. Odahowski)

We get phone calls but not as many as in the past because we have so much information on our web site. (Lita Ugarte Pardi)

We encourage a conversation either before or after the LOI. We want to help guide the grantseeker. (Elizabeth B. Smith)

There are still times when folks will review that material online and they will say, "I am still not quite sure," or they just feel like they would be better served if they had some sort of personal contact before they send the letter. We will speak with them. (David D. Weitnauer)

I really appreciate when people call because in the long run it saves each of us time and effort because if we have a 15 minute conversation we can pretty much figure out if their organization is a good fit. (Bob Wittig)

Letter:

In some cases we will ask for an LOI to see if the nonprofit can make their case cogently in two to three, single-spaced pages. (Doug Bauer)

To those organizations that do not have a relationship established already, the cleanest and fastest way to make contact is to submit the LOI and the request is then assigned to a program officer. A cold call is harder because the program officer's time is really pulled in many directions so it is hard for them to respond to all the different phone calls. (Julie Brooks)

It is basically a mini proposal. What are the goals? What do they want to accomplish? What is the total budget of the program? (Laura H. Gilbertson)

The LOI introduces us to the nonprofit's work so that we can determine whether or not there is a good match with Surdna's funding priorities. (Phillip Henderson)

The LOI introduces the organization and its project to the foundation. It should state the track record in the area for which the nonprofit is seeking support. It can help us anticipate results. It should demonstrate how results are aligned with what the foundation seeks. (Jane B. O'Connell and Karen L. Rosa)

We are considered proactive funders rather than responsive to general letters of inquiry. Our Program Managers have spent a good amount of time in our Building Healthy Communities sites identifying and meeting with organizations and leaders in the community. Based on a community plan developed by community stakeholders, our Program Managers identify organizations that are in position to achieve the goals of the community's vision for health. Program Managers then invite organizations to apply. The same process is used by our statewide policy/advocacy team. Program Managers work with applicants on a Work Plan that serves as the contract for our grants. The Work Plan articulates the applicant's activities, but most importantly, defines the outcomes and how it would be measured. Because we are a health foundation we need to show what the health impact/outcome will be. The online application is a 1,000-word narrative, the Work Plan and the Budget. We purposely are working to simplify the application and review process. (Dianne Yamashiro-Omi)

Various means:

How we identify relationships and folks we want to pursue is through the networks that we have and through the relationships with our current grantee population—there are about 110 grantees or so here in NYC plus what we do in upstate New York. It is really through that network, our network with other funders, and talking with government agencies. There is a lot of informal sharing of information about what is going on out there and who are good groups to support or not to support. (Doug Bauer)

The introduction phase is fairly informal. The nonprofit will send an e-mail with a little information about their program and I will set up a phone call to learn more if they fit the focus areas. Through that phone conversation, we work together to determine if they fall within the grant guidelines. If they do, then they are invited to apply. In this way, the introduction to the organization is not necessarily a letter of intent, rather it is a phone call of intent. (Jessamine Chin)

I try to talk to people first and get a feel for the organization and project. If it is something that is within our guidelines, I immediately ask them to send me an LOI by e-mail. It can be informal—even in the body of an e-mail. But I want to know a little information about the organization and about the project. That way if we want to move on to the application stage, all the basic things are in writing and I can respond to them with something that says we will accept a proposal by this application deadline. (Victoria Kovar)

The best approach depends on how well we know you. Nonprofits never funded by us should go to the web site and follow the described process. Long-time grantees will call and chat a couple of times a year. They will speak with their program officer about a renewal. (Jane B. O'Connell and Karen L. Rosa)

Grantseekeers should try to arrange face-to-face meetings whenever possible, but to be honest, grantmakers simply don't have the time for personal visits with all interested parties. Partnerships with nonprofits are built through much back-and-forth conversation about a shared agenda and goals. (Christine Park)

Once a proposal is pending, is it acceptable for the grantseeker to call you to check on the status of the request or to share information? Is it okay to send additional materials?

If the grantseeker wishes to call and find out when the proposal will be reviewed, that is fine. (Paula Boyce)

It is always a little challenging because any program officer has multiple requests in front of them at any given time. I would say that if an organization has important additional information, I would encourage them to reach out to the funder and tell them that something has changed or that they have another letter of support or there is a new dimension to their thinking about their proposal that they would like us to consider. That sort of pertinent information should go to the funder as soon as the organization has it, but I would not bug the funder about what they think of your proposal. (Kathleen Cerveny)

We get a lot of questions about whether or not they are likely to get a grant. We also get requests to visit their organization, which we always do for an organization we have not funded before. (Curtland E. Fields)

Communication with us once the proposal is in place is critical. Don't drop off the radar screen. (Marilyn Gelber)

I appreciate it when folks share information. It builds rapport.
(A. Thomas Hildebrandt)

I welcome interaction and feel that anybody who goes through the effort of putting together a proposal can call me if they want to figure out where I am. It is a good sign of real interest and an indicator of their passion into not just the solicitation at hand but their work to accomplish their mission.
(Robert B. Jaquay)

We welcome it. There are often a couple of months between the application deadline and when our board will review the application. If there are other pending requests out there, we encourage people to let us know the outcome of those decisions. If there is a major thing that changes in the interim, I think it is completely appropriate to contact the foundation and let them know that something has changed. I think it should really relate to the proposal unless it is something monumental like a leadership staff change.
(Victoria Kovar)

Put us on the mail list or e-mail blast. We don't want to be inundated but let us know key information. It is nice for us to know the grant made a difference. (J. Andrew Lark)

If we have reviewed the LOI and requested a proposal, or indicated that a proposal is going to the board, grantseekers are welcome to call and check on its status and of course send along new materials that are pertinent. (Jane B. O'Connell and Karen L. Rosa)

Do not be a worrywart about this. You cannot be a pest. The more communication the better. We always want to know: Has anything changed? Does the project reflect current need? It is reassuring to get updates. (David A. Odahowski)

No, I do not expect to hear from them. What I tell groups after a meeting is that they will submit their proposal and what we will do from there is to have a reading period and a writing period. It takes us several weeks to read all the proposals and do reports on them. On the day of our board meeting or the following day, I will call them and let them know what the result of the meeting was. And if we have any questions between now and then, we will reach out to them. (Danielle M. Reyes)

Absolutely, stay in touch. (Amy Scop)

During the review process, it is always helpful if applicants keep us informed if something comes up. For example, if the Executive Director leaves or is planning to leave, or if the financial status of the organization shifts dramatically, we need to know about it. There is nothing worse than hiding something from the Program Officer. This would not be a good way to build a trusting relationship. (Dianne Yamashiro-Omi)

Once a proposal is pending, is it okay if one of the nonprofit's board members contacts one of your board members directly?

We do not tell people they cannot talk to our board members. But we do say that it makes it difficult for our board to be lobbied by external parties. And it is up to them if they want to take a chance in exerting some influence or actually distancing a board member as a result of the lobbying. (Kathleen Cerveny)

There is a lot of crossover. Certainly anybody is welcome to talk to anybody about anything. Our board, if they have that type of conversation, will instruct the nonprofit to contact the staff. I do think our board is out there and attuned to what is going on in the community and if there is an exciting opportunity for the foundation, I think they want to be alert to those things. (Victoria Kovar)

I tend to think of that as sort of an end-run around the process, which is a little bit awkward. It is awkward for our board members to receive those calls. If one of our staff members gets a call from a board member, that is fine. If they have skin in the game and they would like to see the foundation helping out their group, that is fine and that is reasonable. But a grantseeker talking to a board member who is not already very actively involved with them is probably not helpful. (J. Andrew Lark)

The board members of nonprofits are active community leaders. They probably see one another. It is a natural thing for board members of nonprofits to be passionate about a cause. It would be disadvantageous if we did not hear from board members in one way, shape, or form. (David A. Odahowski)

Following the rejection of a proposal, do you speak with the applicant about the reasons why, if they ask you to?

If we have a good close relationship with an organization, I will typically call them up and explain something. And typically this will not come as a surprise to them. If it is an organization we do not know well, we will send a formal decline letter and will offer to talk to them on the phone if they want. If you are going to communicate bad news and it is an easy, comfortable relationship, then you can call and say "well, not this time" and that works okay. But if you do not have a close relationship, then you need to give them some time to absorb it. (Peter F. Bird, Jr.)

I do not contact them voluntarily, but I will speak to them if they call. (Susan M. Carter)

Our decline letter will try to be sensitive and indicate what the rationale was for not providing funding. If the organization wants to call us up and talk about why they were declined, we certainly are responsive to that. We are always open to looking at another request. We never tell an organization: "Do not come to us again." (Kathleen Cerveny)

We will provide feedback on a turndown. (William V. Engel)

It is absolutely okay to call. We encourage it. As a matter of fact, I will put my business card in with the declination letter and say call me! We are more than happy at any stage to tell you why something has been declined. (Roxanne Ford)

The best thing is really the honest conversation. Every time something is declined in this new automated world, the staff member's name, phone number, and e-mail is there. The staff encourages people to call and talk to us about the decline. I want people to have an honest understanding of why we did not fund them because there usually is a good reason why. Sometimes it is money. Sometimes it is not money. Sometimes it is our funding priorities. Sometimes it is geography. (Marilyn Gelber)

Unless our board identified a specific reason, I usually do not give one. (Laura H. Gilbertson)

I am happy to take the calls and discuss feedback about their application or provide insights into our grantmaking process. (Jane G. Hardesty)

In a conversation following the turndown, the nonprofit needs to be in a learning mode: courteous and respectful. Learn what the next step is. (Phillip Henderson)

I encourage conversations and face-to-face, post-declination meetings. A lot of times even a proposal that is vetted and improved to perfection may not get to "yes" for reasons that are more about the expression of the board's grantmaking interests. (Robert B. Jaquay)

You know, it depends on how deeply we have been engaged with the grantseeker. If we have not been that deeply engaged, then we will do an e-mail and sometimes a letter. If we have had lots of conversations, then it is an e-mail followed by a call. And we try to give them the core reason for the turndown. (Matthew Klein)

We try to come up with a paragraph in the rejection that explains exactly why the grant was turned down. Sometimes we struggle with a reason because it is really about the limits of our funding. It is about our lack of money, not your lack of quality programming. (Maria Mottola)

Whenever we make declinations after site visits, we call those organizations before sending an e-mail. We feel it is the nice thing to do to give them a heads-up that unfortunately the board did not approve a grant to them. And once they have had enough time to accept this, we are happy to give them feedback as to the decision and talk about potential funding for the future. (Lita Ugarte Pardi)

I call anybody who has received a full review after the board meeting and will talk to them about the decision, whether it was an approval or a decline. If it is a decline, I will give them as much info as I think is helpful. If it is an administrative decline, meaning an immediate response to an LOI, they just get a letter. Now if somebody phones me after they receive that letter, I am also glad to talk to them. But I am not sure the information I provide is very helpful because it is cut and dry that they are just not a fit. (David D. Weitnauer)

I make a phone call or leave a voicemail. I want them to hear my voice telling them that they have not been funded and if they have any questions I encourage them to call me back and we can have a conversation about it. (Bob Wittig)

Following the rejection of a proposal, what is the best thing an organization can do?

The best thing is if you are still interested in receiving funding, identify those weaknesses and try to improve on them if you really are going to try to come back for funding again. This feedback can come from a conversation with a program officer or in a declination letter. (Julie Brooks)

Call us up and talk to us. We are always open to look at another request— come back! (Kathleen Cerveny)

The best thing would be to call us and ask why they were rejected. (William V. Engel)

We let them know that when the reason for the likely decline is going to be timing, they can withdraw their request before our formal review. We say, if you withdraw this one, it will not go to the board and will not get counted as an ask. We ask them to formally withdraw with an e-mail or letter, and then I write a letter that says "this acknowledges your withdrawal. You are free to come back anytime you want." However, if they are formally declined, then they must wait for 12 months to resubmit. (Bruce H. Esterline)

Even on a decline, I have received some extraordinarily gracious thank-you letters saying "'thanks for spending the time working on this. We have learned so much from the process." It is not necessary, but deeply appreciated. (Roxanne Ford)

An honest conversation with staff is always best. (Marilyn Gelber)

Things like "we did not have the money this year," or "the level of clarity was not right," or "we think your organization needs to have a longer track record of doing this work before we are comfortable funding it," those sorts of things can mean the door is ajar for a conversation down the road. And always ask "well, how much further down the road? Is it a year or six months?" and be respectful of the answer. (Phillip Henderson)

There is an art to accepting a "No." There is nothing wrong with reaching out to the funder to understand why your proposal didn't meet their funding requirements. Find out when and under what circumstances it is appropriate to come back. (A. Thomas Hildebrandt)

Our process is extremely competitive, but if the program officer tells you there was no fatal flaw, and there were simply too many proposals, in our case we are telling you the truth. I tell people the numbers we get and they are shocked. Best: call and ask why you were declined. We will pull the folder and look at what the written comments were. We do not ordinarily call—we send a letter. I encourage people to call. The best thing they can do is to call us and find out why. (Karen Kinney)

I guess the best thing is to understand as much as they can about why they were declined. If they can get the reasons, then ask for introductions to other funders. (Matthew Klein)

The best thing is to send some sort of acknowledgement that you have received the news. If people call and want to talk about why a request was declined, we are happy to have that discussion. (Victoria Kovar)

A polite letter or phone call: "Thank you for considering us. I know there are a lot of requests out there. Is there anything you can think of that we can do to strengthen our proposal itself or our likelihood of getting funded?" That sort of gentle, polite probing is fine. (J. Andrew Lark)

Try again. Sometimes groups forget that unless we have said to them "you do not fit the guidelines," probably the reason we did not fund them is that we did not have enough money. As a grantseeker I made that mistake. I crossed a funder off the list and thought, "well, they rejected me—I do not want to go through this again." (Maria Mottola)

The best thing you can do is to call. It creates an accountability on the part of the nonprofit... If you run a foundation, you have an obligation to nonprofits: to those that you fund and to those that you do not fund. There are important messages that are conveyed about the nature of the request, the quality of the request, the size of the request, and the timing. If I am on the board of a nonprofit, I would want to know this and I would have an obligation to the organization that I serve to find that out and I think both parties learn from that and that produces better communication to set up a relationship. (David A. Odahowski)

Try to ascertain whether you are really a fit. Do not just keep going back. Say thank you. (Elspeth A. Revere)

The very best thing they can do is try to get feedback about why. And if the funder has any other advice in terms of whether it was not a strong fit, or if there is something they can do about restructuring the program, I think you want to get absolutely as much information as possible and to try to figure out "well, would it be reasonable if I try to apply again or is it not really a good use of our time?" (Elizabeth B. Smith)

I think if they have questions, certainly it makes sense that they would call. And sometimes I can give them feedback that is useful to them and sometimes I will tell them something they do not want to hear: "There was a more compelling option in the eyes of our board, or we did not have the budget and yours fell below the line." (David D. Weitnauer)

A good practice would be to call the program officer not to contest the decision but to ask for feedback on what they might have done differently. It needs to be done respectfully and in a way that is not contesting the decision, because that puts the program officer in an awkward spot. It is often a matter of "fit" with the funder's strategic goals and not to be interpreted as the applicant being unworthy of funding. We review a lot of proposals from stellar organizations but have to make decisions based on strategy and our own budget limitations. (Dianne Yamashiro-Omi)

Following the rejection of a proposal, what is the worst thing an organization can do?

Being too pushy. People are getting more aggressive asking why the foundation did not support a certain type of program. They cannot accept the fact that a foundation does not fund "everything," or that a foundation has certain areas of focus, or that a foundation is governed by a trust document as to what may be funded. (Paula Boyce)

If you get feedback from the program officer of why you were turned down, understand the reason. Take it to heart. Do not resubmit the same thing next year. It is not the best thing for your organization to twist and turn or to deviate from your mission and work in order to align with a foundation's mission and work. Do not make yourself something that you are not in order to get the funds. It could put your organization in jeopardy if you do not have the capacity to do it. Know your limitations and move forward. (Julie Brooks)

There are two things that nonprofits should not do after a turndown. The first is to give us another proposal for another program the very next month. The second is for them to approach someone else within the company and try to get through another back door. (Susan M. Carter)

Think carefully about complaining to foundation board members about not getting funding. That puts them in an awkward position and puts you in a bad light. This kind of information tends to get back to staff and it sours the relationship. (Kathleen Cerveny)

Do not call and verbally abuse us or whine. We don't like to turn people down. That is not what we are here for. We have taken time to make these decisions and it is a balancing act. So the last thing we need is for someone to call and whine about this. But if somebody calls and really lights into us, that is a big problem and in extreme cases they may never get a grant again. (William V. Engel)

Take the argument to the CEO level or complain to the board. (Bruce H. Esterline)

Insult us. Get angry. This does not solve anything. (Irene Frye)

The worst thing they can do is to call and complain that they were rejected. We encourage them to call to find out why, but I have had people call and yell. It is unnecessary. It is not good practice. (Karen Kinney)

Worst: argue. I do not blame people for wanting to, but it is not going to do anything and it makes people disinclined to help. (Matthew Klein)

The worst thing to do is to call in anger and argue about the grant decision. It is entirely inappropriate and it sets you up to have a poor relationship with the foundation. This happens very rarely, but it does happen. (Victoria Kovar)

The worst: express anger, indignation and quit. Winston Churchill said "Never, never, never, give up." There are a number of groups that come to us once and if they get a "no" they then just go away. It may not be that they are not fundable. It may be that their initial proposal was not then fundable for whatever reason. It does not necessarily mean that the organization is not fundable. I would try again. (J. Andrew Lark)

You get a "no" but then you approach the boss or somebody else in the foundation to try to secure the grant. There is a value to persistence. Just make sure the persistence is done with a full understanding that there are some significant risks of not endearing yourself to a funder that way. (Darin McKeever)

Being defensive is bad. You should not take it as a mark against your program or something you did. It could literally just be that there is not money for it. (Maria Mottola)

If you tell others how poorly the foundation treated you, it will get back to the foundation and you will have no chance in the future. (David A. Odahowski)

I do not mind and totally understand people being disappointed. If people get angry, that is not so great because the funder often feels really badly anyway and difficult choices have to be made. (Elizabeth B. Smith)

I have talked to other grantmakers who used to make phone calls but they got tired of having people argue with them. (David D. Weitnauer)

Try to persuade us why they should have been funded. Because there is nothing I can do at that point. (Bob Wittig)

If a grant is awarded, what is the best thing an organization can do?

I really think it is a good idea for every organization that gets funded by a foundation or individual to write a formal thank-you. The reason I like those things in writing is that it can be shared. Usually in a funding decision, there are multiple people involved, so to be able to share that thank-you is important. All any donor wants is to make a difference, and if you can let them know with some kind of story or dramatic illustration that their money has made a difference, donors feel really good about that. (Peter F. Bird, Jr.)

There is specific information that comes with the award letter including the guidelines for the interim and final report. The best thing they can do is to be timely in sending in their reports. Address each of the specific questions required in the report, and provide the specific financials that are requested. (Paula Boyce)

The best thing the grantee can do is to read through that grant agreement thoroughly, and understand what is expected of them with that grant. It outlines reporting responsibilities, financial management, intellectual property, audited financial statements, and working with press releases. Make sure they are comfortable with it and can actually fulfill that work in the terms of the grant. We are willing to negotiate terms of the grant agreement before the grant starts. (Julie Brooks)

It is so important to continue the relationship with the grantmaker. Some folks will add you to their newsletter e-mail list or some folks will send a thank-you note or make a thank-you call. Obviously they are jumping at the chance for a post-site visit to continue to interact. It is important to be intentional about a plan of maintaining that relationship. (Matt Carpenter)

Be prompt with the thank-you and receipt letter. Stay in touch with progress reports in order to stay on the grantor's mind. (Susan M. Carter)

Getting paperwork in on time and paying attention to the reporting requirements. Get your paperwork in on time so we can pay you on time. One thing that often happens is that everybody is happy when they get news of the grant, but we have a deadline when an award letter has to be signed before we can release dollars and if we do not have it by that certain date, the grantee has to wait another month and then they are calling us and saying "where is the money?" So paying attention to the paperwork is important. Of course paying attention to the reporting requirements is also important. It takes a lot of staff time to track people down to remind them that a report is due. (Kathleen Cerveny)

We would like to think of us now as being really partners in this enterprise. And partners should keep each other informed and be available to each other. We do not want to wake up and see this partnership on the front page of the paper in some sort of unhappy light. We owe it to each other to be very straightforward and professional. (Bruce H. Esterline)

Sometimes I think it is hard to remember to stay in touch during the key moments, especially if it is an executive transition. At times like this, board and staff are often stressed and unsure of the future of the organization. It is all understandable and due to the stress of transition, but it is important to be in touch to say we are trying to regroup. It does not have to be a phone call—it could be an e-mail. (Julie Farkas)

Try and get up and running as quickly as you can. If it is going to be delayed from the time frame you led us to believe was to be the one in process, then I really need to know that right away. We do not appreciate finding out six to eight to 10 months later that something has not even gotten started because then the directors will quite reasonably say, "well we could have earned interest on that in the meantime." (Roxanne Ford)

Always great to receive an acknowledgement, a phone call or an e-mail that communicates their enthusiasm for being funded, and to return the paperwork with the signatures as soon as you can. Nothing is more annoying than having to wait for a return signature so you can cut a check for an organization that you have gone to bat for or them not cashing the check. It is an auditing nightmare for us. (Irene Frye)

Thank the board member and the foundation. Keep us posted. Keep in touch. Communicate. Send reports. Let us know about changes. (Laura H. Gilbertson)

It is very helpful if they communicate back about what has been accomplished. (Jane G. Hardesty)

A prompt and genuine response is expected and appreciated. Failure to properly acknowledge receipt does not position you well for future opportunities. (A. Thomas Hildebrandt)

For deep and longtime grantees, it is a continuation of dialogue and sharing of information, a continued effort to remain open and transparent with each other, a sharing of the glory as well as the bad side, and being open to a real partnership. In our foundation it is about a partnership that is not overly prescriptive, and hopefully candid in information sharing, one where we are going out as well as welcoming grantees to come here to see us. (Robert B. Jaquay)

Best: to keep the person updated. To continue to ask who else might be helpful. To be in touch separate and apart from the grant. To send occasional, small updates that are particularly tailored to a funder's interests. (Matthew Klein)

Acknowledgement of the grant award right away. To contact the foundation in a way that is appropriate for that foundation, whether it is a phone call or an e-mail or note. It is entirely appropriate to thank the foundation in that way. (Victoria Kovar)

Follow along with timely progress reports and report on good progress and any other good news along the way. Share it periodically. We want good things to happen. That is what a good partnership is all about. If they not only come up with a good project but others are emulating it, sure, we would like to know that too. It gives our grant even longer legs when they can tell other groups about their successes and how they can do it too, and others are seeking to do that. That is terrific. (J. Andrew Lark)

No surprises: I think that is really important. (Darin McKeever)

Stay in touch with us. Keep us apprised of how the project is going. I feel like some groups disappear off the radar screen and leave you scratching your head saying, "oh yeah, we have not heard from them in a while." (Maria Mottola)

The best thing is returning the paperwork promptly and some sort of human touch that is either a phone call or setting up an appointment. For us, you can just walk into our office and the best people occasionally just stop in to say hello. Just stop in and say thank you. How would you want to be treated? (David A. Odahowski)

I really appreciate it when nonprofit partners acknowledge that we "went the extra mile" to create a successful partnership. (Christine Park)

The best thing they can do is to return the signed grant agreement letter, do the work they said they would do, and send a report on time. The reports that we ask for are very important because that is the way we report back to our board. Our board likes to hear the good, the bad, and the ugly on how the grantees are doing their work. (Amy Scop)

The more I get to know the organization the more I can really speak about them to my board in a much richer way. I do not read all the newsletters, but if people call just once halfway through to say "I want you to know what is going on." It is important to determine how you strategically stay in touch with me so I have a relationship with you, because at the end of the day that is really important. (Bob Wittig)

If a grant is awarded, what is the worst thing an organization can do?

Sending this standard letter of acknowledgement for gifts of $250 and more, which says that there are no goods or services in exchange for this gift and here is your standard receipt as required by the IRS. Do not let that substitute as a real human thank-you. And do not combine this standard thank-you with a personal one. (Peter F. Bird, Jr.)

Using the grant award for something other than what it was intended for without first asking us. Not being honest and upfront with us. If there is a project/program with a start and end date, and three months into the project you realize it will not be completed in time, do not wait until the last minute to request an extension on the use of the funds, or to ask if the funds can be reallocated. (Paula Boyce)

Over half of our reports are submitted late or incomplete. I think that is the worst thing you can do because it shows the potential for lack of leadership, for the care of a grant, for the care of a donor's willingness to partner with you. (Matt Carpenter)

If things are not going the way you anticipated and you do not tell us, that could be a very bad thing. We would much rather have a grantee call us and say "Gee, we had these three goals, but we do not think we are going to meet two of them. Can we come and talk to you about why?" And if there are legitimate reasons, we can make adjustments to the reporting expectations, the payment cycles, or whatever because of course what we want is the most successful outcome possible and we recognize that things can change. So if something happens that affects the outcome of your project and you do not tell us about it, it is a very bad thing. (Kathleen Cerveny)

Failure to notify about significant changes ahead of time is bad practice. We have lots of ways to accommodate those changes. We can improve things, we can amend the grant, etc. (Bruce H. Esterline)

The worst thing you can do is either not use the grant as it was originally intended or surprise us because some change has occurred and you did not want to tell us about it. I hate surprises. It is a form of a lack of communication. The failure of regular communication is the worst thing you can do. (Marilyn Gelber)

Complain the gift is not large enough or not what they asked for. Sometimes, it does not happen very often, but if they asked for $50,000, and they only got $10,000, every now and then somebody will complain about that. It is not going to change anything. There was a good reason that we granted them at that level, so it does not really do any good to complain about it. (Laura H. Gilbertson)

When organizations spend grant funds on something other than what they originally asked for without having a discussion with the foundation first, it is a problem. (Jane G. Hardesty)

The notion of taking us for granted and thinking just because you have gotten funding for a few years in a row, it is always going to be there. We have to be careful as an organization that our behavior does not make people think there is a check there every year. (A. Thomas Hildebrandt)

We do not want people to violate the terms of the grant agreement. I also think that if things go awry, that can cause problems. Another bad thing that can happen is if a grant recipient withholds information or bad news and tries to paper it over to the point of being misleading. That rarely happens but it has at times. (Robert B. Jaquay)

Not to talk about changes or challenges because they are going to happen and funders like to know what is going on. (Matthew Klein)

Not responding to the call, letter, or grant contract. It is kind of in the back of my head, "Am I going to have to follow up on this?" We will not pay a grant without a signed contract, and there is a little question mark about whether we are all on board. (Victoria Kovar)

The worst thing a charity can do is to withhold information that the key staff member that was going to direct the project has just left—or other similar bad news. We need to know that up front. Oftentimes we can help— we can say, "okay plan b," "let us extend the grant," or "let us re-think this," rather than have them do it in isolation from us and sort of sheepishly report to us six or eight months later that they never really did start the project. That is a problem. (J. Andrew Lark)

If you are trying to get attention for your work by using the Gates Foundation name, tell us and engage with us in advance on how best to do that. (Darin McKeever)

Not submitting reports, not returning phone calls, not letting us know about big changes that might impact our grant. (Maria Mottola)

The worst thing they can do is to take six to eight weeks to sign the acceptance or not acknowledge the receipt of the award letter. (David A. Odahowski)

The worst thing they can do is to get funding for something and then something really does not work out and they do not let the funder know. Another really bad thing is not to report on the grant. Even if they think they might not get funded again, reporting is really critical. Even if the ball was dropped for whatever reason—and there could be very legitimate reasons for that—I think trying to pick up on that is really important. It is an accountability issue. Usually these problems stem from turnover and a lack of communication. (Elizabeth B. Smith)

To depend on the organization for continuous funding. This dependency is problematic. We have experienced it many times, where organizations will assume that once they get a grant they will get a grant forever. And we can say it till we are blue, "You have to raise funds from other sources. We cannot guarantee that we will be here next year," and then next year comes and they say "We are going to have to close shop if you do not give us funding." It puts us in this very awkward position that we should not have to be in. And all of that speaks to quality management. The other is to misconstrue the relationship as a personal relationship. It is a professional relationship rather than a personal one. A mistake grantees make is assuming it is a personal relationship and trying to massage it with gifts or whatever, and it becomes very uncomfortable. Most foundations have a policy on creating very clear boundaries on what is appropriate behavior between program officers and grantees. (Dianne Yamashiro-Omi)

What role does reporting play in your grantmaking process?

The organization cannot seek a renewal without the report being submitted. (William V. Engel)

The information in a report could affect the next decision. (Laura H. Gilbertson)

The report outlines our return-on-investment. (Jane B. O'Connell and Karen L. Rosa)

We are asking questions that can be answered by any grantee so that we can say what percentage of our grantees made progress toward implementing best practices in different areas of operations and achieving goals from their strategic plans. (Lita Ugarte Pardi)

Reporting is important because it allows directors to report accurately back to the trustees and it may trigger a conversation with the nonprofit. (Christine Park)

What specifically are you looking for in a grant report?

Something that we struggle with is nonprofits not submitting their financial report—their budget versus actual expenses for the grant. We have become stringent about not considering their reporting complete until we receive that financial report. (Julie Brooks)

Have there been changes in your landscape that altered the program? Keep us abreast of obstacles and opportunities. (Julie Farkas)

Here is what we look for: notable accomplishments; unanticipated developments or challenges; other sources of funding; research impacts and other impacts. (Roxanne Ford)

Reporting procedures are included in the award letter. It conveys when reports are due and what should be included and that is tailored to specific requests. We look at the timeline that the applicant has submitted and a determination is made based on when would be logical to hear from them about progress. (Irene Frye)

Eighty-five percent of the time, when a report is late it means that an Executive Director or project leader has left and nobody has been appointed to submit the report. (Laura H. Gilbertson)

In the award letter, we include a progress report form of five questions for them to provide us once the funds have been expended to let us know how the funds were utilized and what they learned and positives or negatives about the project. We are looking for the outcomes and impact measurement to understand the value of what those dollars provided in relation to what was intended. Some of the results are exactly as planned versus others that fall a bit short or well exceed expectations. (Jane G. Hardesty)

In our acceptance letter, we say "we need you to sign below that you agree to report." We ask them to report twice yearly. We do not give them a format. We ask them to let us know what they expected to do and what has been accomplished, pretty straightforward. (Christine Park)

We are looking for a report of project activity and the impact it has had. The report should be a conversational narrative with stories. (Elspeth A. Revere)

No format, but send us what we need to know and anything you would like to tell the board. (Bob Wittig)

We have a template for a report based on the outcomes and indicators. Organizations provide a narrative report and a financial report based on how much money they have spent so far against their budget. (Dianne Yamashiro-Omi)

Beyond the basic information, what else should the proposal contain?

We ask about board procedures. We ask about recent accomplishments. We want to know not just when they were founded but who founded them and why. We ask for their strategic planning process, and the best practices they are implementing, with a link to the Independent Sector site about recommended best practices. (Laura H. Gilbertson)

Do not short-cut information—thinking that you are writing for a specific program officer—others will read it. (Karen Kinney)

The board list is obviously important. It is not so much whether they have a board, but what kind of a board they have. We are looking to see who made this happen. Was it domestic workers themselves? Was it the tenants themselves? Was it laywers? A mix of people? The other common application attachments become important when we are processing the proposal for the purposes of presenting something to the board. (Maria Mottola)

What makes a proposal document stand out?

Clarity is essential. The typical jargon and acronyms and flowery words are not as helpful as getting a sense of what the need is and the potential for impact and benefitting the community. (Matt Carpenter)

Directly respond to things requested in the RFP. What makes a group stand out for Consumer Health Foundation is that they have a strong community base—that the project is organic in a neighborhood or community. (Julie Farkas)

Make every word count. It is getting at the question of impact. Why are the funds needed? What difference will they make? What will they enable? That is the question that potential grantees seem to dance around, or are afraid to answer or are just not clear about in their own minds. (Curtland E. Fields)

The applicant must clearly state the purpose and the objective of the grant right up front. That puts the rest of the information in context. Use simple declarative sentences. Keep the information and the reading level simple. We have a very sophisticated group of board members, but it is important to communicate in the plain language free of jargon. Clear, measurable objectives are very important. What is the need? How are you going to address the need? What do you expect will come from your actions and how will you know what success is like? One of the signs of a great grant application is when the distinctive sections of an application really relate to each other. So in the evaluation section you should refer back to the objectives, to what effect you are anticipating, and provide the measures and strategies you will use to evaluate this work. (Victoria Kovar)

What is often rare and that I really appreciate is an articulation of the risks to the project and what they are planning to do about those things. In my case, I find candor and a demonstration of a deep understanding of their work and what might be hard about it really compelling. I find if they do not address those things, those are the questions that I hone in on. (Darin McKeever)

Do you have any other advice to help the proposal writer succeed?

It is important for an organization to be able to distill their focus, programs, services, and potential ideas or challenges that they face succinctly, and to distinguish themselves from similar providers. (Jane G. Hardesty)

Shorter is better. Clearer is better. (Phillip Henderson)

For an organization that has had a lot of challenges, sometimes I have had to coach people to sort of sell it a little bit more and be confident. You do not want to make it look like, "well, if only we could get this grant from the foundation, then we could do this stuff." You really want to say "here is what we do well and here is why you should invest in us." Funders often think like investors, so you want to articulate 'return on investment' (i.e., the benefits to the community, to your clients, and to your organization) from the funder's grant. (Victoria Kovar)

Be cost-efficient. I do not like the use of messengers, or other expensive couriers, or costly five-color letterheads. (J. Andrew Lark)

Being glossy around a sad issue—this is jarring. (Maria Mottola)

I often tell groups that I would love to hear more and to expand on an issue from the LOI in their proposal. I also tell them, I am actually reading this! It is not necessary to cut and paste one part three times just because the common grant application form makes it seem redundant. Better to say "addressed in section two" or go deeper. If organizations feel that they can make a compelling case in less than eight pages, fantastic. And absolutely no more than eight pages. Though some still send in more than eight pages. (Danielle M. Reyes)

The most important part of the proposal is your strategy. Talk about how your organization is best qualified to achieve success, talk about what other nonprofits you are working with—strategic alliances—and how what you are proposing fits within the foundation's programmatic goals. Make your strongest case to show what you are proposing to do and how it connects to what we are trying to accomplish as a foundation. We are looking for solid partnerships with grantees who can make a difference in the communities they work in. That is more important to us. (Dianne Yamashiro-Omi)

Beyond the basic information, should the appendix contain any other materials?

The number of board members who personally gave; the total amount they gave; the percentage of the board that attend meetings. The management letter and the audit can point out significant issues. (Doug Bauer)

Evidence of employee involvement. Date and amount of past support from the company. Other sources of support. (Susan M. Carter)

The agency's most recent activities. (Kathleen Cerveny)

Cash flow projections. (Julie Farkas)

Environmental sustainability policy. Updated listing on Guidestar. Summary of the strategic plan. (Laura H. Gilbertson)

Address your operating challenges. (Matthew Klein)

Strategic, business, and fundraising plans. (Lita Ugarte Pardi)

Short- or long-term fundraising strategies. Staff or board diversity forms. (Elizabeth B. Smith)

Three-year statistical summary of services. Current strategic plan. (David D. Weitnauer)

Could you say how your web site fits in with your grantmaking procedures?

Our first step was to put the guidelines for the various foundations that we manage on the Internet, which we recently accomplished. The second and third step down the road will be to have grantseekers apply directly online. (Paula Boyce)

Our web site provides transparency. Grantseekers see our guidelines and follow them. (Bruce H. Esterline)

The need to connect to the world about the work we are doing is easily accomplished through the web. The downside is you connect to the world and it may not be the world you want to connect to. Sometimes when organizations seek support, they may think they have found a better fit than exists. (Irene Frye)

Until the last couple of years, it really cut down on the number of unsolicited requests we received. (Laura H. Gilbertson)

We are on the edge of understanding the breakthroughs. There is a tidal wave of complex information—tools to make our work easier and efficient. (Phillip Henderson)

The way we take in information is significantly changing because of technology. When I started 15 years ago, the Executive Director regularly sent along a big pile of clippings. Occasionally you still do send along hard copies of material that is germane. Now being able to read the Cleveland papers online and see the bloggers, and go to the web sites of our organizations, oftentimes it is now framed in "check out this url." (Robert B. Jaquay)

The web site has been helpful to the foundation because it addresses questions, reduces calls and inappropriate requests. (Karen Kinney)

Our web site offers transparency. It is helpful to us if grantseekers give a careful read of what is posted. (J. Andrew Lark)

It is not a sophisticated web site but serves its purpose. (Bob Wittig)

Does your foundation/corporation accept items related to the grant application process electronically?

I would love to be at the stage where we have our LOI, proposals, and reporting all online. We have a variety of different proposals and we are two steps away from having them online. (Julie Brooks)

Right now we accept hard copies. I would love it if we could do the whole application process online. That is something we are exploring but we are not there yet. I am hoping that we will accept online applications. Currently if an application is incomplete, there are many things that can be sent electronically. For example, if the budget is not in the format we require, applicants can e-mail an electronic copy of that. (Irene Frye)

In some ways the online application encourages more applications. Possibly makes applying too easy. (Marilyn Gelber)

We are looking at possibly adopting an online application program. For now, we ask for everything by e-mail because I distribute meeting materials electronically. If they send me an attachment on paper, I have to scan it, so I would prefer to have it e-mailed. (Laura H. Gilbertson)

We are trying to work out our internal capacity so we can accept electronic proposals by the end of this year. For the moment, we require a hard copy be submitted, but that will not always be so. (Robert B. Jaquay)

We are exploring, taking a look at online submissions. It has come a long way, but we still have grantees with technology challenges and we are sensitive to that. (Karen Kinney)

Probably where we will go next is to have a back end that tracks grants, but people will continue to submit mostly via e-mail attachments.
(Matthew Klein)

I do not read the paper copies anymore, but it really took me a long time. I really have a hard time not reviewing on paper. I have adapted and now I do not review the paper copy. Honestly, if we did not have paper records of every grant since '34, I might not ask for a paper copy. We have not been convinced that there is anything archivally that is better than paper and it is hard to stop doing things once you start. (Victoria Kovar)

We are still functioning at a basic level. We do not have an online application platform but are currently researching the possibilities in the hopes of implementing an online application in 2013. E-mail does have its downside, but it has helped facilitate that process and make it quicker.
(Lita Ugarte Pardi)

We now accept all letters of inquiry and proposals online. During our first online grant round we received 248 requests—only two organizations submitted hard copies. We found that not only did the vast majority of nonprofits applying to our foundation have the capacity to submit online, they told us that they prefer it. We have received a lot of feedback about the ease of the process and the facility of being able to edit and upload documents online. It has been a positive change for both sides. (Danielle M. Reyes)

One of the best features of this whole thing is that over time, all previous proposals will be saved, and they will all be in the same system. Hopefully it will be a timesaver for applicants. Funders spend a fair amount of time summarizing a docket. I think one of the reasons we wanted to go to an online system is so that the summary data are online and can be analyzed and reported on more easily. (Elizabeth B. Smith)

I love getting proposals by e-mail. It is just much easier for me. I have everything I need electronically. (Bob Wittig)

Do you use e-mail to communicate with grantseekers?

We discourage e-mails and faxes, but we will use them if we initiate them. We would much rather a phone call. We are not wild about having a follow-up or inquiry initiated by a grantee via e-mail. (William V. Engel)

We have really gone electronic. Whatever can possibly be e-mailed to me, I want it e-mailed. (Laura H. Gilbertson)

We rely heavily on e-mail communications to collect all necessary information and to clarify any questions. (Jane G. Hardesty)

E-mail tends to play two roles: one is a scheduling function and two is a way to send attachments, but the actual connection happens in conversation, whether on the phone or in person. E-mail is a tool to enable those conversations to happen and to be grounded in some document that lays out an idea. (Jacob Harold)

I try to do as much electronically as I can. So I will actually send via e-mail a PDF letter that invites the proposal and gives very specific criteria. (Bob Wittig)

What do you look for in your review of grant proposals?

The most important thing is leveraging, looking at the likelihood of a sustainable outcome so that we are not getting into an endless funding pattern here. And I think we are pretty enlightened among grantmakers in recognizing that sustainability in many cases may require multiyear grants, so it is not an incredibly onerous requirement, but we want to see some kind of business plan that suggests a sustainability model. (Edmund J. Cain)

The first step is just trying to get a clear understanding of the information that is presented. (Matt Carpenter)

We have a pretty rigorous process here. The organization submits an inquiry; we review those inquiries on a weekly basis to determine whether we will move forward on the inquiry, request a full proposal, or decline. If it makes it through the next phase, and we ask for a full proposal, we have the meeting with the organization and then we do an internal staff review. Then the responsible program manager will have to do more fact checking or call the organization asking for additional information. (Kathleen Cerveny)

After we have established that they are organizationally fit and competent and programmatically apt, we look at the business plan, the financial side of it— is it as equally strong and convincing? And we are not going to be the only funder for a number of reasons, so where is the rest of the money coming from? (Bruce H. Esterline)

There are three things we look for: the organic nature of the project, the need, and a clear project plan. We offer logic model training to make it possible for all groups to develop clear plans for their work—ideally to level the playing field so that whether an organization has a development staff or just a director who is wearing 20 different hats, everyone can submit a clear proposal. We typically have a primary and a secondary reader for all proposals. (Julie Farkas)

Due diligence is an area where institutions can help us considerably because it helps if we know an institution. Then when we receive their application we do not have to learn from scratch. If we know they have been through a hard time but we have met their president—great. We know where they stand now. If it is financial difficulties, or whatever the problems have been—if they keep us up to speed as they move through issues, it makes it so much easier to report adequately to our directors. (Roxanne Ford)

Due diligence feels softer and more qualitative than one might expect.
It is rare that Surdna deals with an organization that has not established
a reputation and networked with other foundations. It is really about
triangulating—by telephone, by site visits, through conversations with other
grantmakers—to give us the sense that they are on solid footing.
(Phillip Henderson)

One of the harder-to-measure goals is whether an organization is going to be
a significant one that is going to have the capacity to influence beyond the
direct client it serves, and affect best practice or policy. So we are trying to get
a sense of if it did work and have an impact, does that contribute anything to
the field? (Matthew Klein)

Each Monday, the program staff gathers to discuss the proposals received and
reviewed during the prior week. We talk about why the organizations and
their requests are or are not a fit for our guidelines and priorities; we get ideas
from each other, and we utilize the shared knowledge of our staff.
(Jane B. O'Connell and Karen L. Rosa)

There are a few things that are absolutely key: the fit with our funding
guidelines and what we are trying to accomplish. If we see that, we obviously
look at issues related to the program, and at the comprehensiveness of the
activities that are going on and the thoughtfulness of them and whether or
not they represent best practices or evolving best practice because we have
groups that are small and building. We look to see whether there is an active
board and whether there is financial accountability within the organization—
even if it is a small one. (Elizabeth B. Smith)

What else is part of your "due diligence" process?

Speaking to other funders

I do speak or meet with other donors around 1) exciting projects;
2) problems; 3) issues facing the city; or, 4) problem nonprofits—how we
can help the client if the nonprofit cannot be saved. (Peter F. Bird, Jr.)

What a foundation funds or does not fund, usually has no bearing on another
foundation; however, foundation people talk to each other, and nonprofits
need to realize this. Being honest with funders is critical. (Paula Boyce)

As for speaking to other donors: it depends on the grant. Program staff are definitely looking at who else is funding the work. Program staff will call other funders and get their feedback. What is their relationship with the grantee? How much funding has been provided? Have they been able to complete the work? (Julie Brooks)

It often happens that a project is submitted to more than one funder and when we see that sometimes we invite the face-to-face meeting to be a joint meeting, if it works for the other funder's timetable. If we feel another funder knows an organization better than we might, we might make that inquiry of them. (Kathleen Cerveny)

Sometimes we actively look for other funders to support a project if they like it. (Bruce H. Esterline)

We would love to be able to talk to other funders in more cases than we do. However, we do it mainly in cases where we have heard something negative or we are on the fence. We are a small team so we do not have a chance to be as involved with our organizations as we would like. In many cases we will call the Victoria Foundation and say, "Are you guys still funding this organization and what do you think and how do you read recent events?" It tends to be more of an exception basis that we will seek the insights of our peers. (Curtland E. Fields)

There has been communication with other funders on occasion, especially if it is a large project reliant on other funders to make it happen. So yes, it does happen when appropriate. (Irene Frye)

There are a couple of colleagues at other foundations—in my case the Packard, Mott, and Gates Foundations—that have similar grantees, and in one way or another I am talking to them every month if not more often. And often during a conversation we will touch on three common grantees or applicants we are looking at, or in some cases, where we are co-funding. And twice a year, grantmakers that fund nonprofit infrastructure informally get together in person and talk about those issues. (Jacob Harold)

There is an increasingly collaborative working environment among funders that puts many heads into the due diligence process. In a process sense it makes this more complicated, trying to schedule meetings and making sure people are copied on e-mails, etc. But if constructively structured and diligently pursued, this oftentimes ends in a better result. (Robert B. Jaquay)

We will call other funders, particularly for new grantees. Who are they and what do they do? I always encourage people to send in letters of support if we have never seen a proposal from them or it is a new program that they want to try. I always encourage letters of support and not ones that say the same thing from four different people. (Karen Kinney)

Beyond the standard review of the organization's documentation, due diligence really depends on whom we are dealing with and how well we know them. We may ask questions that go beyond looking at the financial reports or board lists to questions of their own internal processes. Like, "describe for me what your cash handling and internal control processes are in your office," "how often does your board meet?," "how often does your board review financial statements?," and "who prepares your financial statements?" There is a whole list of things we go over with organizations, especially if they are new to us, to see whether what is happening on the back end of the organization seems appropriate. (Victoria Kovar)

Libby Costas tends to speak to other funders more than I do, but I am interested to see if it is an ongoing project and who has funded it before. Libby is the one who will certainly pick up the phone and talk to some other funders and say "I have seen that you have funded this group, at least in general, maybe not this particular program. Can you tell us about them and give us some background?" It can help to give a leg up to a group, and we hope that some of our grants will, in turn, give a leg up to that group, when other funders see that the Cummings Fund has supported that charity. I think that the Cummings Fund has a reputation for doing our homework and that if we have given a grant, even if it is not the largest grant in the world, it is sort of a stamp of approval. (J. Andrew Lark)

We talk to other grantmakers, we talk to other community leaders, and we talk to elected officials. That is really important because if a nonprofit organization is the best-kept secret in town and nobody knows them, that is an issue. (David A. Odahowski)

I do some checking with other foundations, particularly when it is an organization I really know nothing about. (Christine Park)

If they are a group I am on the fence with and I have some concerns, and they mention to me that they are being considered by foundation A, and I know foundation A very well, I will call or e-mail them and say "hey, I am struggling a bit. Where are you with funding them?" Or if they are brand-new to us and I know other groups have funded them or declined them, I will speak to other funders. It is a much stronger case if I feel good about a brand-new organization and I know that three other foundations have already funded them. (Bob Wittig)

Speak to other knowledgeable nonprofits

We not only talk to the nonprofit itself but also other nonprofits that are in the same business or the same community. (Matt Carpenter)

We might send a proposal, based on the subject area, out for an external review by an expert in the area. That is determined by the program officer. (Irene Frye)

Google/web site/oversight agencies

We certainly check their 990s all the time with Guidestar. Sometimes we use Guidestar's analysis, but we require all our arts organizations to submit reports from the Ohio Cultural Data Project [created by Pew Charitable Trust]. It is a way that arts organizations can produce very sophisticated reports for free that they can use themselves within their own organization, but they can also very quickly populate a funder's reporting requirements or application process with financials and operational details so we can look at arts institutions in an apples-to-apples sort of way. (Kathleen Cerveny)

Staff almost always looks at the organization's web site. Not having an Internet presence raises a flag—"hmm, I wonder why they have not taken advantage of that." And the url goes to the board so they can check out the sites when they review the write-up. (Bruce H. Esterline)

One should assume that if the nonprofit is on the Internet we will find it. (Roxanne Ford)

Always look at their web site, and I Google them, too. And I use that as a way to evaluate their capacity. If they have a calendar on their site that is two years old, it is obviously not a priority for them. (Laura H. Gilbertson)

We check Guidestar and we check the organization's tax-exempt status. I am not sure if those are new trends. I am seeing an increased use of the Guidestar rating by grantees in their proposals, if they are highly rated. (Robert B. Jaquay)

I often go on the agency web site. Sometimes the language is clearer there than it is on the proposal. I have Googled in the past. It is not something we typically do, but if they are new, I might Google them. (Karen Kinney)

I always look at the web site and often Google. (Victoria Kovar)

The Internet has provided us with so much access. Between Guidestar and an organization's web site, we learned so much about prospects and we were able to solicit opinions from others—donors, nonprofits, and board members. (Richard M. Krasno)

I do turn to Guidestar occasionally to view 990s. I turn to the Foundation Center to better understand other funders of the organization and what level of support they provide. (Darin McKeever)

There is more responsibility now on the part of grantmakers to go online and do searches. I can go online and get a 990 [and sometimes audited financials], and read news accounts or video clips of these organizations. Sometimes executive directors are doing something personally in some online community that catches my attention. If board members ever saw some of this stuff, they would ask themselves "Who is running these organizations?" (David A. Odahowski)

I will go to Guidestar only if there is something questionable—something incomplete in the LOI or if I notice that four of the board members all have the same last name. I might go to Guidestar and look at the 990. Otherwise, no. I use Google frequently. I search the organization, sometimes Google an Executive Director's name. I have also found things I don't want to find. That is not common, but it's out there. (Danielle M. Reyes)

I use Guidestar a lot. Guidestar is fabulous because I can look at their financials. And I can make sure they are current with their IRS filings. (Bob Wittig)

Financial review

We have become increasingly careful about looking over audits and we ask increasingly detailed questions. A lot of people will look at 990s. We look at audits and if we see problems, we will go back two or three years and really examine carefully where things stand. Though we will make some allowances these days, institutions have to show that they can be around another year. (Roxanne Ford)

In looking at financials, one of the things I encourage is to help us understand how a budget deficit is being addressed. Give us a half-page narrative that says "here is how we have addressed this shortfall and provide examples of specific changes." They need to show how they are dealing with it now, addressing it going forward, and hopefully preventing further holes that they might see coming. (Jane G. Hardesty)

Where we are going to spend a lot of the initial time is the financial reports. (Victoria Kovar)

We have a financial review: we ask for three years of audits. We partnered with an organization called the Nonprofit Finance Fund to help train our staff in reviewing financial documents. We have a tool that we use that we plug numbers from the audits to show us trends over the last three years. That is one part of due diligence. The other is that we review everything that we get. There is a team for each cycle and the team reviews all the final applications and all the attachments. We feel it is really important for everyone to read everything because then nobody is advocating more strongly for one organization not having read the rest of them. (Lita Ugarte Pardi)

There is a financial checklist. Internally, I look at the audit and the 990s. If it is an old audit, I will request updated financials. With our financial checklist, we are looking for a few core things: one is that revenue meets or exceeds expenses and that the audit was clean, that cash flow looks healthy, that they are not out of bounds in terms of funds toward lobbying, who prepares financial info to be presented to the board, who presents it, and how frequently it is presented, and what sort of internal controls and procedures they have. If they do not have any, we ask them to do that before going through the process. That it should be written down and everybody on the board should be aware of it. (Danielle M. Reyes)

What is the role of your board in the proposal review process?

The staff will make a recommendation to the president for grants up to $250,000. Anything above $250,000 is reviewed and approved by the Board of Trustees. (Julie Brooks)

We have a one-page executive summary—the major categories that we have are the organizational basics, the basics of the request, other support for the request, our own history with the organization or similar organization, financial information analysis, and a staff comment or recommendation.

Sometimes we bleed over to two pages. All the full information is available to our trustees, including the proposal and the staff report on the site visit. (Matt Carpenter)

Anything that is over $10,000 is reviewed at our quarterly board meeting. So we put a docket together with information on what the request is, how much is requested, a history of past giving to the organization, ratings from various watchdog agencies like Charity Navigator, and other sources of support that have been received for the project. I will also include any employee involvement with the organization for disclosure purposes. (Susan M. Carter)

Our board meets 10 times per year—they must review board packets of 100 pages or more for each meeting—just proposals—in addition, they receive analyses, minutes, treasurers reports, decline lists, grant updates, etc. Board review sheets have the "approve without discussion" and "favor discussion" options, which moves meetings along more quickly if discussion is not required. (Bruce H. Esterline)

Staff prepare write-ups—proposal summaries and analyses—which are reviewed by our program committee, and the committee's recommendations go to our board. Most of our board is on our program committee, which is great because they are intested and engaged in our work on the ground. Our write-ups have evolved over the years to become much more laser-focused. We present matrices which convey all the critical information in a succinct way because our board members are busy people. It is enough information that they can read it and ask questions at the meeting. And they do! (Julie Farkas)

Staff reads an application and can send a recommendation and evaluation to the board along with the full application in three categories in "recommended," "not recommended," and "special conditions." Then the board knows how we feel about it and then they read to determine if they agree with our proposal and the rationale. Since many of the board members live in the area that we fund, some of them may know an organization directly and will be able to say, "this is a really good one" or "they have had some problems, we should think twice or go visit them." (Curtland E. Fields)

They review the proposal along with a four- to eight-page summary from the staff about the request. And that provides information about past grants and results that have occurred. It provides commentary on the evaluation and dissemination plans and the merits of the proposal. There is a vote that goes out to the trustees so they vote in advance. If it is a unanimous vote, that is a consent agenda. If there is not a unanimous vote, it may or may not be open for discussion and a re-vote. Any of the trustees has the authority to request that the proposal get discussed at the meeting. Our board meetings are generally two days long. (Irene Frye)

I do a summary or coversheet for the proposal, which is a very brief description of what they are asking for, a history of the grants they have received from us in the past, and a list of what is attached. On the other side I summarize their audit and their budget. Then the trustees receive the cover letter, the proposal narrative, and the proposal budget, as well as the summary of the strategic plan and the environmental impact statement and the board list, and they do really look at those things. They ask a host of questions—applicants are always surprised by the types of questions that come up in the board meetings. Grantseekers are always surprised by how thoroughly our board reviews each proposal. Not a consent agenda. Unanimity not required. (Laura H. Gilbertson)

Most of our grants go through the board on a three-times-a-year cycle— three dockets that we present to the board. They almost always approve. Very very rare exceptions when they do not. We are allowed to make some grants totaling no more than 10 percent of our budget, or no more than $400,000 through a process called presidential discretionary grants, which only requires the signature of the president and does not require board approval. (Jacob Harold)

Usually if it makes our final agenda, there is a good chance it will get funded. We go through all proposals and the advisory board member who is present at our site visits gives the introductory comments and the reasons for funding or not funding and opens discussion up to the whole group, so everything is given a full hearing. (J. Andrew Lark)

After site visit, staff meets and compiles three-page recommendations. We put together, based on the amount of funding we have available, a docket of recommendations that we present to our board committee. They discuss those and make recommendations to the full board. Once they are approved, the announcements are made. Other staff are invited to sit in on the recommendation committee meeting and provide input. (Lita Ugarte Pardi)

Every foundation is different. For us, the board only reviews and approves grants over $1 million. They also look at conflicts of interest and are deeply engaged in determining policies and strategic direction of the foundation. They hold our executive leadership accountable, oversee our expenditures and grants budget, are committed to executing our mission, and have a deep passion for improving the health of our underserved communities. (Dianne Yamashiro-Omi)

Usually if we have invited a proposal, the request is going to the board. Only rarely do we invite a proposal and then decide not to advance it to the board. We might ask a group to withdraw upon getting more information. This happens when it is something we really want to do but the organization is just not ready. We try not to advance groups that would get declined at a board meeting. We prepare one-page write-ups for the board. The board has a chance to look at the write-ups and e-mail any questions or ask them at the board meeting. At the board meeting, they have the opportunity to ask any questions. Often there is a question or two, but not about every single organization. We really go into those meetings prepared. Our staff has a reputation for our level of due diligence. Many small foundations and funding partners will consider a group if we are funding them because they know we did the due diligence. (Anonymous)

Do you meet with prospective grantees, and if so, why?

We do wander in unannounced if we hear about problems and have called repeatedly without an answer, or have troubling reports from third parties. But by and large, if there is no reason for concern or suspicion, we arrange meetings in advance. I am interested in seeing hands-on staff to see what their philosophy of service delivery is, to get a sense of their leadership, how well they staff, and whether they pursue certain quality initiatives. (Curtland E. Fields)

We try to accomplish a greater understanding of the project and how it relates to our key interests and our mission. (Irene Frye)

We have been trying to meet with more applicants, especially new ones. At the very least we have a phone conversation with all applicants so we always have some personal connection. (Victoria Kovar)

It is the groups in the middle that we sort of fret over. We fill our calendar to the maximum degree in terms of how many groups we can do site visits with, either at our office, or if it is a group we are not familiar with or if it is a heavily staff-dependent proposal, we will want to actually go out and see that staff and location. (J. Andrew Lark)

What do you look for in the course of a site visit?

We try to see some of the programs in action, but some of that can be very stilted. It is not that they are rolling out the red carpet, but they have clearly informed everyone that a funder is going to be present. In many cases, I just want to see how the organization works. What is the condition of the facility? What is the interaction among staff? I am very interested to see how connected the Executive Director is to his or her staff. Does he or she know them by name? How does the relationship look and feel? I am also very interested to see how engaged the board chair is, and whether they are on the same wavelength as the executive director. (Doug Bauer)

Staff observes programs in action. You can talk to somebody about it, but actually seeing how they run it is even better. (Marilyn Gelber)

I would like to see the organization at work. I would like to see what participants are doing, and the people they are serving and how they are being served. You want to see that passion for the work. (Karen Kinney)

If we do not know the program yet but they have written a proposal, there can be a disconnect. Going out and eyeballing the facility, talking to the staff, meeting a board member, and seeing at least some of the clients served are all-important. (J. Andrew Lark)

When I first started, I made site visits to all the grantees. There are times when I find it helpful to do a site visit, but I do not see it as due diligence but rather as relationship-building. There is something very useful about showing up and seeing their offices. I suppose it does help with due diligence, but it also creates a deeper sense of empathy that hopefully will lead to a more candid, trusting relationship. (Darin McKeever)

I want to see the people closest to the work. It does not help me much if I am going to see a large organization and see the executive director and the development director but not actually get to meet the program staff that actually do the work. That is not as helpful. For smaller groups, having board members there is really helpful. Seeing one energetic, dynamic founder is okay, but knowing that there are also stakeholders that are rooting for that person is important, especially for startups. Sometimes having community partners there is helpful. It is important to see the neighborhood, schools, and businesses that make the context in which the organization operates. (Maria Mottola)

What I have done by the time I get there, a review of all the materials. I am really just asking questions for clarification, and getting a feel for the leadership and taking a look around the premises. (David D. Weitnauer)

Site visits are really important because they make the organization come alive that much more. At a site visit, I can hear them tell me about their organization and program in person. As much as possible, I try to meet clients and/or see the program in action. For me, a proposal is based on the people that are there. That is an important part and you cannot get that from a paper proposal. It is just like interviewing for a job, it is a chance for the employer to learn more about you. You can learn so much more in person, I think. (Bob Wittig)

Whom do you want to meet with representing the grantseeking organization?

It need not be the chairman of the board but my preference would be an experienced board member who is present during our site visit. Sometimes if you have a board chair you encounter an entrenched view, and it is not as helpful as somebody who is in the middle—not quite part of the status quo, but someone who has a good working knowledge of the board. Because it really is important to know if the board is active. Are they involved in the agency's strategic planning? Fortunately more groups are doing strategic planning. But then we also ask "how" they are doing their planning. Too often it is overly staff-driven, which is not that helpful. We prefer that the initial strategic plan be kicked off by a board retreat—or at least an extensive board-driven brainstorming session. (J. Andrew Lark)

The Executive Director and board chair are required and we suggest that they have somebody from the board or staff who is well versed in the organization's finances and any other board or staff leader that they feel can add to the conversation. I like to limit it to four people. I think that is more than enough. (Lita Ugarte Pardi)

We really do not want a performance. We do not want to make it more difficult for the applicant. We want to make it as smooth a process as possible, so really we just want to have one or two key people participate in the site visit. (Amy Scop)

We always want to have a board member there. Typically the Executive Director is there. We do not fund really large organizations so we would like not only the Executive Director but the person who is actually overseeing the work—a lead organizer or lead program person. And we ideally like to talk to people who are being served or affected by the program. (Elizabeth B. Smith)

The CEO and it is helpful to have at least one board member. But more than that is not helpful. Sometimes we will go and there will be two or three board members and that has never really struck me as a good use of people's time. But with one trustee, you can usually ask questions about board function and committees and those types of things. But we do not require a board member be present. We let them dictate that. The main person I want to meet with is the executive director. Typically, unless it is a very large enterprise, I will not just meet with a development person. (David D. Weitnauer)

It is especially beneficial for new board members. I typically see the Executive Director, but it is really helpful for me to meet and talk to the person who is running the program we may be supporting because they have more on-the-ground information depending on the size of the agency. It is always a fine line about meeting the clients because I do not want it to be a dog-and-pony show but it has also been helpful to actually talk to the clients for 10 or 15 minutes to hear their story and find out why the program is important to them. I always tell board members it is a great way to be engaged, to learn about the organization, and connect to the mission. And I always tell Executive Directors it is a great way to engage your board membes in a very helpful way without them having to do a whole lot. (Bob Wittig)

Do you have any tips for nonprofits preparing for a meeting with your foundation?

Be prepared to answer a lot of questions about the project, and the finances. I cannot remember a time where there was a bad impression, or when that had any particular sway. People have anxiety about being friendly and deferential, but I would sort of downplay the anxiety around issues around impressing us and just know the subject more than worrying about the personality. We are cognizant of the fact that there is a big power differential in the room. So we work very hard at being very real, very sincere, and leveling the playing field. We are able to sort of get real with folks. (Bruce H. Esterline)

Do not make it a red carpet tour. A dialogue is more important that a "red carpet tour of the program," which can be disruptive, and not always as frank. (Maria Mottola)

Here are a few tips: 1) be yourself, 2) be able to engage, and 3) time is critical—be well structured. (Jane B. O'Connell and Karen L. Rosa)

Appendix A: Sample Proposal

ENACT

A Request for Funding to Early Riser Fund

Submitted By:
Diana Feldman
Founder, Executive Director
ENACT, Inc.
630 Ninth Avenue, Suite 301
New York, NY 10036
Phone: (212) 741-6591
www.enact.org

EXECUTIVE SUMMARY

ENACT requests the renewed support of the Early Riser Fund through a $10,000 grant for our **School Workshop Program** which serves an average of 5,000 at-risk students on an annual basis.

ENACT's work began twenty years ago to help New York City public school students learn social-emotional skills through creative drama and drama therapy techniques. ENACT uses trained actor instructors to lead classroom-based activities and special role play exercises which enable young people to recognize, reflect on, and regulate their own emotions and behavior. A trusted partner of the Department of Education, ENACT annually serves nearly 15,000 students, school staff, and parents through long-term and short-term school partnerships, parent and teacher workshops, summer and after school programming, and performances.

A recent report from an outside evaluator, funded through The Ford Foundation, determined that:

- ENACT staff and teaching artists were **highly effective at engaging students.**

- Students learned how to **respect** each other's differences and work together effectively.

- Teachers noted **improvement in students' behavior** and respect for one another.

- ENACT teaching artists engaged students who were initially resistant. Students began to **better understand their emotions**, express themselves and **take ownership of their behavior.**

At the core of ENACT's programming is a powerful **School Workshop Program** which partners with the New York City Department of Education to provide in-school workshops. As funding allows, ENACT also provides parent and teacher workshops to have a greater impact on our partnering schools. At a time when the struggles of underserved New York City communities are increasing, The Seth Sprague Educational and Charitable Foundation's renewed support will ensure our ability to continue to serve thousands of at-risk youth in the next year.

NEED ADDRESSED AND POPULATION SERVED

The graduation rate in the United States has been called a silent epidemic. Overall, nearly one-third of all high school students in the nation drop-out of school. When looking at New York City specifically, that rate climbs up to 50 percent. Even worse, when the data is disaggregated to account for ethnicity, statistics show that approximately 70 percent of black and Latino students in New York City do not graduate. The stated reasons for why these students do not complete high school are various and complex.

ENACT serves students who are at the greatest risk of dropping out. Across the board, our partnering schools educate students who live in economically depressed communities where poverty has brought high rates of violence, crime, drug and alcohol abuse, and teen pregnancy. Many of the young people served by ENACT lack positive role models, family and community supports, and even a basic sense of physical security. A significant number of youth are also victims of abuse and neglect, live in foster care settings, or have a history of homelessness. The school environment exacerbates the situation in which overcrowded classrooms, high teacher turnover, violence, gang activity, and negative peer pressure are the norm rather than the exception. As a result of such hopeless environments, students are unmotivated to learn, apathetic, and disconnected from school.

ENACT's research-based method teaches at-risk students six core skills of positive social/emotional behavior: focus, engagement, reflection, self-management, self-discipline and self-awareness. It is widely documented that social-emotional education has a strong impact on positive growth and academic achievement. ENACT's proven method has also been recognized as a powerful dropout prevention tool.

Ninety-five percent of the youth served by ENACT in 2008–09 were between the ages of 12 and 19. In terms of ethnicity, 50 percent were African American, 40 percent were Hispanic, and 10 percent were of other ethnic groups. Currently 40 percent of ENACT's work is in the South Bronx, 40 percent is in Brooklyn, and the remaining work takes place in high-poverty areas of Queens.

PROGRAM DESCRIPTION

Our renowned School Workshop Program helps students build the skills they need to make positive life choices. The program operates annually from September through June. The timeframe and length of individual partnerships vary depending on each school's needs and the availability of funding.

In each workshop, a team of two professionally trained actor-instructors who are overseen by our drama therapist and mental health professionals provide direct services to students in a classroom setting. ENACT's teaching artists build scenes that parallel students' issues and concerns drawing from their toolkit of activities. The teaching artists then engage students in reflective discussions about the conflict depicted in the scene. In the process of engaging the students, the teaching artist focuses on topics such as managing emotions, communicating effectively, and making responsible decisions. Students then reconstruct the scene with alternate outcomes to practice the skills they are learning, and rehearse for the situations they face in real life. Each partnership includes:

Advance Planning/Curriculum Design: ENACT meets with school administrators to gain an understanding of the needs of students, teachers, and families. ENACT then meets with classroom teachers to discuss the students' interests and needs. The ENACT curriculum is then adapted accordingly.

The Right Team of Teaching Artists: Teaching artists are selected based on expertise, experience, ethnicity, and languages spoken. ENACT has a fully-trained cadre of 50 acting professionals.

Supervision: All teaching artists and ENACT staff receive ongoing training and support from social workers, psychologists, psychiatrists, and educational specialists. To ensure that students receive the proper care, staff members are trained to identify children whose issues require special attention, and to make referrals to the appropriate clinical staff.

Counseling Support: When students are disruptive to the safe environment or when they demonstrate issues that are beyond the role of the teaching artist, they are referred to the social worker, who determines the appropriate form of counseling. This strategy has proven highly effective in helping students identify their core issues and in reintegrating them into the classroom as soon as they are ready.

Collaboration with School-Based Support Staff: To ensure that students receive the necessary support, ENACT develops close working relationships with school social workers and guidance counselors. All ENACT staff are trained to maintain the confidentiality of students and their families.

Teacher and Parent Workshops: Teacher workshops introduce the ENACT method, as well as to provide additional communication and problem-solving strategies to help teachers offer guidance and support. ENACT offers Parent Workshops in English and Spanish to best meet the needs of all family members.

Learning Outcome Celebration: During the final week of the program, the ENACT team and school staff organize an event to celebrate the students' new skills. The main feature is a play or video created jointly by the students and the teaching artist.

EVALUATION, OBJECTIVES & PROJECTED OUTCOMES

The School Workshop Program is evaluated by ENACT's program staff to measure the effectiveness of our school programs and teaching artists using a combination of evaluation methods including:

- Pre-Assessment Interviews that are one-on-one with teachers to assess student behavior, evaluate the overall classroom "climate", and outline student needs and challenges.

- Mid-Program and Final Program Evaluations to compare with initial assessments.

- Program Impact Surveys, Questionnaires and Focus Groups with teachers, students, administrators and Teaching Artists to evaluate the effectiveness of the program, the program's ability to achieve goals and to develop recommendations for strengthening the partnership.

- Rubric for Assessing Group Behavior and Likert Scales are the two major quantitative tools that ENACT uses. The Group Rubrics are used by Teaching Artists to measure changes in students' demonstrated respect, behavior, self-control, feelings/emotions, and self-confidence, assessing the change from the beginning of the residency to the end. Classroom Teachers use the Likert Scales to assess student change.

ENACT works toward the following annual objectives: 1) Contract at least 450 workshops with the Department of Education; 2) Work with approximately 5,000 students to help them develop coping strategies, and communication and problem solving skills; and 3) Provide training to nearly 1,300 school staff and 300 parents.

Specific outcomes we aim to achieve include: 1) 80 percent of participating students will exhibit positive behavioral change through participation in ENACT's social-emotional curriculum; and 2) 85 percent of classroom teachers will report improved behavior among students during other classroom activities.

FUNDING AND SUSTAINABILITY

The total budget for our School Workshop Program is $557,861. Although ENACT does receive important funding from the New York City Department of Education for its workshops, this funding does not cover the true cost of service. The cost of each workshop is $1,200 which includes high level planning and staff training. ENACT is reimbursed at a maximum of $750 per workshop; in some cases, less. As ENACT conducts an estimated 465 workshops annually (including student, parent, and teacher workshops) we need to raise over $150,000 to cover non-reimbursed costs each year.

For this reason, ENACT continually researches and approaches appropriate foundation and corporate prospects to underwrite the cost of our services. Current funders of the School Workshop Program include: the American Chai Trust, the Countess Moira Charitable Foundation, The Barker Welfare Foundation, Ronald McDonald House Charities, the Rite Aid Foundation, and the Glickenhaus Foundation.

STAFF AND QUALIFICATIONS

Led by founder and Executive Director Diana Feldman, ENACT's 12-member staff includes a Director of Operations, Director of Research and Programs, Director of Research and Training, and Director of Partnerships. Complementing their expertise are the members of the Advisory Committee, all of whom have outstanding credentials and extensive experience in psychology, drama therapy, evaluation, and training. Staff members and teaching artists receive in-depth, ongoing training from the clinical staff, Advisory Committee members, and outside experts which includes: Seth Aronson from Mount Saini Hospital, psychotherapist and leader in the field of adolescent health, Robert Landy Ph.D., Professor and Program Director of Drama Therapy at New York University, Linda Lantieri, conflict resolution specialist of Resolving Conflict Creatively, Sarah Suatoni, bodywork specialist, and conflict resolution specialist, Martha Eddy Ph.D., a movement therapist and, Lisa Sazuki, a multicultural expert and professor of applied psychology at New York University.

All of ENACT's teaching artists who conduct the School Workshop Program are working actors with impressive theatre, film, and television credentials. With masterful improvisational skills and tremendous energy, these individuals create the dynamic engagement with students that serves as the foundation for teaching and learning. Currently ENACT's Board of Trustees has ten members, all of whom have demonstrated a high level of commitment to the organization and its mission.

ORGANIZATIONAL INFORMATION

In addition to our School Workshop Program, ENACT provides the following programs and services:

Long-term Attendance Improvement Dropout Prevention Programming: In partnership with the United Way of New York City ENACT has developed long-term partnerships in which teaching artists and program coordinators work as full partners with teachers, parents and administrators to provide direct service to students who meet state mandated selection criteria. Many of these partnerships span across a twelve-month or multi-year period and allow ENACT to have a greater impact on the school community. In 2007 ENACT expanded this program through funding from the New York City Council, serving six of the City's lowest performing schools. Based on the success of this programming, the City Council renewed it support in 2008-09, however, because of budget cuts, ENACT received two-thirds of what was received last year. ENACT is currently raising funds to make up for this funding gap.

After School and Saturday Programs: ENACT's After School Programs serve an average of 600 students on an annual basis; approximately 50 percent of students served also work with ENACT through our school day partnerships. These programs operate in collaboration with the New York City Department of Education, the United Way of New York City and The After School Corporation. ENACT also offers its workshops for students, staff and parents during Saturday hours.

Performances: ENACT offers four popular performance pieces which address important issues students face and are used to generate powerful discussions. Current performances include A Day in the Life for grades 1–5, 2:45 for grades 6–8, Cooked for grades 7–12, and Finding the Words for grades 9–12.

ENACT's Training Institutes: Over the years, ENACT created a Training Institute which teaches other youth service providers the core elements of the ENACT method. Attendees of ENACT's past training workshops include: the New School for Social Research's faculty; Roundabout Theatre Company; Arts Genesis, Inc.; Irondale Theatre Company; and Arts Connection.

CONCLUSION

ENACT's School Workshop Program helps students to cope with their chaotic home, school and community environments and learn to manage their behavior. We hope the Early Riser Fund will partner with us once again through a $10,000 grant as we continue to work toward our mission "to help New York City's neediest public school students learn social-emotional skills through creative drama and drama therapy to empower them to make positive life choices."

ENACT
School Workshop Program

EXPENSES

Teaching Artist #1 (@ 100%)	$175
Teaching Artist #2 (@ 100%)	$175
Extra fees (Travel, meetings, rehearsal, etc)	$100
Fringe @ 15%	$68
Total Teaching Artist Expenses	**$518**
Artistic Director	$110
Manager of Business Affairs	$70
Program Manager	$70
Director of Training	$70
Program Manager-Parent Services	$30
Program Assistant/Office Manager	$20
Assist. Director of Training	$20
Fringe (@ 28%)	$109
Total Administrative Expenses	**$499**
Supplies	$15
Food	$10
Travel (not travel stipend)	$5
Training	$25
Marketing	$10
Accounting	$15
Insurance	$15
other	$50
Indirect Costs	$38
Total Expenses per Workshop	**$1,200**
Projected Number of Workshops*	465
Projected Total Expenses	**$558,000**

*This number includes student, parent, and teacher workshops and is calculated based on the average number of workshops held in previous years.

Appendix B:
Selected Resources on
Proposal Development

Books

Barber, Daniel M. *Finding Funding: The Comprehensive Guide to Grant Writing.* 2nd ed. Long Beach, CA: Bond Street Publishers, 2002. This handbook provides advice for writers of proposals to government agencies, foundations, and corporations. It includes a section on responding to a request for proposals and instructions for creating a letter proposal.

Browning, Beverly A. *Perfect Phrases for Writing Grant Proposals.* New York, NY: McGraw Hill, 2008. Provides sample phrases to help proposal writers select the right wording to describe their organizations or projects.

Carlson, Mim and Tori O'Neal-McElrath. *Winning Grants Step by Step.* 3rd ed. San Francisco, CA: Jossey-Bass Publishers, 2008. Contains instructions to help with proposal development for foundation and corporate funding. Provides a number of sample documents and worksheets.

Chapin, Paul G. *Research Projects and Research Proposals: A Guide for Scientists Seeking Funding.* New York, NY: Cambridge University Press, 2004. Directed to scientists who wish to design and write proposals to funding agencies. Includes project planning, information about specific government funders (as well as more general recommendations about researching private foundations), and grants management.

Clarke, Cheryl A. *Storytelling for Grantseekers: The Guide to Creative Nonprofit Fundraising.* 2nd ed. San Francisco, CA: Jossey-Bass Publishers, 2009. Clarke puts forward the notion that proposals share much with great stories: characters, setting, and plot. She shows proposal writers how to craft documents that include elements of drama. The book also covers the research process and cultivation. Includes sample letters of inquiry, letter proposals, as well as information on packaging the proposal.

Geever, Jane C. and Silvia R. Sanusian (trans.) *Guía para escribir propuestas.* New York, NY: Foundation Center, 2008. A Spanish translation of *The Foundation Center's Guide to Proposal Writing,* 5th ed. Appendix lists Foundation Center libraries and Cooperating Collections where Spanish is spoken and where materials in Spanish are available.

Gitlin, Laura N. and Kevin J. Lyons. *Successful Grant Writing: Strategies for Health and Human Service Professionals.* 3rd ed. New York, NY: Springer, 2008. Covers many aspects of proposal development and grantsmanship including identifying competitive projects, composing a budget, and grants management for both public and private agencies.

Howlett, Susan C. *Getting Funded: The Complete Guide to Writing Grant Proposals.* 5th ed. Seattle, WA: Word & Raby LLC, 2011. This proposal writing guide explains how to prepare your organization to compete for grants, identify suitable grantmakers, describe projects persuasively, and maintain strong relationships with funders. Includes stories and advice from funders, examples based on best practices, and numerous checklists/worksheets.

Johnson, Victoria M. *Grant Writing 101: Everything You Need to Start Raising Funds Today.* New York, NY: McGraw Hill, 2011. The author provides no-frills grant writing essentials and tricks. Chapters cover choosing the correct type of grant, preparation, researching funders, the waiting process, and handling acceptances and rejections. Includes a grant deadlines matrix template as well as sample letters, proposals (short, medium, and long), and budgets.

Koch, Deborah S. *How To Say It—Grantwriting: Write Proposals That Grantmakers Want to Fund.* New York, NY: Prentice Hall, 2009. This guide explains how to identify potential funders and develop proposals that grantmakers would be interested in supporting. Discusses project development and specific proposal components, such as the letter of inquiry, cover letter, and the budget. The appendix includes sample proposals to a major foundation, community foundation, and a federal agency.

Margolin, Judith B. and Elan K. DiMaio, eds. *The Grantseeker's Guide to Winning Proposals.* New York, NY: Foundation Center, 2008. The third volume in the *Foundation Center's Guide to Winning Proposals* series includes 35 proposals in a variety of formats. Each proposal includes a critique by the decision-maker who approved the grant. Winning proposals cover general operating support, program development, staff salaries, program evaluation, and other needs.

Miner, Jeremy T., Lynn E. Miner, and Jerry Griffith. *Collaborative Grantseeking: A Guide to Designing Projects, Leading Partners, and Persuading Sponsors.* Santa Barbara, CA: Greenwood, 2011. This book delves into the humanistic aspects of designing and leading successful collaborative projects, and gives detailed advice on writing persuasive proposals to fund them. Chapters cover collaboration types, generating ideas for collaborative grants, and program evaluation. Provides analyses of four successful collaborative grant proposals responding to RFPs issued by corporate foundations and government funders.

New, Cheryl Carter and James Aaron Quick. *How to Write a Grant Proposal.* Hoboken, NJ: John Wiley & Sons, 2003. The authors cover the key elements of standard proposal formats, including the executive summary, need statement, project description, evaluation, and budget. Each chapter contains examples and checklists.

Robinson, Andy. *Grassroots Grants: An Activist's Guide to Proposal Writing.* 2nd ed. San Francisco, CA: Jossey-Bass Publishers, 2004. The writer provides step-by-step guidance on how to create successful proposals, design projects, and manage grants. Several sample proposals are included.

Rosenberg, Gigi. *The Artist's Guide to Grant Writing: How to Find Funds and Write Foolproof Proposals for the Visual, Literary, and Performing Artist.* New York, NY: Watson-Guptill Publications, 2010. Targets writers, performers, and visual artists who want to learn how to fundraise successfully and write winning proposals. Chapters include tips from successful grant writers, grant officers, and fundraising specialists, and cover the application process, step-by-step proposal writing, crafting an artist statement, and budgeting (with sample).

Smith, Nancy Burke and E. Gabriel Works. *The Complete Book of Grant Writing: Learn to Write Grants Like a Professional.* Naperville, IL: Sourcebooks, Inc., 2006. This book explains how to write proposals to both government and private funders, and includes a brief treatment of responses to requests for proposals. Numerous sample proposal documents are provided, some of which focus on specific components of proposals. The authors also discuss grantwriting as a career.

Teitel, Martin. *"Thank You for Submitting Your Proposal": A Foundation Director Reveals What Happens Next.* Medfield, MA: Emerson & Church, 2006. In this behind-the-scenes account of the daily life of a foundation, Teitel (the executive director of the Cedar Tree Foundation) provides advice to grantseekers about proposal fundamentals, the use of letters of inquiry, site visits, communications with funders, and the reality of board decision-making.

Tremore, Judy and Nancy Burke Smith. *Grant Writing: A Complete Resource for Proposal Writers.* Avon, MA: Adams Media Corporation, 2009. Chapters cover numerous topics including government grants, foundation grants, letters of inquiry, letters of support, statements of need, action plans and timelines, evaluations, budgets, capital-grant proposals, and other areas.

Wells, Michael K. *Proven Strategies Professionals Use to Make Their Proposals Work.* (Grantwriting Beyond the Basics Series). Portland, OR: Portland State University, 2005. Provides a treatment of specialized concerns related to the proposal, such as evaluation methods, project development, researching the need section, and effective use of attachments. Includes a sample proposal.

W.K. Kellogg Foundation. *Evaluation Handbook.* Battle Creek, MI: W.K. Kellogg Foundation, 1998. (wkkf.org/knowledge-center/resources/2010/W-K-Kellogg-Foundation-Evaluation-Handbook.aspx.) Part one outlines the W.K. Kellogg Foundation's expectations for evaluations by grantees, and part two delineates the steps in project evaluations.

Wholey, Joseph S, Harry P. Hatry, and Kathryn E. Newcomer, eds. *Handbook of Practical Program Evaluation.* San Francisco, CA: Jossey-Bass Publishers, 2004. Each chapter is contributed by a specialist. The book is divided into sections on evaluation design, practical data collection procedures, data analysis, and planning and managing for maximum effectiveness.

York, Peter. *A Funder's Guide to Evaluation: Leveraging Evaluation to Improve Nonprofit Effectiveness.* St. Paul, MN: Fieldstone Alliance, 2005. Evaluation is one capacity-building tool that funders can put into practice, and the book explains how the process can be implemented. Noting that both nonprofits and foundations benefit from this management tool, York provides step-by-step methods and many sample worksheets for assessing grantees.

Online Resources

The Corporation for Public Broadcasting (cpb.org/grants/grantwriting.html): Offers a variety of grant proposal writing tips for preparing and writing a grant proposal. This information is general in nature and would apply to various types of projects.

GrantSpace (grantspace/Skills/Developing-Proposals): The "Developing Proposals" section of this Foundation Center web portal contains links to multimedia content, discussion forums, sample documents, and articles.

The Idea Bank (theideabank.com/onlinecourse/samplegrant.php): The site provides a number of proposals online for fire and safety organizations (indicating which ones have been successfully funded).

The Minnesota Council on Foundations (mcf.org/nonprofits/successful-grant-proposal): The document "Writing a Successful Grant Proposal" includes sections on the problem description, work plan, outcomes, and budget. Frequently asked questions are addressed.

School Grants (k12grants.org/samples/samples_index.htm): Provides a number of education-focused, successful, sample proposals. Most are directed to corporate or government funding sources and can be downloaded in PDF format.

Appendix C: Resources of the Foundation Center

Established in 1956, the Foundation Center is the leading source of information about philanthropy worldwide. Through data, analysis, and training, it connects people who want to change the world to the resources they need to succeed. The Center maintains the most comprehensive database on U.S. and, increasingly, global grantmakers and their grants—a robust, accessible knowledge bank for the sector. It also operates research, education, and training programs designed to advance knowledge of philanthropy at every level. Thousands of people visit the Center's web site each day and are served in its five regional library/learning centers and its network of more than 450 funding information centers located in public libraries, community foundations, and educational institutions nationwide and around the world.

ONLINE DATABASES

FOUNDATION DIRECTORY ONLINE SUBSCRIPTION PLANS
To meet the needs of grantseekers at every level, *Foundation Directory Online* (FDO) offers five plans—each with monthly, annual, and two-year subscription options. With every plan, subscribers can choose from indexed search terms or keyword search; and search for grantmakers geographically by county, metropolitan area, congressional district, and ZIP code, as well as by state and city.

Professional

FDO *Professional* is acclaimed as the best grantseeking tool on the market. Only *Professional* provides immediate access to nine comprehensive databases, updated weekly: grantmakers, companies, grants, and IRS 990s...all with indexed search terms and fully keyword-searchable, plus news, jobs, RFPs, PubHub reports, and nonprofit literature. *Professional* features interactive maps and charts displaying a foundation's giving patterns, and unique funder portfolios with abstracts from *Philanthropy News Digest*, the grantmaker's latest RFPs, job postings, and key staff affiliations.

$179.95: ONE MONTH
$1,295: ONE YEAR

Platinum

The *Platinum* plan includes profiles of all U.S. foundations, corporate funders, and grantmaking public charities in addition to their recently awarded grants and an index of trustee, officer, and donor names.

$149.95: ONE MONTH
$995: ONE YEAR

Premium

The *Premium* plan features profiles of the nation's top 20,000 funders and an expanded database of recently awarded grants...fully searchable. With indexed trustee, officer, and donor names, it's a popular starting point for mid-size nonprofits.

$59.95: ONE MONTH
$595: ONE YEAR

Plus

Search two databases: the nation's 10,000 largest foundations and recently awarded grants. *Plus* includes an index of trustee, officer, and donor names. A terrific value.

$29.95: ONE MONTH
$295: ONE YEAR

Basic

Gain access to profiles of the nation's 10,000 largest foundations. FDO *Basic* includes an index of trustee, officer, and donor names. A great tool for beginning grantseekers.

$19.95: ONE MONTH
$195: ONE YEAR

TO SUBSCRIBE, VISIT FOUNDATIONCENTER.ORG/FDO

CORPORATE GIVING ONLINE

For nonprofits seeking grants or in-kind donations of equipment, products, professional services, and volunteers from U.S. company-sponsored foundations and giving programs, *Corporate Giving Online* includes three databases, updated weekly: companies, grantmakers, and grants.

$59.95: ONE MONTH
$595: ONE YEAR

TO SUBSCRIBE, VISIT CGONLINE.FOUNDATIONCENTER.ORG

FOUNDATION GRANTS TO INDIVIDUALS ONLINE

Need a scholarship, fellowship or award? Visit the new *Foundation Grants to Individuals Online,* built specifically for students, artists, researchers, and individuals like you!

$19.95: ONE MONTH
$36.95: THREE MONTHS
$59.95: SIX MONTHS
$99.95: ONE YEAR

TO SUBSCRIBE, VISIT GTIONLINE.FOUNDATIONCENTER.ORG

MAP OF CROSS-BORDER GIVING
Who is making a difference outside of the U.S.?

The Map of Cross-Border Giving is an online, interactive mapping tool that lets you see over 45,000 grants totaling more than $13 billion—invaluable for quickly finding U.S. foundations and corporations that support non-U.S. organizations.

$59.95: ONE MONTH
$595: ONE YEAR

TO SUBSCRIBE, VISIT CROSSBORDER.FOUNDATIONCENTER.ORG

NONPROFIT COLLABORATION DATABASE

This database provides hundreds of real-life examples of how nonprofits are working together.

PLEASE VISIT FOUNDATIONCENTER.ORG/GAINKNOWLEDGE/COLLABORATION

PHILANTHROPY IN/SIGHT®
A grantmaker's essential planning tool.

Philanthropy In/Sight® is an interactive mapping platform designed for grantmakers, policymakers, researchers, academics—virtually anyone interested in the impact of philanthropy around the world today.

$195: ONE MONTH
$1,495: ONE YEAR

TO SUBSCRIBE, VISIT PHILANTHROPYINSIGIIT.ORG

TRASI (TOOLS AND RESOURCES FOR ASSESSING SOCIAL IMPACT)

Browse or search the TRASI database for proven approaches to social impact assessment, guidelines for creating and conducting an assessment, and ready-to-use tools for measuring social change. TRASI also features a community page where individuals can connect with peers and experts.

FREE

PLEASE VISIT TRASI.FOUNDATIONCENTER.ORG

GRANTMAKER DIRECTORIES

THE CELEBRITY FOUNDATION DIRECTORY, 3RD DIGITAL EDITION

This downloadable directory (PDF) includes detailed descriptions of more than 1,600 foundations started by VIPs in the fields of business, entertainment, politics, and sports.

SEPTEMBER 2011 / ISBN 978-1-59542-375-7 / $59.95

THE FOUNDATION DIRECTORY, 2012 EDITION

Key facts include fields of interest, contact information, financials, names of decision makers, and over 55,000 sample grants. Convenient indexes are provided for all *Foundation Directories.*

MARCH 2012 / ISBN 978-1-59542-402-0 / $215 / PUBLISHED ANNUALLY

THE FOUNDATION DIRECTORY PART 2, 2012 EDITION

Thorough coverage for the next 10,000 largest foundations, with nearly 40,000 sample grants.

MARCH 2012 / ISBN 978-1-59542-403-7 / $185 / PUBLISHED ANNUALLY

THE FOUNDATION DIRECTORY SUPPLEMENT, 2012 EDITION

This single volume provides updates for thousands of foundations in *The Foundation Directory* and the *Directory Part 2.* Changes in foundation status, contact information, and giving interests are highlighted in new entries.

SEPTEMBER 2012 / ISBN 978-1-59542-407-5 / $125 / PUBLISHED ANNUALLY

FOUNDATION GRANTS TO INDIVIDUALS, 20TH EDITION

The only publication devoted entirely to foundation grant opportunities for qualified individual applicants, this directory features over 9,500 entries with current information: foundation name, address, contact, program description, grant amount, application guidelines, and more.

JULY 2011 / ISBN 978-1-59542-374-0 / $75 / PUBLISHED ANNUALLY

GRANT GUIDES

Designed for fundraisers who work within specific areas, 25 digital-edition *Grant Guides* list actual foundation grants of $10,000 or more. Guides include a keyword search tool and indexes to pinpoint grants of interest to you. As a special bonus, each grantmaker entry contains a link to its Foundation Finder profile for even more details, all in a convenient PDF format.

2011 EDITIONS / $39.95 EACH

TO ORDER, VISIT FOUNDATIONCENTER.ORG/MARKETPLACE/GRANTGUIDES

GUIDE TO FUNDING FOR INTERNATIONAL & FOREIGN PROGRAMS, 11TH EDITION

Profiles of more than 2,200 grantmakers that provide funding for international relief, disaster assistance, human rights, civil liberties, community development, and education.

MAY 2012 / ISBN 978-1-59542-408-2 / $125

NATIONAL DIRECTORY OF CORPORATE GIVING, 17TH EDITION

The *National Directory of Corporate Giving* offers comprehensive profiles of nearly 4,400 companies, nearly 1,700 corporate giving programs, and over 11,400 sample grants.

AUGUST 2011 / ISBN 978-1-59542-368-9 / $195 / PUBLISHED ANNUALLY

THE PRI DIRECTORY, 3RD EDITION

Charitable Loans and Other Program-Related Investments by Foundations
This directory lists leading funders, recipients, and project descriptions, and includes tips on how to secure and manage PRIs. Foundation listings include funder name and state; recipient name, city, and state (or country); and a description of the project funded.

PUBLISHED IN PARTERNSHIP WITH PRI MAKERS NETWORK.

JULY 2010 / ISBN 978-1-59542-214-9 / $95

FUNDRAISING GUIDES

AFTER THE GRANT

The Nonprofit's Guide to Good Stewardship
An invaluable and practical resource for anyone seeking funding from foundations, this *Guide* will help you manage your grant to ensure you get the next one.

MARCH 2010 / ISBN 978-1-59542-301-6 / $39.95

THE FOUNDATION CENTER'S GUIDE TO PROPOSAL WRITING, 6TH EDITION
Author Jane Geever provides detailed instructions on preparing successful grant proposals, incorporating the results of interviews with 40 U.S. grantmakers.
JUNE 2012 / ISBN 978-1-59542-404-4 / $39.95

FOUNDATION FUNDAMENTALS, 8TH EDITION
Expert advice on fundraising research and proposal development.
A go-to resource in academic programs on the nonprofit sector. *Foundation Fundamentals* describes foundation funding and provides advice on research strategies, including how to best use *Foundation Directory Online*.
MARCH 2008 / ISBN 978-1-59542-156-2 / $39.95

THE GRANTSEEKER'S GUIDE TO WINNING PROPOSALS
A collection of 35 actual proposals submitted to international, regional, corporate, and local foundations. Each includes remarks by the program officer who approved the grant.
AUGUST 2008 / ISBN 978-1-59542-195-1 / $39.95

GUÍA PARA ESCRIBIR PROPUESTAS
The Spanish-language translation of *The Foundation Center's Guide to Proposal Writing*, 5th edition.
MARCH 2008 / ISBN 978-1-595423-158-6 / $39.95

SECURING YOUR ORGANIZATION'S FUTURE
A Complete Guide to Fundraising Strategies, Revised Edition
Author Michael Seltzer explains how to strengthen your nonprofit's capacity to raise funds and achieve long-term financial stability.
FEBRUARY 2001 / ISBN 0-87954-900-9 / $39.95

NONPROFIT MANAGEMENT GUIDES

THE 21ST CENTURY NONPROFIT
Managing in the Age of Governance
This book details the significant improvements in nonprofit management practice that have taken place in recent years.
SEPTEMBER 2009 / ISBN 978-1-59542-249-1 / $39.95

AMERICA'S NONPROFIT SECTOR
A Primer
The third edition of this publication, by Lester Salamon, is ideal for people who want a thorough, accessible introduction to the nonprofit sector—as well as the nation's social welfare system.
MARCH 2012 / ISBN 978-1-59542-360-3 / $24.95

THE BOARD MEMBER'S BOOK
Making a Difference in Voluntary Organizations, 3rd Edition
Written by former Independent Sector President Brian O'Connell, this is the perfect guide to the issues, challenges, and possibilities facing a nonprofit organization and its board.

MAY 2003 / ISBN 1-931923-17-5 / $29.95

EFFECTIVE ECONOMIC DECISION-MAKING BY NONPROFIT ORGANIZATIONS
Editor Dennis R. Young offers practical guidelines to help nonprofit managers advance their mission while balancing the interests of trustees, funders, government, and staff.

DECEMBER 2003 / ISBN 1-931923-69-8 / $34.95

FOUNDATIONS AND PUBLIC POLICY
This book presents a valuable framework for foundations as they plan or implement their engagement with public policy.

PUBLISHED IN PARTNERSHIP WITH THE CENTER ON PHILANTHROPY & PUBLIC POLICY.

MARCH 2009 / ISBN 978-1-59542-218-7 / $34.95

INVESTING IN CAPACITY BUILDING
A Guide to High-Impact Approaches
Author Barbara Blumenthal helps grantmakers and consultants design better methods to help nonprofits, while showing nonprofit managers how to get more effective support.

NOVEMBER 2003 / ISBN 1-931923-65-5 / $34.95

LOCAL MISSION—GLOBAL VISION
Community Foundations in the 21st Century
This book examines the new role of community foundations, exploring the potential impact of transnational evolution on organized philanthropy.

PUBLISHED IN PARTNERSHIP WITH TRANSATLANTIC COMMUNITY FOUNDATIONS NETWORK.

AUGUST 2008 / ISBN 978-1-59542-204-0 / $34.95

PHILANTHROPY'S CHALLENGE
Building Nonprofit Capacity Through Venture Grantmaking
Author Paul Firstenberg explores the roles of grantmaker and grantee within various models of venture grantmaking. He outlines the characteristics that qualify an organization for a venture grant, and outlines the steps a grantmaker can take to build the grantees' organizational capacity.

FEBRUARY 2003 / SOFTBOUND: ISBN 1-931923-15-9 / $29.95

HARDBOUND: ISBN 1-931923-53-1 / $39.95

WISE DECISION-MAKING IN UNCERTAIN TIMES
Using Nonprofit Resources Effectively

This book highlights the critical challenges of fiscal sustainability for nonprofits, and encourages organizations to take a more expansive approach to funding outreach.

AUGUST 2006 / ISBN 1-59542-099-1 / $34.95

RESEARCH REPORTS

ACCELERATING CHANGE FOR WOMEN AND GIRLS:
The Role of Women's Funds

Philanthropy by and for women has increased since the 1970s, calling attention to critical women's issues like human trafficking and domestic violence. Published in partnership with the Women's Funding Network, this report examines patterns of giving by women's funds and their role in spearheading social change.

JUNE 2009 / ISBN 978-1-59542-262-0 / $19.95

ARTS FUNDING IV
An Update on Foundation Trends

This report provides a framework for understanding trends in foundation funding for arts and culture through 2001, based on a sample of over 800 foundations.

JUNE 2003 / ISBN 1-931923-48-5 / $19.95

FOUNDATIONS TODAY SERIES 2011

The *Foundations Today Series* provides the latest information on foundation growth and trends in foundation giving.

THREE-BOOK SET / $95

Foundation Giving Trends: Update on Funding Priorities
Examines recent grantmaking patterns of more than 1,000 large U.S. foundations and compares current giving priorities with trends since 1980.

JULY 2011 / ISBN 978-1-59542-364-1 / $45

Foundation Growth and Giving Estimates: Current Outlook
Includes the new top 100 foundations list and the outlook for 2010.

APRIL 2012 / ISBN 978-1-59542-406-8 / $20

Foundation Yearbook: Facts and Figures on Private and Community Foundations
The growth in number, giving amounts, and assets of all active U.S. foundations from 1975 through 2009.

DECEMBER 2011 / ISBN 978-1-59542-366-5 / $45

THE GLOBAL ROLE OF U.S. FOUNDATIONS

This study looks at private foundations as growing political actors with great potential as global players pursuing foreign policies and focuses in particular on how foundations have addressed five major global challenges: health disparities, poverty, climate change, democracy and civil society, and peace and security—and raises important questions regarding the assessment of foundation impact, the role of foundations in global governance, and institutional accountability.

MAY 2010 / ISBN 978-1-59542-312-2 / $19.95

INTERNATIONAL GRANTMAKING IV

This report examines grantmakers' international giving strategies and practices, assesses the outlook for future funding, and documents trends based on grants awarded by over 1,000 of the largest U.S. foundations.

DECEMBER 2008 / ISBN 978-1-59542-211-8 / $40

SOCIAL JUSTICE GRANTMAKING II

This research report includes an analysis of social justice giving by private and public foundations, and examines the evolving nature of social justice funding through interviews with leading grantmakers.

AUGUST 2009 / ISBN 978-1-59542-213-2 / $40

ASSOCIATES PROGRAM

For just $995 a year or $695 for six months, the Associates Program experts will answer all of your questions about foundation giving, corporate philanthropy, and individual donors.

You will receive online access to several lists that are updated monthly, including new grantmakers and grantmaker application deadlines. In addition, you will receive most results within the next business day.

JOIN NOW AT FOUNDATIONCENTER.ORG/MARKETPLACE/ASSOCIATES

ADDITIONAL ONLINE RESOURCES

foundationcenter.org

- Philanthropy News Digest is a daily digest of philanthropy-related articles. Read interviews with leaders, look for RFPs, learn from the experts, and share ideas with others in the field.

- PubHub provides links to reports and white papers covering the full scope of philanthropic activity in the United States.

- FC Stats provides thousands of tables of national, state, and metropolitan area data on U.S. foundations and their grants, including assets and giving, grant distribution patterns, and top recipients.

- Access research studies to track trends in foundation growth and giving in grantmaker policies and practices.

- To stay current on the latest research trends visit foundationcenter.org/gainknowledge.

glasspockets.org

Learn about the online transparency and accountability practices of the largest foundations, and see who has "glass pockets." Transparency Talk, the Glasspockets blog and podcast series, highlights strategies, findings, and best practices related to foundation transparency.

grantcraft.org

GrantCraft, a former project of the Ford Foundation, operates under the leadership of the Foundation Center in New York and the European Foundation Centre in Brussels. GrantCraft's signature approach has been to tap the "practical wisdom" of a diverse group of experienced grantmakers to improve the practice of philanthropy. Find real-life examples and tested solutions for overcoming hurdles faced by funders. Learn about grantmaking tools and techniques through guides, case studies, videos, surveys, workshops, and translations.

grantspace.org

GrantSpace, the Foundation Center's learning community for the social sector, features resources organized under the 13 most common subject areas of funding research—including health, education, and the arts. Dig into the GrantSpace knowledge base for answers to more than 150 questions asked about grantseeking and nonprofits. Stay up-to-date on classes and events happening in person and online with the GrantSpace training calendar. Add your voice and help build a community-driven knowledge base: share your expertise, rate content, ask questions, and add comments.

About the Author

Jane C. Geever is chairman of the development consulting firm, J. C. Geever, Inc. The firm, founded by Ms. Geever in 1975, was the first woman-led fundraising company admitted into membership in the American Association of Fund Raising Counsel (AAFRC).

Among her achievements, she assisted in the creation of the certificate program in fund raising at New York University, spearheaded the first jobs bank at the Association of Fundraising Professionals' International Conference and Fundraising Day in New York, and was appointed to the Independent Sector's ad hoc committee on Values and Ethics. Ms. Geever is a member of the Philanthropic Advisory Council for the Better Business Bureau in New York and the advisory council for the national project *Funding Fundraising* at Baruch College, and is active in the Independent Sector's *Give Five* program in New York. She has been a member of the board and officer of the National Society of Fundraising Executive Institute and of the AAFRC. Ms. Geever is also an instructor at Columbia University's Master of Science Program in fundraising management.

Ms. Geever holds a master's degree from the New School for Social Research, and she has done post-graduate study in business management at Stanford University. She delivered the May 1989 commencement address at the 71st commencement of her alma mater, Seton Hill College in Greensburg, Pennsylvania, at which time she received an honorary Doctor of Humane Letters degree.

Ms. Geever is a nationally recognized author and lecturer. She teaches seminars in association with the Foundation Center on proposal writing and approaching foundations and corporate funders.